© Ward Lock Limited 1974, 1984
© Michael Kilgarriff 1982, 1983, 1984

This edition first published in Great Britain in 1984
by Ward Lock Limited, 82 Gower Street, London
WC1E 6EQ, a Pentos Company.

Reprinted 1984

Printed in Finland

British Library Cataloguing in Publication Data
3001 jokes for kids
    1. Wit and humour, Juvenile
    2. English wit and humour
    I. Kilgarriff, Michael
    828'.91402'080928   PZ8.7
ISBN 0-7063-6291-8

3001 JOKES FOR KIDS

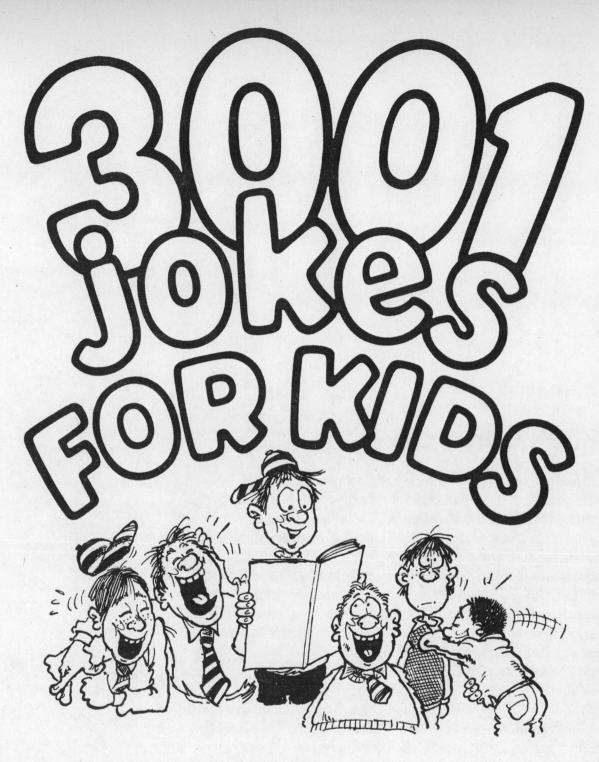

by
Michael Kilgarriff

illustrated by
David Mostyn

WARD LOCK LIMITED · LONDON

ACKNOWLEDGMENTS

I would like to express my gratitude to the following for so kindly permitting me to invade their classrooms and meetings in quest of the material for this book: the Headmistress, Mrs James, the staff and pupils of Beacon House School, London W5; the Headmaster, Mr V.S. McQueen, the staff and pupils of Montpelier Middle School, London W5; the Headmistress, Miss M.J. Percy, of Notting Hill and Ealing High School (G.P.D.S.T.), and Miss Ross and the girls of Skipton House; the Headmistress, Mrs Ashe, and Mr Peter Farrington and the boys and girls of Uxendon Primary School, Kenton, Middlesex; the Headmaster, Mr J. Nisbett and the children of Blagh Primary School, Coleraine, Northern Ireland; Brown Owl (Mrs O'Shaughnessy) and the girls of the 20th Ealing (St Benedict's) Brownie Pack; the Captain (Miss Julia Shipton) and the girls of the 20th Ealing (St Benedict's) Guide Troop; the girls of the 3rd Ealing (Christ the Saviour) Guide Company and their Captain, Mrs Margaret 'Magpie' Lyall; Mrs Sylvia Merrikin (Akela) and the boys of the 8th Ealing Cub Pack; Akela (Mr Ken Frith) and the boys of the 9th Ealing Cub Pack; Mr David Lewis (Captain) and the boys of 10th Ealing Coy., The Boys' Brigade; Mr P. Rankmore (Lieutenant in Charge) and the boys of 4th Ealing Coy., The Boys' Brigade; the members of Gemini Theatre Company and their director, Liz York; and the children of Portsmouth, Cardiff, Glasgow and Dorset.

My thanks are also due to my father, Joseph C. Kilgarriff, for his valuable assistance; and to all my friends and acquaintances, especially my daughter Rebecca and her pals, for their funny stories.

Michael Kilgarriff
1983

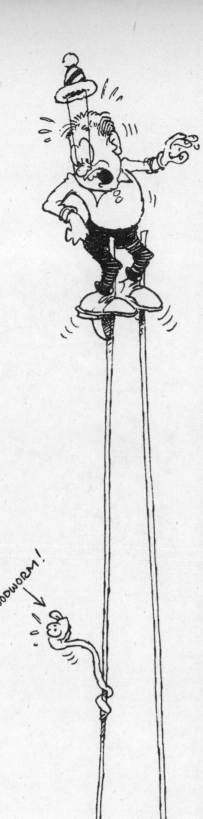

WOODWORM!

CONTENTS.

Contents

Lucky Dip

'Did you hear about the fool who keeps going round saying No?'
  'No.'
  'Oh, so it's you!'

In an apple-eating contest Sue ate ninety apples and Selena ate a hundred and one. How many more apples did Selena eat than Sue?
Answer: Ten — Selena ate a hundred and *won!*

Say to a pal 'What's this?' Then wave your hand in a snake-like motion. Your pal will say 'I don't know', so then you wave your other hand in a similar manner and say 'Nor do I — but here comes another one!'

A man committed suicide by hanging himself from a high beam in a remote barn. There was no way to climb up to the beam, and the only thing the police found in the barn was a puddle of water beneath the body. How did he get up to the beam in order to hang himself?
Answer: He stood on a block of ice!

A deaf and dumb man went into an ironmonger's shop to buy a hammer. He couldn't speak so he mimed hammering... then another deaf and dumb man went in wanting a screw-driver, so he mimed putting in a screw...Then a blind man went into the shop and he wanted a saw. So what sort of mime did he do?
  He didn't mime at all — he just asked for it!

Two boys were born on the same day, on the same date, to the same set of parents. They look alike, talk alike, think alike and behave alike — yet they are not twins! How can this be?
Answer: Because they are two of a set of triplets!

I saw Esau sitting on a see-saw — how many S's in that?
  There aren't any S's in THAT!

A man is in a prison cell with no doors and no windows; there are no holes in the ceiling or trapdoors in the floor, yet in the morning the warders find him gone. How did he get out?
Answer: Through the door*way* — there were no doors, remember?!

Is it 'nine and five *is* thirteen' or 'nine and five *are* thirteen'? Neither — nine and five are fourteen!

What was the tallest mountain in the world before Mount Everest was discovered?
Answer: Still Mount Everest — the fact that it was undiscovered makes no difference, it was still the highest mountain in the world.

If a dog is tied to a rope fifteen feet long, how can it reach a bone thirty feet away?
Answer: The rope isn't tied to anything!

How can you drop an egg three feet on to a concrete path without breaking it?
Answer: Drop it *four* feet. It will certainly be smashed, but only after dropping *more* than three feet!

A frog is lying on a lilypad in the middle of a pond. If he is six inches from the north edge, six inches from the south edge, and four inches from the east and west edges, in which direction will he jump to get out of the pond?
He won't jump at all because he's dead.

A diesel train enters a tunnel running due north-south. If the train enters the tunnel at the north end, which way does the smoke blow?
Diesel trains don't have smoke!

'Why doesn't the Queen wave with this hand?' (*Wave your left hand*)
'I don't know. Why?'
'Because it's *my* hand!'

'Let's have a race to say the alphabet.'
'All right.'
'The alphabet — beat you!'

'What's five Q and five Q?'
'Ten Q.'
'You're welcome!'

A man with a cat, a mouse and a lump of cheese has to cross a river in a small boat, but he can only take one thing with him at a time. So how does he get them all across without the cat eating the mouse or the mouse eating the cheese?
Answer: First he crosses with the mouse, then he crosses with the cat and returns *with the mouse* which he leaves behind while he crosses with the cheese, finally returning for the mouse!

As I was going to St Ives,
I met a man with seven wives.
Every wife had seven sacks,
Every sack had seven cats.
Every cat had seven kits —
Kits, cats, sacks, wives,
How many were going to St Ives?
Answer: Only me — all the rest were coming *from* St Ives!

'Which would you rather be—half-drowned or saved?'
   'Saved, of course.'
   'But if you're only half-drowned you *are* saved!'

A tropical lily is growing in a pond. If it doubles its size
every day and takes twenty-two days to fill the entire area of
the pond, how far will it have reached on the twenty-first
day?
Answer: Half-way — because it doubles its size every day!

What is frozen water? Ice.
What is frozen cream? Ice-cream.
What is frozen tea? Iced tea.
What is frozen coffee? Iced coffee.
What is frozen ink? Iced ink. (I stink).
You'd better go and have a bath, then!

'You still owe me twenty pence for that honey.'
   'What honey?'
   'I never knew you cared!'

If there are fifty-two weeks in the year how many seconds
are there?
Twelve — January 2nd, February 2nd, March 2nd, etc., etc.

Which month in the year has twenty-eight days? All of
them...

What's your favourite colour? Red? And what is your
favourite animal? A cat? And what is your favourite
number? Seven? So when did you last see a red cat with
seven legs...?!

If you have an umpire in cricket and a referee in football,
what do you have in bowls?
   Goldfish.

If an aeroplane crashed on the borders of England and
Scotland, where would the survivors be buried?
   Nowhere, 'cos any survivors wouldn't be dead!

Put down ten matches to make the word WET. How can you remove two matches yet still have a three-letter word? You simply remove the first two matches, leaving the word VET!

Before WET After VET

Say to a friend: Do you know Shakespeare's stamp? *Your friend will say 'No' and you then say* Shake . . . *(shaking him by the shoulders)* . . . spear . . . *(spearing him)* . . . stamp! *(Stamping on his toe!)*

If it takes ten men four days to dig a hole, how long will it take five men to dig half a hole? There's no such thing as half a hole!

A boy wanted to cross a river from south to north; he couldn't swim, no boats were available, and the only bridge was watched over by a guard who came out of his hut every five minutes. As it took ten minutes to walk across the bridge how did the boy achieve his goal?
Answer: He walked across from south to north; as the guard emerged from his hut the boy turned round and pretended he was walking from north to south. The guard then ran after him and shooed the boy back the way he thought he had come — i.e. to the north side of the river!

How can a cock lay an egg on barbed wire?
Cocks don't lay eggs, only hens!

If a man rides into an inn on Friday and stays three days, how can he ride out on Friday?
Answer: Friday was the name of his horse!

A donkey wanted to cross a stream in order to eat the lush grass in the meadow opposite. There was no bridge, no boat, and the donkey couldn't swim. So how did he cross? . . . You give up? . . . So did the donkey!

Three boys called Peter, Paul and Pardon went to play by the river. Peter and Paul fell in and were drowned: who was left? *(You will of course receive the reply 'Pardon', at which you repeat loudly:)* Three boys called Peter, Paul and Pardon . . . etc.

Try this on a friend. Ask 'Would you kiss a tramp for £1?' The answer will of course be 'No!' Then you ask 'Would you kiss a tramp for £5?' And again the answer will be 'No!' You then ask 'Would you kiss a tramp for £10?' And for the third time the answer will be in the negative. But then you say, 'What would you kiss a tramp for?' The answer you receive this time will probably be, 'Nothing.' To which you reply, 'Oh, so you'd kiss a tramp for nothing, would you?!' Or the reply might be, 'I wouldn't kiss a tramp for anything!' to which you can respond, 'So you would kiss a tramp for something, then!'

After many years of searching, the wicked Abanazar finally found the magic cave which he hoped would contain the wonderful lamp, the possession of which would make him master of the universe. He stood before the rock which sealed the entrance to the cave, spread his arms wide, and in a commanding voice said 'Open Sesame!' And from within the cave a ghostly voice answered, 'Open says-a who?'

Two boys camping out in a back-garden wanted to know the time, so they began singing at the tops of the voices. Eventually a neighbour threw open his window and shouted down at them, 'Hey! Less noise! Don't you know what the time is? It's three o'clock!'

'Tell me,' said the hiker to the local yokel, 'will this pathway take me to the main road?'
  'No, zur,' replied the rustic, 'you'll have to go by yourself!'

'I didn't come here to be insulted!'
  'No? Where do you usually go?'

'No, no, no!' said the enraged businessman to the persistent salesman. 'I cannot see you today!'
  'That's fine,' said the salesman. 'I'm selling spectacles!'

A very grand lady made her very first visit to a post office— previously one of her servants had always gone for her, but on this occasion curiosity got the better of her, and in she went to purchase a postage stamp. Gazing at the small gummed piece of paper she said haughtily to the clerk,
  'Have I got to stick this on myself?'
  'No, lady', came the reply. 'You stick it on the envelope!'

Two lorries, one carrying a load of red paint and the other a load of purple paint, crashed on a desert island. The drivers are now marooned.

A man just released from prison was so elated after five years behind bars that he ran down the street shouting, 'I'm free! I'm free!' And a small boy on the corner said, 'So what — I'se four!'

Mr Timpson noticed his neighbour, Mr Simpson, searching very hard for something in his front garden. 'Have you lost something, Mr Simpson?' asked Mr Timpson. 'Yes,' replied Mr Simpson. 'I've mislaid my spectacles.' 'Oh dear,' said Mr Timpson, 'Where did you last see them?' 'In my sitting-room,' said Mr Simpson. 'In your sitting-room?' queried Mr Timpson. 'So why are you looking for them in your garden?' 'Oh,' replied Mr Simpson, 'there's more light out here!'

Newsflash: Forty pedigree dogs stolen from kennels. Police say they have no leads.

'Do you know the quickest way to the station?'
'Yes — run!'

Think of the numbers two, four, seven, and eight . . . now, shut your eyes . . . dark, isn't it?!

Behind the counter of a sweet shop served a woman who was seven feet tall and sixty inches wide. What did she weigh? Sweets.

A man standing on a canal bridge saw a barge passing below. What's the bargemaster's name? Watt.

Charlie and Farley saw two men at a river bridge fishing in a most peculiar manner. One was holding the other over the parapet by his ankles and the second was hooking the fish out of the water with his hands! Strange though this angling technique may have been it was remarkably successful, and the man being held over the bridge was throwing up big fish every few seconds. 'Let's try that!' said Charlie to Farley, and Farley agreed. So on they walked till they came to another bridge, where Charlie held on to Farley's ankles and waited for his friend to throw up lots of fish. But five minutes went by and Farley had caught nothing; ten minutes, twenty minutes — an hour, then two hours, and still no fish. Then suddenly Farley called out, 'Charlie, pull me up quick! There's a train coming!'

But Charlie let go of Farley, who was run over by the train and seriously injured. 'Charlie!' yelled out Farley, 'don't just stand there. Call me an ambulance!' 'All right,' said Charlie. 'You're an ambulance!'

'What are you doing with that manure?' said the nutter to the gardener. 'I'm putting it on my rhubarb,' replied the gardener. 'Really?' said the nutter. 'Where I live we put custard on it!'

In 1800 an Irishman invented the lavatory pan . . . in 1900 an Englishman invented a hole in it . . .

Customer: This restaurant must have very clean kitchens.
Manager: Thank you, sir. What makes you say that?
Customer: Everything tastes of soap!

A motorist in his car with his two sons was involved in a collision. He and one of his sons were killed outright, and the other son was taken to hospital, where the doctor said, 'This is my son.' How can this be?
Answer: The doctor was his mother.

In the school the backward children were placed in a classroom on the ground floor, the stupid children on the first floor, the naughty children on the second floor, and the really thick tearaways on the third floor. What was on the top floor? The teachers' staff-room!

Three men visited a wizard's castle to ask for help. 'If you can spend one hour in my horrible dungeon,' the wizard replied, 'you will be granted your heart's desire. But you have one wish each, and only one, so choose carefully.' In went the first man to the horrible dungeon, to find his nostrils assailed by the most awful, vile smell he had ever experienced. Doing his best to ignore the fetid stench he concentrated on his wish — 'I want to be a doctor! I want to be a doctor!' And sure enough after an hour he emerged a doctor. The second man entered and also managed to think safely of his heart's desire despite the dreadful smell. 'I want to be a lawyer! I want to be a lawyer!' And he too emerged after an hour a fully-qualified lawyer. But when the third man entered he immediately said, 'Pooh!' and straightaway was turned into a bear . . .

News Flash: 1,000 Wigs stolen in Cumbria. Police are combing the area.

Why did the lady have her hair in a bun?
  'Cos she had her nose in a cheeseburger!'

How do you define agony?
  A man with one arm hanging from a cliff-top and an itchy behind!

News Flash: Eminent plastic surgeon dies. He sat on a radiator and made a complete pool of himself.

The salesgirl in a chemist's shop one freezing cold winter's day was surprised to see a small girl come in with bare feet. 'Aren't you chilled with nothing on your feet?' she asked. The little girl looked down and said, 'Oh, I thought I was in Boots!'

Did you hear about the idiot stunt-man who tried to jump over two dozen motor-bikes in a double-decker bus? He might have succeeded but someone rang the bell.

Two children were admiring the famous statue by Rodin entitled 'The Thinker'. 'What do you suppose he's thinking about?' said one, to which the other replied, 'I should imagine he's thinking about where he put his clothes!'

Stan had bravely climbed a tall tree but now found himself unable to get down. 'Why don't you come down the same way you went up? called out his pal.
  'No fear!' shouted back Stan. 'I came up head first!'

'How's your new guitar?'
  'Oh, I threw it away.'
  'Why?'
  'It had a hole in the middle!'

Did you hear about the woman who was so mean she kept a fork in the sugar-bowl . . . ?

Tarzan had climbed to the top of a mountain in the middle of the Amazon jungle. At the summit he was immediately surrounded by hideous monsters, ghouls and demons of every kind. Do you know what he said? 'Boy, am I in the wrong joke!'

What's this?

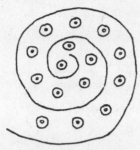

Fifteen Mexicans walking down a mountain path.

I wouldn't say Robert is stingy but every time he takes a coin out of his pocket the Queen blinks . . . and he's so suspicious! He doesn't even trust himself — both his eyes watch each other all the time.

'I don't think these photographs you've taken do me justice.'
    'You don't want justice — you want mercy!'

Claud isn't exactly stupid, but when he went to a mind-reader he got his money back.

'I understand you buried your cat last week?'
    'Had to. She was dead.'

The workmen had just finished laying a huge wall-to-wall carpet when one of them noticed a small lump right in the centre. 'Oh, those must be my cigarettes,' he declared. 'I was wondering where they had got to.' So rather than take up the carpet and go through the difficult and tedious process of relaying it he simply took a large mallet and banged the offending protuberance flat. Just then in came the lady of the house, carrying a tray. 'I've brought you some tea,' she said. 'And I think one of you left these cigarettes in the kitchen . . . oh by the way, have any of you seen my little boy's hamster?'

Two friends were out hunting grouse. A bird suddenly flew out of the bracken right before their eyes; one of the men raised his gun and fired. The grouse uttered a despairing squawk, its wings folded and it fluttered to the ground. 'You needn't have shot it!' said the other man. 'The fall would have killed it!'

In the swimming competition the first high diver announced that he would attempt a triple somersault with one and a half twists. The second diver arrived on the top board carrying a fish. 'And what are you going to do?' asked the judge, to which the diver answered 'A somersault with pike!'

Telephone Operator: 'Is that the lunatic asylum?'
Superintendent: 'Yes, but we're not on the phone.'

'I'm holding a match and a lighter. Which is the heavier?'
  'The match of course.'
  'No, 'cos they're both lighters!'

Two Irishmen looking for work saw a sign which read TREE FELLERS WANTED. 'Oh, now, look at that,' said Paddy. 'What a pity dere's only de two of us!'

'Are your teeth checked?'
  'No, sort of off-white...'

A man went into the Post Office with some jelly stuck in one ear and some cream cake stuck into the other. The man behind the counter said, 'Why have you got jelly in one ear and cream cake in the other ear?' To which the customer replied, 'You'll have to speak up — I'm a trifle deaf!'

The convicted murderer was about to be shot. 'Do you have any last request?' asked the prison warden. 'Yes,' replied the criminal, 'I'd like to sing a song.' 'Very well,' said the warden, and the condemned man began to sing: 'Nine hundred and ninety-eight thousand, three hundred and twenty-eight bottles, hanging on the wall...'

'Why are you so angry?'
  'It's all the rage.'

'Do you like my new swimming-pool?'
  'It's marvellous. Must have cost you a fortune!'
  'Yes, it did at that.'
  'But why isn't there any water in it?'
  'I can't swim.'

A man in a cinema left his seat to buy an ice-cream. On his return he said to an old lady sitting at the end of the row, 'Did I step on your toe just now?' 'You certainly did!' she said crossly. 'Oh, good,' came the heartless reply, 'this is my row.'

The woman in a theatre box-office was surprised one evening just before the show at the behaviour of a patron. He bought a ticket, went away, and then returned a few minutes later to buy another one; he went away again, returned and bought a third ticket. Then he went away yet again, returned yet again and bought a fourth ticket. By this time the show had started, so the woman in the box-office said, 'I hope you don't mind my asking, sir, but why do you keep coming back and buying more tickets?'
  'Every time I try and get into the auditorium,' the hapless patron replied, 'some chap takes my ticket and tears it in half!'

The private detective was reporting to his boss. 'I traced the woman to Manchester, sir,' he said, 'but then she gave me the slip. Then I traced her to Glasgow, and again she gave me the slip. I picked up her trail in Cardiff, where again she gave me the slip.'

'This is getting monotonous, Holmes,' said the boss. 'What happened then?'

'I found her in Birmingham, sir and there — '

'She gave you the slip?'

'No, sir. In Birmingham she gave me the frock.'

Did you hear about the pop-singer who got his shoelaces tangled up in his hair? When he stood up he broke his neck.

'There's a leaky roof in my office.'

'Won't the landlord repair it?'

'Repair it? He's so mean he's charging me an extra £5 a week for the use of the shower!'

Did you hear the tragic event at the supermarket? A customer was leaning over the frozen food counter when five fish fingers reached up and strangled him.

'This watch,' said the very superior person, 'is shockproof, waterproof, antimagnetic, and will function perfectly for one hundred years. I paid no less than £400 for it!'

'Did you really?' said his humble friend. 'I bought a watch ten years ago for no more than 50p; two days after buying it I dropped it in the river and its been running non-stop ever since.'

'The watch?'

'No, the river!'

Sign in stationery shop window:
Calendars and Diaries
All with 1 Year's Guarantee

Mr Grouch was enraged when young Joe from next door began throwing stones at his greenhouse. 'I'll teach you, you young imp of Satan!' roared the furious neighbour. 'I'll teach you to throw stones at my greenhouse!'

'I wish you would,' said the cheeky lad. 'I've had three goes and I haven't hit it yet!'

One very hot day an extremely small man went into a cafe, put his newspaper on a table and went to the counter. But on returning with his cup of tea he saw that his place had been taken by a huge, bearded ferocious-looking man of some twenty-two stone in weight and six feet nine inches in height. 'Excuse me,' said the little man to the big man, 'but you're sitting in my seat.'

'Oh, yeah?' snarled the big man. 'Prove it!'

'Certainly. You're sitting on my ice-cream.'

One late autumn evening two boys, having collected a sackful of conkers, decided to share them out in a graveyard. On their way in one of the boys dropped the sack and two of the conkers rolled out. 'We'll get those later,' he said, and in they went to divide up the remainder. As they were counting them out a small girl happened to be crossing the graveyard, and to her horror she heard from behind a bush a voice say, 'One for you, one for me. One for you, one for me!' In terror she rushed to the gate and bumped into a policeman. 'What's the matter, little girl?' he asked, for she was obviously in great distress.

'Oh, Mr Policeman!' she wailed, 'there's ghosts in the graveyard, and they're sharing out the dead bodies! Listen!' And as she held a trembling finger to her lips they heard a voice say, 'One for you, one for me. And we mustn't forget those two by the gate!'

The Teddy Bear had gone to work on a building site clearing the ground for a new block of offices. But he had only been there an hour when he sought out the foreman.

'Someone's stolen my pick!' he said angrily.

'I'm not surprised,' said the foreman. 'Didn't you know? Today's the day the Teddy Bears have their picks nicked!'

'My girlfriend's one of twins.'
  'How can you tell them apart?'
  'Her brother's got a beard.'

'How do you do?'
  'Do what?'

Why did the golfer wear an extra pair of trousers?
  In case he got a hole in one.

Supporter: 'I know you lost ten goals to nil but why did you have to clout that little boy?'
Footballer: 'He's our good luck mascot!'

'Want to try some of this? I've just invented it.'
  'What is it?'
  'My new truth drink. One sip and you tell the truth.'
  'All right, I'll have a go...ugh! That's paraffin!'
  'And that's the truth!'

'Do you like this dress? It's seventy years old!'
  'Did you make it yourself?'

A boy riding his bicycle knocked over an old lady; she wasn't hurt, just shaken up and furious. 'You wretched boy!' she fumed, dusting herself down. 'Don't you know how to ride that bike?'

'Yes,' he replied, 'but I don't know how to ring the bell!'

The inmates of a prisoner-of-war camp asked whether they might be permitted to play a series of football matches against their captors. 'Certainly!' said the Camp Commandant. 'And everyone must practise hard! My men will practise on the bottom field, my officers will practise on the top field, and you prisoners will practise on the minefield!'

'Care to come to my birthday party on Saturday, Jill?'
  'Thanks, Trevor. Where do you live?'
  'Number thirty-eight, London Road. Just push the bell with your elbow.'
  'Why with my elbow?'
  'You're not coming empty-handed, are you?'

Postman: 'Is this letter for you, sir? The name is all smudged.'
Man: 'No, my name is Allsop.'

Three biscuits were crossing the road when the first one was knocked down and then a second was knocked down. What did the third biscuit say as he reached the pavement in safety? 'Crumbs!'

'Even when my pocket's empty I've still got something in it.'
  'What's that?'
  'A hole!'

'Why do you keep doing the back-stroke?'
  'I've just had lunch and don't want to swim on a full stomach!'

Jemima's new shoes were too squeaky for the irritable librarian, and as Jemima tip-toed past the 'Silence' sign the librarian yelled out, *'QUIIIIEEEEEETTTT!'*

'Throw the baby down!' shouted the man to a woman on top of a blazing building.
  'I daren't!' she yelled back. 'You might drop him!'
  'No, I won't!' he shouted back. 'I'm a professional goal-keeper!'
Reassured, the woman dropped her baby to the footballer, who immediately bounced it three times and kicked it over the garden wall...

Paddy and Mick went duck-hunting with their dogs but without any success. 'I know what it is, Mick,' said Paddy. 'I know what we're doing wrong.'
  'What's that, then, Paddy?'
  'We're not throwing the dogs high enough.'

'My neighbours bang on the wall at all hours.'

'Doesn't that keep you awake?'

'No, but it doesn't half interfere with my trumpet practice!'

'Is that Cohen, Cohen, Cohen & Cohen?'

'Yes, madam.'

'May I speak to Mr Cohen, please? It's very important.'

'I'm afraid Mr Cohen is on holiday.'

'Oh...may I speak to Mr Cohen, then? It's extremely urgent.'

'I'm afraid Mr Cohen is off sick.'

'Oh, dear...what about Mr Cohen? It's a matter of life and death!'

'Mr Cohen is in Brussels on business.'

'Oh, Lord, I'm desperate!' Can I speak to Mr Cohen, then?'

'Speaking.'

'What shall I sing next?'

'Do you know "Loch Lomond"?'

'Yes, I do.'

'Then go and jump in it!'

'I've got over 5,000 records.'

'Over 5,000! Gosh, you must be very fond of music.'

'Oh, I don't play them. I just collect the holes in the middle.'

'What steps would you take,' roared the sergeant-instructor, 'if one of the enemy came at you with a bayonet?'

And a small voice in the rear rank muttered, 'Dirty great *big* ones!'

'Why were you late back to camp, Frank?' asked the Scoutmaster.

'I'm sorry, Skip,' replied the Scout. 'But as we crossed that field of cows my beret blew off and I had to try on forty before I found it.'

An old soldier was visiting the site of one of his past battles. 'I remember this spot so vividly,' he said to his wife, his eyes misting over with nostalgia. 'It was just here that my Commanding Officer fell.'

'Was he shot?' she asked gently.

'No. Blind drunk as usual.'

Flying instructor: 'Tomorrow you will fly solo.'

Trainee pilot: 'How low?'

How do you stop a cold going to your chest?
Tie a knot in your neck.

'That girl looks like Helen Green.'
  'She looks even worse in red.'

'There's a man outside with a big bushy beard.'
  'Is it a naval beard?'
  'No, it grows on his chin.'

Two boys were watching television when the fabulous face and figure of Bo Derek appeared on the screen. 'If ever I stop hating girls,' said one to the other, 'I think I'll stop hating her first.'

How can one plus one equal a window?

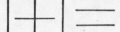 Put these together and you get

'Dark in this cave, isn't it?'
  'Dunno — I can't see to tell.'

Did you hear about the farmer's boy who hated the country? He went to the big city and got a job as a shoe-shine boy, and so the farmer made hay while the son shone!

'Imagine you're on a hike,' said the Scoutmaster to Eric the Tenderfoot, 'and you're facing north. Now, what is on your right?'
  'East, Skip,' said Eric.
  'Correct. And what is on your left?'
  'West, Skip.'
  'Correct again. And what is at your back?'
  'Er — my rucksack, Skip.'

Sign in shop window:

FOR SALE
Pedigree Bulldog.
House trained. Eats anything.
Very fond of children.

Advertisement in newspaper:

WANTED
Lad to trace gas leaks with
lighted candle.
Must be willing to travel.

'How old were you last birthday?'
  'Nine.'
  'I see. So you'll be ten on your next birthday.'
  'No, I won't. I'll be eleven.'
  'How can that be?'
  'I'm ten today.'

'Why are you jumping up and down?'
'I've just taken my medicine and I forgot to shake the bottle.'

'This morning my Dad gave me soap-flakes instead of corn-flakes for breakfast!'
'I bet you were mad.'
'Mad? I was foaming at the mouth!'

'Did you hear about Charlie Evans' diet? The doctor said he could only have bananas and coconut milk. For three months that was all he had — bananas and coconut milk!'
'Did he lose any weight?'
'No, but he can't half climb trees!'

'Some girls think I'm handsome,' said the young Romeo, 'and some girls think I'm ugly. What do you think, Sheila?'
'A bit of both. Pretty ugly.'

'Why are you covered in bruises?'
'I started to walk through a revolving door and then I changed my mind.'

Top of the pops:
She Left Her Electric Blanket On, And Now She's The Toast Of The Town
Don't Throw The Cat In The Washing-Machine, Mother, Or You May Get A Sock In The Puss
They're Moving Father's Grave To Build A Sewer
Meet Me Under The Clothes-Line, Darling, 'Cos That's Where I Hang Out
Vesuvius Please Don't Blow Your Top, or, Lava Come Back To Me

'This morning,' said one pilot to the other, 'I made a perfect three-point landing.'
'That's nothing,' came the reply. 'This morning I made a perfect one-point landing.'
'How did you manage that?'
'I got stuck on the church steeple!'

A lady in a pub noticed a man in the corner of the bar rapidly getting drunker and drunker. 'I've seen you in here before,' she snapped at him, 'and you're always drunk. Why do you drink so much?'
''Cos o' my problem, lady,' he said mournfully as he downed another double Scotch.
'And what problem do you have, may I ask?'
'I drink too much.'

'You're ugly!'
'And you're drunk!'
'Yes, but in the morning I'll be sober!'

Good news! I've been given a goldfish for my birthday... the bad news is that I don't get the bowl till my next birthday!

'You have to be a good singer in our house, you know.'
    'Why's that?'
    'There's no lock on the lavvy door.'

Did you hear about the woman who dreamed she was chewing her pillow?
    In the morning she was all right, just a little down in the mouth.

'Is it possible to eat soup politely with a big moustache?'
    'Yes, but it's a big strain.'

'I'd like to buy a dog.'
    'Certainly, sir. Any particular breed. A red setter, perhaps?'
    'No, not a red setter.'
    'A Golden Labrador?'
    'No, not a Golden Labrador. I don't want a coloured dog. Just a black and white one.'
    'Why a black and white one, sir?'
    'Isn't the licence cheaper?'

Good news! At school today there will be free Coca-Cola for everyone...the bad news is that the straws are 50p each!

Good news! My Dad's just bought me a smashing model railway engine...the bad news is that he forgot to buy the track!

As the fire engine pulled away from the station with its siren blaring — DA! *Da!* DA! *Da!* DA! *Da!* — the crew became aware of a boy running alongside. The fire appliance accelerated, surging through the traffic — DA! *Da!* DA! *Da!* DA! *Da!*—but still the lad managed somehow to keep up. Eventually the driver turned on to a motorway where he could put his foot right down, but still the boy was there running alongside!
    Mile after mile the fire engine tore along — DA! *Da!* DA! *Da!* DA! *Da!* — but the boy miraculously kept pace with the speeding vehicle. His superhuman running finally unnerved the driver, who, despite the urgency of the call, slowed and stopped. 'Hey, sonny!' he shouted to the boy who had also stopped. 'What in blazes do you want?'
    'A 30p Mr Whippy, please,' came the reply, 'and no chocolate flake!'

'Last winter during the dark nights I dressed all in white so that the traffic would see me.'
'Did that keep you safe?'
'No. I got knocked down by a snow-plough.'

'Young man,' said the old lady to the Boy Scout, 'can you see me across the road?'
'I dunno,' replied the lad. 'I'll go and have a look.'

'When's your birthday?'
'August 26th.'
'What year?'
'Every year.'

A man unable to stop himself stealing asked the doctor for help and advice.
'Try these pills,' said the doctor. 'They should help.'
'But what if they don't?' asked the wretched patient.
'Then see if you can get me a video, will you?'

1st Eskimo boy: 'Where's your Mum come from?'
2nd Eskimo boy: 'Alaska.'
1st Eskimo boy: 'Don't bother — I'll ask 'er myself.'

The new Guide was asked by her father whether she learned how to tie any knots.
'Oh, yes, Dad,' replied the keen Guide. 'And next week we're going to learn how to untie the Captain!'

What's this?

A koala climbing up a tree.

Why is a tree surgeon like an actor?
'Cos he's always taking boughs.

Which burns longer — a black candle or a white candle?
Neither. They both burn shorter.

'That new restaurant has an interesting item on the menu.'
'Oh — what's that?'
'Soup in a basket!'

Advertisement in the window of a dry-cleaners:
We'll clean for you   We'll press for you
We'll even dye for you

Advertisement in the window of a chemist's:
Got a cold? Try Chesto Cough Drops
We guarantee you'll never get better

Monkey Business

We call our dog Carpenter 'cos he's always doing little odd jobs around the house.

What happens when the frog's car breaks down?
  He gets toad away.

What is a crate of ducks?
  A box of quackers.

A mouse went into a music shop, jumped on to the counter and, to the astonishment of the owner, said 'Can I have a mouse-organ, please?'
  The music shop owner gulped and said, 'This is quite extraordinary. I've been here for thirty-five years and no mouse has ever asked for a mouse-organ until today — and you are the second! There was another mouse here just an hour or so ago, also asking for a mouse-organ.'
  'Ah yes,' said the mouse, 'That'll be 'Armonica . . .'

Why do cats and dogs turn round and round before sleeping?
  Because one good turn deserves another.

What do people in Mozambique call little black cats?
  Little black kittens.

What is a musical fish?
  A piano-tuna.

What does a frog do with bad eyesight?
  Hops to the hoptician.

Why are wolves like playing-cards?
  They both come in packs.

What birds hover over people lost in the desert?
  Luncheon vultures.

How can you get a set of teeth put in for free?
Smack a tiger.

What did the goat say when he only had thistles to eat?
'Thistle have to do.'

If a peacock lays an egg in your garden, who owns the egg?
No one — peacocks don't lay eggs, only peahens.

How do you shoe a horse?
Say 'Giddy-up!'

Where does a two-ton gorilla sit when he goes to the theatre?
Anywhere he wants to!

'We had roast boar for dinner last night.'
'Was it a wild boar?'
'Well, it wasn't very pleased.'

Where do you find wild boar?
Depends where you leave them.

What was the tortoise doing on the motorway?
About 150 metres an hour.

Why did the whale let Jonah go?
He couldn't stomach him.

Why can't you play jokes on snakes?
'Cos you can never pull their legs.

A man standing at a bus-stop was eating fish and chips. Next to him stood a lady with her little dog, which became very excited at the smell of the man's supper and began whining and jumping up at him. 'Do you mind if I throw him a bit?' said the man to the lady. 'No, not at all,' she replied. Whereupon the man picked up the dog and threw him over a wall . . .

Which shop do sheep like to visit?
The baaaber's!

What's worse than a crocodile with tooth-ache?
A centipede with bunions.

What's the definition of a caterpillar?
A worm with a fur coat.

What is the animal with the highest intelligence?
  A giraffe.

Why can't you trust an Indian leopard?
  'Cos it's a cheetah.

What happened at the badly organized milking contest?
  There was udder chaos.

Why was the camel unhappy?
  'Cos it had the hump.

Why are skunks always arguing?
  'Cos they like to raise a stink.

What animal are you like when you take a bath?
  A little bear.

If there are five partridges in a pear tree and a hunter shoots three, how many are left?
  None — the others flew away.

If twenty dogs run after one dog, what time is it?
  Twenty after one.

A man walked into a pub with a huge, vicious looking Alsatian. 'Sorry, sir,' said the landlord, 'but that dog looks dangerous to me. You'll have to leave him outside.' So the Alsatian owner took his dog outside, then came back into the bar and ordered a drink. He was just finishing when a young woman came in and said, 'Whose Alsatian is that outside?'

'Mine,' said its proud owner.

'I'm afraid,' said the young woman, 'that my dog's just killed him!'

'Killed him!' said the man in disbelief. 'What kind of dog do you have then?'

'A Chihuahua,' said the young woman.

'But how could a little Chihuahua kill my enormous Alsatian?'

'She got stuck in his throat and choked him.'

A woman bought two parrots, one of whom she was warned was extremely aggressive. And it was, too! When she took the cover off the cage the morning after bringing them home the aggressive parrot had killed the other stone dead! To teach it a lesson she then bought a condor — and again when she took the cover off the cage the next morning the parrot had put paid to the intruder. Determined not to be beaten the woman then bought an eagle! In the morning she took the cover off — and there was the eagle, dead on the floor of the cage! But this time the parrot was completely denuded of feathers! It stood on its perch, totally featherless, cocked its head on one side, looked at its mistress and said, 'I really had to take my coat off to that one!'

A family of tortoises went into a cafe for some ice-cream. They sat down and were about to start when Father Tortoise said, 'I think it's going to rain. Junior, will you pop home and fetch my umbrella?' So off went Junior Tortoise for his father's umbrella, but three days later he still hadn't returned. 'I think, dear,' said Mother Tortoise to Father Tortoise, 'we'd better eat Junior's ice-cream before it melts.' And a voice from the door said, 'If you do that I won't go!'

What does a cat turn into when the lights go out?
   The dark.

'Who's been eating my porridge?' squeaked Baby Bear. 'Who's been eating *my* porridge?' growled Father Bear. 'Don't get all excited,' said Mother Bear. 'I haven't made it yet!'

Why do bees hum?
   'Cos they don't know the words.

A man buying a camel was advised that to make it walk he should say 'Few!', to make it run he should say 'Many!', and to make it stop he should say 'Amen!' At his first ride all went well. 'Few!' he called, and off the camel went. 'Many!' he shouted, and the camel began to run — straight for the edge of a cliff. But the new owner had forgotten the word to make the camel stop! As the cliff edge came closer and closer he called out in terror, 'Lord save me! Lord save me! Amen!' And of course the camel stopped — right on the very edge of the precipice. Whereupon the rider mopped his brow in relief and said, 'Phew, that was clo-AAAAGH!''

Two fish were swimming in a stream when it began to rain. 'Quick!' said one fish to the other, 'Let's swim under that bridge, otherwise we'll get wet!''

What animal is like a nursery rhyme?
   Ee, Aw, Marjorie Daw . . . !

'Who's been eating my porridge?' squeaked Baby Bear.
'Who's been eating *my* porridge?' cried Mother Bear.
'Burp!' said Father Bear . . .

'My dog died of 'flu.'
'But dogs don't get 'flu.'
'Mine flew under a bus.'

Which animal goes to sleep with its shoes on?
   A horse.

If a farmer stands in a field with his dog and forty pigs, how many feet have they got between them? Two — only the farmer has feet!

'My dog's got no legs. I call him Cigarette.'
'Why?'
"Cos every night I take him out for a drag.'

'I did have a shock yesterday with my Binkie.'
'You mean your budgie?'
'Yes, poor little thing. I'd filled my lighter just before letting him out of his cage for his exercise, and I hadn't noticed that I'd spilled some of the fuel on the sideboard. Well, Binkie spotted it and before I could stop him he'd flown on to the sideboard and taken two or three beakfuls!'
'What happened?'
'Well, he gave a strangled squawk, flew straight up and hit the ceiling, and then flew three times round the room, going faster and faster!'
'Oo-er!'
'Then he flew out into the hall, into the kitchen, out of the kitchen back into the hall, up the stairs and into the bathroom. He flew straight at the mirror, smacked his little head – crack! – against the glass and then fell into the wash-basin. And there he lay, prone, not moving!'
'Was he dead?'
'No, he'd just run out of petrol.'

The loud-mouthed frog said to the giraffe, 'What do you eat, Mr Giraffe?' 'Leaves,' said the giraffe. The loud-mouthed frog then said to the antelope, 'And what do you eat, Mr Antelope?' 'Grass,' said the antelope. So the loud-mouthed frog then said to the crocodile, 'And what do you eat, Mr Crocodile?' 'Loud-mouthed frogs,' said the crocodile, to which the loud-mouthed frog replied, *(with your mouth tightly shut)* 'Oh, you don't get many of those round here!'

Last time Horace went to the zoo he got into trouble for feeding the monkeys ... he fed them to the lions.

Two flies were on a cornflakes packet. 'Why are we running so fast?' asked one.
'Because,' said the second, 'it says "tear along dotted line"!'

'Do you serve Scotsmen?' asked the man in the pub.
'Of course we do, sir,' replied the barman.
'Right. A pint of beer for me and two Scotsmen for my crocodile here.'

'I see you've got a new dog. Is he a watch dog?'
'Yes, he watches television.'
'Have you had him long?'
'Only two weeks and already he's a one-man dog. He only bites me.'

What is the difference between unlawful and illegal? Unlawful means against the law and illegal is a sick bird.

The huge lion was stalking proudly through the jungle when he came upon a leopard. 'Leopard!' snarled the lion menacingly, 'who is the King of the Jungle!'

'You are, Lion!' said the leopard nervously, and slunk away. Further down the jungle path the lion met a monkey. 'Raaaarrrrgh!' roared the lion. 'Monkey! Who is the King of the Jungle?'

'Oh, you are, Lion,' said the monkey, cowering away, 'no question about it!'

Further still down the jungle path the lion confronted an elephant. With his tail lashing, his magnificent mane bristling, his teeth bared and his claws fully exposed, the lion glared aggressively at the grey lumbering beast.

'Elephant!' commanded the lion, 'who is the King of the Jungle?'

And without a word the elephant picked up the lion in his trunk and hurled him smack against a tree; he then picked up the dazed lion again and slammed him down on the ground – two, three, four times – and finally threw the by now semi-conscious lion into a thick bramble patch.

'All right, all right!' mumbled the bleeding, battered, crumpled lion, 'no need to get cross just because you don't know the answer!'

Her Ladyship: 'Charters, there is a mouse in the west drawing-room.'
Butler: 'Very good, me lady. I'll ascertain whether the cat is at home.'

'I used to think I was a dog, but the doctor cured me.'
'So you're alright now.'
'Yes, I'm fine. Here – feel my nose.'

A policeman strolling on his beat one day was astonished to see a man walking towards him with a fully-grown African lion on a lead.

'Hey!' said the policeman, 'you can't walk around with a lion like that. Take him to the Zoo.'

'Oh, all right, officer,' said the lion owner, and away he went.

But the next day the policeman was again confronted with the man and his fully-grown African lion walking along the pavement.

'Hey, you!' yelled the policeman, 'I thought I told you yesterday to take that lion to the Zoo?'

'I did,' came the reply, 'and today I'm taking him to the pictures.'

Why are parrots always clever? Because they suck seed (succeed).

Why are there no aspirins in the jungle? Because the parrots ate 'em all. (Paracetemol)

'Peter! Stop pulling the dog's tail like that!'
　'But it's him that's doing the pulling, Mum!'

Why is it dangerous to play cards in the jungle? 'Cos there are too many cheetahs about.

'My new horse is very well-mannered.'
　'That's nice.'
　'Yes, isn't it? Every time we come to a jump he stops and lets me go first!'

A large sailing-ship was at anchor off the coast of Mauritius, and two dodos watched the sailors rowing ashore. 'We'd better hide,' said the first dodo.
　'Why?' asked the second.
　'Because,' said the first, 'we're supposed to be extinct, silly!'

Name nine animals from Africa. Eight elephants and a giraffe.

Name four animals of the cat family. Mummy cat, Daddy cat and their two kittens.

When is a man-eating tiger likely to enter a house? When the door is open.

'My budgie lays square eggs.'
　'That's amazing! Can it talk as well?'
　'Yes, but only one word.'
　'What's that?'
　'Ouch!'

'Daddy, there's a man at the door with a bill.'
　'It must be a duck with a hat on.'

The swing doors of the Wild West saloon crashed open and in came Little Pete, black with fury. 'All right!' he raged, 'all right! Who did it? What goldarned varmint painted my horse blue?'
　And the huge figure of Black Jake, notorious gunfighter and town baddie, rose from a chair by the door.
　'It was me, shrimp,' he drawled, bunching his gigantic fists, 'what about it?'
　'Oh, well, er,' stammered Little Pete wretchedly, 'all I wanted to say was ... er ... when are you going to give it another coat?'

Why do prairie dogs howl all night long? 'Cos there aren't any trees on the prairie ... just cactus.

Did you hear about the baby mouse who saw a bat? He ran home and told his mother he'd seen an angel ...

The psychiatrist was surprised to see a tortoise come into his office.

'What can I do for you, Mr Tortoise?' asked the psychiatrist.

'I'm terribly shy, doctor,' said the tortoise, 'I want you to cure me of that.'

'No problem. I'll soon have you out of your shell.'

'I love watching tennis,' said the cat to his friend.

'Why?'

'I've got two brothers in that racket.'

Why was the young kangaroo thrown out by his mother? For smoking in bed.

'Mummy,' said the baby polar bear, 'am I one hundred per cent pure polar bear?'

'Of course you are, son,' said his Daddy. 'Why do you ask?'

''Cos I'm flipping freezing!'

'Oi 'ad a larf last Sat'day,' said the farmhand to his mates in the village pub.

'Whoi, what did'ee do?' they asked.

'Oi emptied a bottle o' Scotch in the cows' drinkin' water!'

'Did 'ee, now? What 'appened to 'em?'

'They was all roight – lapped it up! But next day they didn't alf 'ave an 'angunder!'

'I tried washing my parrot in Daz.'

'Any good?'

'No, it died. It wasn't the Daz that killed him, though.'

'What was it, then?'

'The spin drier.'

'Why are you crying, little boy?'

'I was thirsty – sob! sob! – and I swapped my dog for a bottle of lemonade! Boo-hoo!'

'And now you wish you had him back, eh?'

'Yeeesss! Waaaa!'

'Because you realise now how much you love him?'

'No – sob! – 'cos I'm thirsty again!'

'My dog's bone idle.'

'Is he?'

'Yesterday I was watering the garden, and he wouldn't lift a leg to help me!'

How do you stop a skunk smelling? Put a clothes peg on his nose!

Two little skunks called In and Out were playing in the woods. Out went home, and his mother said, 'Where's In? Go and get him, there's a good boy.' So Out went back into the woods and returned very shortly after with his brother.

'That's a good boy,' said Mother Skunk, 'how did you find him so quickly?'

'Easy,' said the little skunk, 'In stinked ...'

Two fleas were walking out of a cinema when they discovered it was raining hard.

'Shall we walk?' said one flea.

'No,' said the other, 'let's take a dog.'

What did one germ say to the other germ? 'Keep away – I've got a dose of penicillin.'

Two sheep, walking in opposite directions, met in a country lane.

'Baaa,' said the first sheep.

'Hee-haw!' said the second.

'Baaa!' said the first again, in a surprised tone.

'Hee-haw!' repeated the second.

'What are you up to?' asked the first sheep. 'Sheep don't go "hee-haw".'

'But I'm a stranger round here,' said the second.

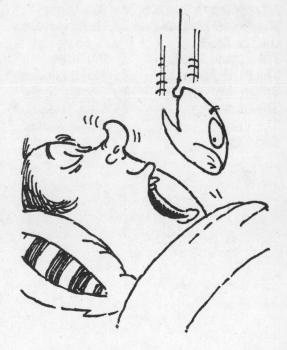

'Doctor, doctor!' said the panic-stricken woman, 'my husband was asleep with his mouth open, and he's swallowed a mouse! What shall I do?'

'Quite simple,' said the doctor calmly. 'You just tie a lump of cheese to a piece of string and lower it into your husband's mouth. As soon as the mouse takes a bite – haul it out.'

'Oh, I see. Thank you, doctor. I'll go round to the fishmonger straight away and get a cod's head.'

'What do you want a cod's head for?'

'Oh – I forgot to tell you. I've got to get the cat out first!'

Who would win a fight between an African lion and an African tiger? Neither – there aren't any tigers in Africa.

'Look at that speed!' said one hawk to another as the jet fighter plane hurtled over their heads.

'Hmph!' snorted the other. 'So would you fly fast if your tail was on fire!'

'Look over there!' said the frightened skunk to his pal, 'There's a human with a gun, and he's getting closer and closer! What are we going to do?'

To which the second skunk calmly replied, 'Let us spray ...'

From Our Bookshelf

Swimming the Channel *by* Frances Near
At the North Pole   *by* I. C. Blast
At the South Pole   *by* Ann Tarctic
The Bullfighter   *by* Matt Adore
The Farmer's Wife   *by* Mike Howe
The Water Diviner   *by* Hazel Fork
The Tiger's Revenge   *by* Claud Body
Rice Growing   *by* Paddy Field
Aches and Pains   *by* Arthur Ritis

Drunk and Disorderly   *by* Honour Bender
A Schoolboy's Troubles   *by* Ben Dover
The Cannibal's Daughter *by* Henrietta Mann
On The Beach   *by* C. Shaw
The Broken Window   *by* Eva Brick
The Earthquake   *by* Major Disaster
British Workmen   *by* General Strike
The Insomniac   *by* Eliza Wake
The Burglar   *by* Robin Banks
Springtime   *by* Teresa Greene

The Naughty Farm Boy *by* Enid Spankin
The Unknown Author   *by* Ann Onymous
The Post-script   *by* Adeline Extra
Road Transport   *by* Laurie Driver
Jungle Fever   *by* Amos Quito
Tea for Two   *by* Roland Butta
The Long Hot Summer *by* I. Scream
Try and Try Again   *by* Percy Vere
It Pays to Advertise   *by* Bill Sticker
The Barber of Seville   *by* Ray Zerr
The Calypso Band   *by* Lydia Dustbin
The Drawing Lesson   *by* Art Master

A Cliff-top Tragedy.   *by* Eileen Dover
Moving Day   *by* Ivor Newhouse
Noisy Nights   *by* Constance Norah
Drums and Trumpets   *by* Major Headache
African Pygmies   *by* R. U. Short
Influenza   *by* Mike Robe
My Most Embarrassing Moment *by* Lucy Lastick
Simple Mathematics   *by* Algy Brar
The Rifle Range   *by* Bob Downe
Stranded on the Motorway   *by* Buster Tyre
Gretna Green   *by* Marion Secret
The Return of the Prodigal Son *by* Gladys Back

Waiter Minute!

I say, waiter!   There are some coins in my soup!
Well, you said you wanted some change
in your meals.

- I've only got one piece of meat!
All right, I'll cut it in two for you.

- What about meat balls?
I've never been to any.

- There's a button in my lettuce!
That must be from the salad dressing.

- This egg's bad!
Don't blame me. I only lay the table.

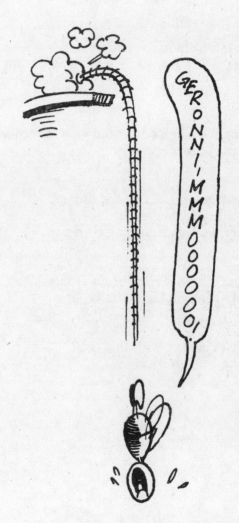

- How long will my pizza be?
We don't do long ones, sir. Only round.

- What's this fly doing in my soup?
Looks like backstroke, sir.

- I've just found a maggot in my salad!
That's better than finding half a maggot, isn't
it?

- There's a fly in my soup!
You'll have to get it out yourself. I can't swim.

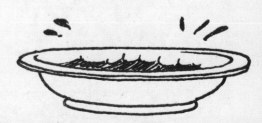

- What's this fly doing in my wine?
You did ask for something with body in it.

- You've brought me the wrong order!
Well, you did say you wanted something
different.

- Why is my food all mushed up?
You did ask me to step on it, sir.

– Bring me a dragon sandwich.
  Sorry, sir. We've run out of bread.

– What's this fly doing in my soup?
  Looks like he's trying to get out, sir.

– There's a cockroach in my soup!
  That's strange – it's usually a fly.

– There's a frog in my soup!
  Yes, sir. The fly's on holiday.

– There's a fly in my soup.
  That's all right, sir. There's a spider on your roll.

– Bring me a crocodile sandwich immediately.
  I'll make it snappy, sir.

– What do you charge for dinner?
  £5 a head, sir.
  Very well. Just bring me an ear.

– What's in this Hungarian Goulash?
  Only genuine Hungarians, sir.

– What's wrong with this fish?
  Long time, no sea.

– There's a fly playing about in my saucer!
  Yes, sir. Next week he hopes to be playing in the cup.

– This plate's dirty.
  The thumb mark's mine but the egg-stain's from yesterday.

– There's a fly in my alphabet soup!
  I expect he's learning to read.

– There's a fly in my soup!
  The little rascals don't care what they eat, do they?

– There's a fly in my soup!
  Yes, the chef used to be a tailor.

– There's a fly in my soup!
  That's not a fly – it's the last customer. The chef's a witch-doctor.

– what do you call this?
That's bean soup, sir.
I don't care what it's been – what is it now?

– send the chef here. I wish to complain about this disgusting meal.
I'm afraid you'll have to wait, sir. He's just popped out for his dinner.

– I'll have the pie, please.
Anything with it, sir?
If it's anything like last time I'd better have a hammer and chisel.

– do you call this a three-course meal?
That's right, sir. Two chips and a pea.

– I'll have my bill now.
How did you find your steak, sir?
Oh, I just moved the potato and there it was.

– this soup tastes funny.
So why don't you laugh?

– what do you call this?
Cottage pie, sir.
Well, I've just bitten on a piece of the door.

– there's a dead fly in my soup.
What do you expect for 5p – a live one?

– Waiter, would you say you were an independent-minded person?
I would, indeed, sir. I don't take orders from anyone.

– Do you play tennis?
Oh, yes. I really know how to serve.

– There's a fly in my soup!
Don't worry, sir, he won't drink much.

– There's a spider in my soup!
Oh, really? That's 10p extra.

– This soup is terrible! Call the manager!
He won't eat it either, sir.

Ghost Gags

Who said 'Shiver me timbers!' on the ghost ship?
    The skeleton crew.

Why are a monster's fingers never more than eleven inches long?
    'Cos if they were twelve inches they'd be a foot.

Why is a turkey like an evil little creature?
    'Cos it's always a-gobblin' . . .

Where did Dracula keep his money?
    In a blood bank.

How does a witch tell the time?
    With a witch watch.

Why was Frankenstein never lonely?
    He was good at making friends.

Why did the skeleton go to the party?
    For a rattling good time!

Can a toothless vampire still bite you?
    No, but he can give you a nasty suck!

Why did the landlord of a wine bar refuse to serve gin to a ghost?
    'Cos he didn't have a licence to serve spirits.

What do ghosts like to play at parties?
    Haunt and seek.

'Don't eat with your fingers, dear' said the Mummy ghost to the little ghost. 'Use the shovel!'

Why did the baby monster push his father in the freezer?
    'Cos he wanted frozen pop.

Why are monsters forgetful?
    'Cos everything you tell them goes in one ear and out the others.

What is the best way to speak to a monster?
    From a long distance.

Where do monsters study?
    At ghoullege.

What do you call a friendly and handsome monster?
    A failure.

What has webbed feet and fangs?
    Count Quackula.

Why did Frankenstein's monster give up boxing?
    'Cos he didn't want to spoil his looks.

Why is Baron Frankenstein good fun at parties?
    'Cos he'll have you in stitches.

What do vampires cross the sea in?
    Blood vessels.

What is the best thing to do if a monster breaks down your front door?
    Run out through the back door.

What do monsters put on their roast beef?
    Grave-y.

What is a ghost's favourite drink?
    Demonade.

Did you hear about the stupid ghost?
    He climbed over walls.

Where do monsters travel?
    From ghost to ghost.

Why is Dracula so unpopular?
    'Cos he's a pain in the neck.

What did the vampire say to the dentist after he'd had all his teeth out?
    'Fangs for the memory!'

What do ghosts eat for dinner?
  Spook-etti.

What do short-sighted ghosts wear?
  Spook-tacles.

What did the Mummy Ghost say to the Baby Ghost?
  'Spook when you're spooken to.'

What do you call a drunken ghost?
  A methylated spirit.

Why couldn't the skeleton go to the ball?
  'Cos he had nobody to go with.

What do you do if you see a skeleton running across a busy road?
  Jump out of your skin and join him.

What do ghosts wear in the rain?
  Boo-oots and ghoul-oshes.

What do ghosts eat for breakfast?
  Dreaded wheat.

Why do ghosts like tall buildings?
  'Cos they have lots of scarecases.

What did the ghost guard say?
  'Who ghosts there?'

What do baby ghosts like chewing?
  Booble gum.

What did the baby ghost say when he wanted his favourite food?
  'I scream.'

Why did the baby monster push his father's finger into the light socket?
  'Cos he wanted Fizzy Pop.

What is the best way for a ghost-hunter to keep fit?
  He must exorcise regularly.

What do you call twin ghosts who keep ringing doorbells?
  Dead ringers.

Why are ghosts bad at telling lies?
 'Cos you can always see through them.

Why are vampires mad?
 'Cos they're bats.

What did the policeman say when he met the three-headed monster?
 ' 'Ello, 'Ello, 'Ello!'

What is a gargoyle?
 Something you take for a sore throat.

Where do you find giant snails?
 On the end of giants' fingers.

What is the monsters' favourite football team?
 Slitherpool.

What is Dracula's favourite pudding?
 Leeches and scream.

What is Dracula's favourite breakfast?
 Readyneck.

The Ghost teacher was showing the Kiddie Ghosts how to walk through walls. 'Now did you all follow that, Ghosties?' she asked. 'If not, I'll just go through it again...'
'

Why does Dracula live in a coffin?
 'Cos the rent is low.

Who put their point of view at the ghosts' press conference?
 A spooksman.

What does a monster eat after a tooth extraction?
 The dentist.

What trees do monsters like best?
 Cemetrees.

If you were surrounded by Dracula, Frankenstein's monster, a ghost and a werewolf, what would you be hoping?
 That you were at a fancy-dress party.

Where do witches live by the sea?
Sand-witch.

Why do witches fly about on broomsticks?
Because vacuum-cleaners don't have long enough cords.

What is Dracula's favourite sport?
Batminton.

What is a ghost's favourite music?
Haunting melodies.

What job did the lady ghost have on an aeroplane?
An air ghostess.

Where do ghosts like to swim?
In the Dead Sea.

Why was the Mummy Ghost worried about Baby Ghost?
'Cos he was always in good spirits.

What is the ghosts' favourite Western Town?
Tombstone.

What do ghosts like to ride on at the fair-ground?
The Roller Ghoaster.

Where do ghosts live?
In a far distant terror-tory.

What is the ghosts' favourite stretch of water?
Lake Erie.

What did one ghost say to the other ghost?
'I simply do not believe in people.'

Was Dracula ever married?
No, he was a bat-chelor.

What is the ghosts' favourite pub?
The Horse and Gloom.

How does a ghost count?
One *Boo* Three Four Five Six Seven *Hate* Nine Frigh*ten*!

What did the Hungarian ghost have for lunch?
Ghoulash.

The Old Jokes At Home

'Why is your brother called Flannel?'
  'Cos he shrinks from washing!'

One little boy's family were so poor they used sugar sacks for nappies. He had to take the rough with the smooth. He was ten before he realized his name wasn't Tate & Lyle...

'Any luck with your advertisement for a husband?'
  'Yes, I've had sixteen replies. And they all say the same thing.'
  'What's that?'
'You can have mine!'
  'You can have mine!'

Why did the comedian's wife sue him for divorce?
  He kept trying to joke her to death.

'My Dad's in hospital. Last week he went down the garden to cut a cabbage for our dinner. The knife slipped and he stabbed himself.'
  'Gosh! What did your Mum do?
  'Opened up a tin of peas.'

'Mummy, may I leave the table?'
  'Well, you certainly can't take it with you!'

Despite his big brother's warnings, little Jasper insisted on walking along the top of a high wall. 'Well,' said big brother, 'if you fall and break both your legs, don't come running to me!'

'Daddy, I don't like cheese with holes.'
  'Just eat the cheese and leave the holes on the side of your plate.'

'Grandma, what's a weapon?'
  'A weapon is something you fight with.'
  'You mean like Grandad?'

'Kevin,' said little Ernie to his big brother, 'what does that big L on the car mean?'

'It means I'm learning to drive,' said Kevin.

A few weeks later Kevin had passed his test and was preparing to take his car to France; to the rear of the car he affixed the customary GB sticker.

'Kevin,' said little Ernie, 'does GB mean you're getting better?'

Sandra and Simon were arguing furiously over the breakfast table. 'Oh, you're stupid!' shouted Simon. 'Simon!' said their father, 'that's quite enough of that! Now, say you're sorry.'

'All right,' said Simon. 'Sandra, I'm sorry you're stupid.'

'Is your brother fat?'

I'll say! He's so fat he had mumps for three weeks before we found out!'

'Mummy, I don't want to go to France!'
'Shut up and start swimming . . .'

'Mummy, why can't we have a dustbin like everyone else?'
'Shut up and keep eating.'

The family seated in a restaurant had finished their dinners when Father called over the waiter. 'Yes, sir?' said the waiter.

'My son has left quite a lot of meat on his plate,' explained Father. 'Could you give me a bag so that I can take it home for the dog?'

'Gosh, Dad!' exclaimed the excited boy. 'Have we got a dog then?'

'How was it you were born in Sheffield?
' 'Cos my mother wanted me near her.'

Why was the Egyptian girl worried?
'Cos her Daddy was a Mummy.

Why did Grandpa put wheels on his rocking-chair?
'Cos he wanted to Rock'n'Roll.

'Katie, have you finished your alphabet soup?'
'Not yet, Mum. I'm only up to the Ks . . .'

Little Helen and her Mummy were in the cinema. After half an hour or so of the main feature, Helen whispered 'Mummy, is your seat comfortable?' 'Yes, thank you, dear,' replied her mother. 'Can you see the screen all right?' 'Yes, thank you, dear.' 'Are you sitting in a draught?' 'No, dear.' 'Then can I swap places with you?'

Did you hear about the three daughters in the kitchen?

One washed up, one dried up, and the third picked up the pieces.

'Mrs Finnegan!' said her neighbour crossly, 'Have you told your son to stop imitating me?'

'Yes, I've told him to stop acting the fool!'

'Stephen, it's time for your violin lesson.'

'Oh, fiddle!'

'Stephen, it's time for your drum lesson.'

'Oh, smashing!'

Little brother: 'Look, Sis, I've got a pack of cards.'
Big sister: 'Big deal!'

Father: 'Well, Susie, did you have a good time at school today?'
Susie: 'Only home time!'

For her tenth birthday Jessica received a bottle of perfume and a recorder. For supper that evening were two old friends of her parents, and as she sat between them at table she confided, 'If you hear a little noise and smell a little smell — it's me!'

'Steve, you've been fighting again, haven't you?'

'Yes, Mum.'

'You must try and control your temper. Didn't I tell you to count up to 10?'

'Yes, but Vic's Mum only told him to count up to five so he hit me first!'

Amos asked his mother whether they could have a video.

'I'm afraid we can't afford one,' sighed his mother.

But on the following day in came Amos, staggering beneath the weight of a brand-new video.

'How on earth did you pay for that?' gasped his mother.

'Easy, Mum,' replied Amos. 'I sold the television!'

Why did Henry put a frog in his sister's bed?

'Cos he couldn't catch a mouse.

A Yorkshire man whose wife died instructed the stonemason to carve on her headstone the words 'She Was Thine'. But when he went to inspect the result the mason had put 'She Was Thin'. The grieving widower angrily informed the artisan that he had left an E out. 'Sorry,' said the stonemason, 'Ah'll put it reet for thee, never fear. A'll put t'E in tomorrow.' But when the widower went to see the tombstone the legend now read, 'E, She Was Thin . . .'

'I'm divorcing my wife for smoking in bed.'
  'That doesn't sound all that serious.'
  'Oh, she doesn't smoke cigarettes.'
  'What does she smoke, then?'
  'Bacon.'

It didn't take long to wind up Grandad's estate. All he left was a cuckoo clock.

'Will you love me when I'm old and ugly?'
  'Darling, of course I do.'

'We never wanted for anything when I was a kid.'
  'That's nice.'
  'All except my Uncle Colin, that is. He was wanted for burglary.'

When Mr Maxwell's wife left him he couldn't sleep. She took the bed.

'Grandad, is it fun being ninety-nine?'
  'Certainly it is. If I wasn't ninety-nine I'd be dead.'

The housewife answered a knock on the door and found a total stranger standing on the step. 'Excuse me for disturbing you, madam,' he said politely, 'but I pass your house every morning on my way to work, and I've noticed that every day you appear to be hitting your son on the head with a loaf of bread.'
  'That's right.'
  'Every day you hit him on the head with a loaf of bread, and yet this morning you were clouting him with a chocolate gateau . . .?'
  'Well, today's his birthday.'

Jack met Claud in the street and noticed that Claud was carrying a small parcel.
  'Been shopping then, Claud?' he asked.
  'Yes,' replied Claud, 'I've just been to the chemist to buy a present for the wife's birthday tomorrow.'
  'Oh, yes?' said Jack, 'what did you get her, then?'
  'A bottle of toilet water. Very expensive – this little bottle cost me £15!'
  '£15 for a bottle of toilet water?!' said Jack in amazement. 'Why don't you come home with me? You can have all you want for nothing!'

'I forgot my sister's birthday.'
  'Crikey! What did she say?'
  'Nothing . . . for six weeks.'

The son of a businessman had agreed to join the family business, and on his very first day at the factory his father took him on to the roof and said, 'Now, my son, I am about to give you your first lesson in business. Stand on the edge of the roof.'

'On the edge, Dad?' said the puzzled youth.

'On the very edge.'

'Very well, Dad,' and the obedient son did as he was told.

'Now, when I say "Jump!"' said his father, 'I want you to jump.'

'But it's a twenty foot drop!'

'My boy,' said the father, 'you want to learn the business, don't you?'

'Yes, Dad.'

'And you trust me?'

'Yes, Dad.'

'Right. Then do as I say – "Jump!"'

And the boy jumped, only to crash painfully to the ground twenty feet below. His father ran down the stairs to where the youth was lying, bruised, battered and winded.

'Now, my son,' said his father, 'you have just learned your first lesson in business – *never trust anybody*!'

Mrs McLean had such an ugly baby she didn't push the pram – she pulled it.

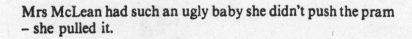
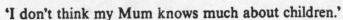

'I don't think my Mum knows much about children.'

'Why do you say that?'

'Because she always puts me to bed when I'm wide awake and gets me up when I'm sleepy.'

'I hear you've got a new baby sister,' said Jonathan to his friend William.

'Yeah.'

'Is she fun to play with?'

'Nah.'

'Well, why don't you change her?'

'We can't,' explained William, 'we've used her a week already.'

'How old is your Grandad?'

'I dunno, but we've had him a long time.'

'There were fifteen of us kids when I was a youngster.'

'Fifteen! That's a big family.'

'It sure is. There were so many nappies hanging up we had a rainbow in the hall.'

It is truly said that children brighten a home – they never turn the lights off.

'One of my ancestors fell at Waterloo.'

'Really?'

'Somebody pushed him off platform five.'

'My sister's taking cookery lessons,' said little Nick. 'Last night she made some soup – ugh! – it was awful. This morning some pygmies came over from Africa to dip their darts into it ... and for lunch today she gave us cold boiled ham. That's ham boiled in cold water.'

'My Dad,' said the vain girl loftily, 'says that when I grow up I'll be a raving beauty.'

'Why?' asked her catty friend, 'is he going to put you in a lunatic asylum?'

'Certainly not! He says I'm sure to have lots of men at my feet.'

'Very likely – chiropodists!'

'Hello, Ginger!' her brother called cheerily to his sister.

'Don't call me Ginger!' she snapped furiously. 'My hair is the colour of gold.'

'Yeah,' he replied with a jeer, 'twenty-two carrots!'

The welfare worker was paying his first visit to a problem family in his area, and the door was opened by a small girl.

'What'ja want?' she asked suspiciously.

'Is your mother in?' asked the welfare officer.

'Nah,' answered the moppet, 'she's in a 'ome for nutters, ain't she?'

'Oh ... well, is your father in?'

'Nah. 'E's in the nick, ain't 'e?'

'Oh dear ... what about your brother?'

'E's in Borstal.'

'Good gracious. Is there a big sister locking after you, then?'

'She was until last week but now she's at Oxford University.'

'Your mother's in an asylum, your father's in gaol, your brother's in Borstal and your sister's at university?'

'S' right.'

'What is she studying?'

'She ain't. They're studyin' 'er!'

Where does a goose come from? A gooseberry bush.

The neighbour was congratulating Mrs Smith on the arrival of her new baby. 'And I bet your Peter's pleased,' she said, referring to Mrs Smith's six year old son.

'Oh yes, he is,' replied the new mother, 'now he can stop teasing the cat.'

Father's Day is just like Mother's Day only you don't have to spend so much ...

It was local election time and the candidate was calling round all the houses in his area. At one house the door was answered by a small boy. 'Tell me, young man,' said the politician, 'is your Mummy in the Labour Party or the Conservative Party?'

'Neither,' said the imp, 'she's in the lavvy.'

DEADLY THUD!!

Old Granny Parkinson had won over half a million pounds on the football pools, but as she was a frail little body her family were concerned that the shock of hearing the news might prove too much for her. Accordingly, they called in the family doctor to ask his advice. 'I'll tell her if you like,' said the doctor. 'I'll lead up to it gradually.' The family accepted his offer gratefully, and showed him into the old lady's bedroom. The doctor pretended to give her a routine examination and then began to chat generally of this and that, carefully leading the conversation round to money.

'Tell me Mrs Parkinson,' he said, 'what would you do if you suddenly came into half a million pounds?'

'Half a million?' said the old lady reflectively, 'well, you've always been very good to me, doctor, so I think I'd give half of it to you.'

And the doctor immediately collapsed and died of shock.

'Mum, can I have 10p for being good?'
'All right, but I wish you could be good-for-nothing!'

'Mum, can I go out and play?'
'What in those clothes?'
'No – in the park.'

Little Jackie's mother was on the telephone to the boy's dentist. 'I don't understand it,' she complained, 'I thought his treatment would only cost £10, but you have charged me £40.'

'It is usually £10, madam,' agreed the dentist, 'but Jackie yelled so loudly that three of my other patients ran away!'

Alfie had been listening to his sister practising her singing.
'Sis,' he said, 'I wish you'd sing Christmas carols.'
'That's nice of you, Alfie,' she said, 'why?'
'Then I'd only have to hear you once a year!'

One small boy was telling his friend about the mysteries of his big sister's make-up. 'She's worried about what she calls her "complexion",' he said, 'so she puts lemon-juice on her face.'
'Lemon juice!?' exclaimed his pal, 'no wonder she always looks so sour!'

'Louisa,' asked her small brother, 'can you help me with my maths homework?'
'Certainly not,' replied Louisa indignantly, 'it wouldn't be right.'
'Maybe not,' said the boy, 'but you could at least try ...!'

Julian was the most advanced boy in his class. He sat in the front.

Cliff had just formed his own pop group, and his little brother said one day, 'Cliff, I wish you and your group could be on the telly!'

'You think we're good, eh?'

'Then I could turn you off!'

'My sister's just got engaged to an Irish chap.'

'Oh, really?'

'No – O'Reilly!'

'What are you learning at school now, Brenda?' asked her Grannie.

'French, German and we've just started Algebra.'

'Really?' said the old lady, impressed. 'I used to learn French and German but I've never heard anyone speak Algebra.'

'Dad, the careers master said that with a mind like mine I should study criminal law.'

'That's wonderful, son. I'm proud of you.'

'He said I had a criminal mind.'

'So,' thundered Stanley's furious father, 'you've been expelled from university, have you?'

'Yes, Dad. I am a fugitive from a brain gang.'

'I saw you kissing my sister last night!' jeered the brat to the embarrassed teenage lad.

'All right, all right! Not so loud,' said the youth. 'Here's fifty pence to keep your mouth shut.'

'Cor, thanks! Wait a minute and I'll give you twenty pence change.'

'Twenty pence change? What for?'

'I like to be fair,' said the youngster, 'and it's the same price for everybody!'

Rebecca's mother found her in her bedroom in floods of tears. 'What on earth is the matter, dear?' she enquired anxiously.

'I've just had a letter from my boyfriend,' sobbed the distraught girl, 'and he's only put two kisses on the bottom!'

'So?'

'I hate being double-crossed!'

Alan had just asked his father for an increase in his pocket money.

'What do you want more money for?' demanded his father.

'Well, I'm thirteen now, Dad,' explained the lad, 'and I'm thinking of going out with girls.'

'Girls? What kind of girls?'

'Girls with money.'

'Mum, now that I'm fifteen, can I wear lipstick and mascara and perfume and pluck my eyebrows and get my hair waved?'

'No, James, you may not.'

'How are you getting on with your football, Peter?'

'Well, Dad, pretty good. The sports master said I was one of the team's greatest drawbacks!'

At a party the old lady was bemoaning the behaviour of the youth of today. 'Look at the girl over there,' she complained, 'I don't know what young girls are coming to! She's wearing boy's jeans, a boy's shirt, and that haircut is so boyish – you wouldn't know she was a girl at all, would you?'

'Well, as it happens, I would,' came the reply, 'because she is my daughter.'

'Oh dear,' said the old lady embarrassed, 'I'm so sorry – I didn't know you were her father.'

'I'm not. I'm her mother.'

The eldest of six boys had just passed his driving-test. His brothers gathered round enviously to congratulate him, to which he replied graciously, 'Thanks, boys. And I tell you what: now that I've got my own car, you can all move up one bike!'

'Larry! Come here!' said his furious mother, putting the telephone down. 'I've just had a call from Mrs Harrison about your behaviour to her Doris at the school dance last night. You wretched, rude boy!'

'I was nice to her, Mum, really I was!' protested the youth. 'I even paid her a compliment when we had a dance.'

'Did you, indeed?' said his mother grimly. 'And what exactly did you say?'

'I said, "Gosh, Doris, you sweat less than any fat girl I've ever danced with"!'

'Daddy, do you think I'm vain?'

'Vain, dear? No, I wouldn't say so. Why do you ask?'

'Because most girls as pretty as me are.'

'You stupid girl!' said her Mother crossly, 'didn't I tell you to watch that saucepan and notice when it boiled over?'

'But I did, Mum. It was half-past ten.'

'I've, made the chicken soup for lunch today,' said big sister proudly to her small brother.

'Thank goodness for that,' said the wart, 'I thought it was for us.'

Sister: 'Try some of my sponge cake.'
Brother: (*Nibbling on a piece*) 'It's a bit tough, isn't it?'
Sister: 'Yes, I can't understand it. I bought the sponge fresh from the chemist this morning!'

Brother: 'You've just backed the car over my bike!'
Sister: 'Serve you right. You shouldn't leave it in the hall.'

Russell couldn't swim, yet when he fell into the river and was floundering around desperately, what did his callous friend say from the safety of the bank? 'Russell – if you don't come up for the third time, can I have your sheath knife?'

Susannah was watching her big sister covering her face with cream. 'What's that for?' she asked.

'To make me beautiful,' came the reply. Susannah watched in silence as her sister then wiped her face clean.

'Doesn't work, does it?' was the moppet's comment.

Harold's big sister was almost in tears over her cooking. 'I don't know what to do,' she moaned, looking at yet another unsuccessful batch of cakes. 'What can I do to make my cakes light?'

'I tell you what, Sis,' said Harold helpfully, 'why not soak them in paraffin!'

'Are you from a large family?'

'Yes, I'm the fourteenth of thirteen children.'

'Are you married?'   'What does your Dad do?'

'Yes.'   'He's a Government artist.'

'Children?'   'What does he draw?'

'Three boys and six girls.'   'The dole!'

'That's nine altogether.'

'No – one at a time.'

'My boyfriend', said Miss Vanity, on her nineteenth birthday, 'says I have a skin like a peach!'

'Is that so?' said her insolent little brother. 'And who wants to look like a nineteen-year-old peach . . . ?!'

'What would you like for your birthday, Sis?'

'I'd like a dress to match the colour of my eyes.'

'Would you? Where am I going to get a bloodshot frock?'

'My boyfriend says I look like a dishy Italian!' said Miss Conceited.

'He's right,' said her brother.

'Sophia Loren?'

'No – spaghetti!'

'Is my dinner hot?' asked the excessively late husband.

'It should be,' said his furious wife, 'it's been on the fire since seven o'clock!'

'I think it's true when they say television causes violence,' said the small boy.

'What makes you think that?'

''Cos every time I switch it on my Dad clouts me.'

The insurance salesman was trying to persuade a housewife to take out a life insurance policy. 'Now supposing your husband were to die,' he said, 'what would you get?'

'Oh, a Labrador, I think,' replied the housewife. 'They're always good company!'

'Now, Sam,' said the wife to her rather uncouth husband, 'we've got company to tea on Sunday, so I want you on your best behaviour.'

'What are you on about, woman?' demanded the aggrieved husband.

'Well, for a start, I don't want you drinking your tea out of the saucer like you usually do.'

'Then what shall I drink it out of?'

'Out of the cup, of course!' said his wife, exasperated.

'Out of the cup? But if I do that I'll get the spoon in my eye!'

Damien was being severely ticked off by his father for fighting. 'Now, Damien,' said his angry parent, 'this will not do! You must learn that you can't have everything you want in this life. There must always be give and take.'

'But there was, Dad!' protested the aggressive youngster. 'I gave him a black eye and took the apple!'

'Eat up all you spinach, Jemima. It'll put colour in your cheeks.'

'But who wants to have green cheeks?'

'Last night my sister fell out of her bedroom window.'

'Golly! Did she hurt herself?'

'No – we live in a bungalow.'

'Donovan! How many more times? Don't eat with your knife!'

'But, Mum! My fork's got a leak!'

'Dad, there's a man at the door collecting for the new swimming-pool.'

'Give him a glass of water!'

'Mum! All the kids at school call me Bighead!'

'Never mind what those stupid children say, dear. Now, go to the greengrocers and get me five pounds of potatoes in your cap.'

'When I was a lad,' said Grandpa, 'all the railway trains were steam-powered.'

'Really, Grandpa?' said his wide-eyed grandchild. 'Does that mean they were in black and white?'

And do you like your new school?' asked grandmother fondly.

'Well, sometimes, Granny,' said little Jacob.

'And what times are those?'

'When it's shut!'

Lines for Loonies

These are the graves of three poor sinners,
Who died after eating Grange School dinners.

Doctor Bell fell down the well,
And broke his collar-bone;
A doctor should attend the sick,
And leave the well alone!

There once was a great big cat,
Who swallowed a whole cricket bat;
He swallowed the ball,
The stumps, bails and all —
So the cricket team clobbered him flat!

Here come the bride,
Sixty inches wide;
Look at her now as she wobbles,
Up the centre aisle.
Here comes the groom,
Biting his nails in gloom,
He's looking as thin as a dressmaking pin,
And never again will he smile.

There once was an old man of Ealing,
Who had an expectorant feeling.
But a sign on the door,
Said DON'T SPIT ON THE FLOOR,
So he looked up and spat on the ceiling.

Little birdie flying high,
Dropped a message from the sky.
'Oh,' said the farmer wiping his eye,
'Isn't it lucky cows don't fly!'

I like my little school,
It's a nice little school,
It's built of bricks and plaster.
The only nasty thing,
In my nice little school,
Is the cross-eyed, bald-headed maths master!

Latin's a dead language,
As dead as dead can be;
It killed off all the Romans,
And now it's killing me!

*(The author's Latin master at school was
for some obscure reason known as Charlie,
which gave rise to the following ode —
substitute your own teacher's
name suitably Latinized.)*
Charlibus sittibus
On the deskinorum.
Deskibus collapsibus —
Charlie on the floorum!

Julius Caesar broke his beezer,
Playing squash with a lemon-squeezer!

Don't eat school dinners,
Just throw them aside.
A lot of kids didn't,
A lot of kids died.
The meat's made of iron,
The spuds are of steel,
And if *they don't* kill you,
The pudding will!

(To the tune of Frère Jacques)
School dinners! School dinners!
Concrete chips! Concrete chips!
Semolina pudding! Semolina pudding!
I feel sick — bathroom quick!

There was a young girl called Nelly,
Who was always watching the telly.
Her eyes grew square,
But she didn't care,
So they packed her off to Pwllheli.

(To the tune of My Darling Clementine)
Build a bonfire! Build a bonfire!
Put the teachers on the top;
Put the Headmaster in the middle,
Then burn the flippin' lot!

We go up and we go down,
We don't care if the school falls down;
No more English,
No more French,
No more sitting on the old school fence.
If the teacher interferes,
Tie her up and box her ears;
If that doesn't serve her right,
Blow her up with dynamite!

Row, row, row your boat,
Gently down the stream;
Throw the teacher overboard,
Then you'll hear her scream!

November the Fifth has come and gone,
But thoughts of it still linger.
I held a banger in my hand –
Has anybody seen my finger?

The Dachshund's a dog of German descent;
Whose tail never knew where his front end went.

Mary had a little lamb,
It had a touch of colic.
She gave it brandy twice a day –
And now it's alcoholic.

Mary had a little lamb,
It leapt around in hops.
It gambolled in the road one day,
And finished up as chops.

Mary Rose
Sat on a pin.
Mary Rose.

'Twas in a cafe that they first met,
Romeo and Juliet.
And there he first ran into debt –
For Rome-owed for what Juli-ate!

A famous painter
Met his death;
Because he couldn't
Draw his breath.

Martini Hand Is Frozen

Knock! Knock!

— Who's there?
Adolf.
Adolf who?
A dolf ball hid me in der moud and I can't dalk proper!

—Who's there?
Soup.
Soup who?
Soup-erman!

— Who's there?
Egbert.
Egbert who?
Egbert no bacon.

— Who's there?
Cows.
Cows who?
Cows go 'moo' not 'who'!

— Who's there?
Noah.
Noah who?
Noah good place to eat?

— Who's there?
Bet.
Bet who?
Bet you don't know who's knocking on your door!

— Who's there?
Juno.
Juno who?
Juno what the time is — my watch is broken?

— Who's there?
Europe.
Europe who?
Europe early this morning.

— Who's there?
Sal.
Sal who?
(Sing) Sal-ong way to Tipperary . . .

— Who's there?
Arfur.
Arfur who?
Arfur got.

— Who's there?
Police.
Police who?
Police let me in — it's cold out here!

— Who's there?
Mickey.
Mickey who?
Mickey's stuck in the door!

— Who's there?
Wendy.
Wendy who?
(Sing) Wendy red, red robin comes bob, bob, bobbin' along

— Who's there?
Luke. Luke who?
Luke through the keyhole and you'll see.

— Who's there?
Ken.
Ken who?
Ken I come in?

— Who's there?
Dishwasher.
Dishwasher who?
Dishwashn't de way I shpoke before I had falsh teeth!

— Who's there?
Aardvark.
Aardvark who?
(Sing) Aardvark a million miles for one of your smiles, My Mammy . . .

— Who's there?
Bella.
Bella who?
Bella not-a work so I knock-a on-a de door!

— Who's there?
Dismay.
Dismay who?
Dismay be a joke but it doesn't make me laugh!

— Who's there?
Toby.
Toby who?
Toby or not to be . . .

— Who's there?
Martini.
Martini who?
Martini hand is frozen so let me in!

— Who's there?
Rupert.
Rupert who?
Rupert your left arm in, your left arm out . . .

— Who's there?
Dawn.
Dawn who?
Dawn leave me standing out here in the cold. Or (Sing) 'Dawn laugh at me 'cos I'm a fool . . .'

— Who's there?
Capfitz.
Capfitz who?
Capfitz you not who.

— Who's there?
Zephyr.
Zephyr who?
Zephyr de doctor, I got a code id de node.

— Who's there?
Amos.
Amos who?
Amosquito.

— Who's there?
Owl.
Owl who?
Owl you know unless you open the door?

— Who's there?
Anna.
Anna who?
Annather mosquito.

— Who's there?
Phyllis.
Phyllis who?
Phyllis up with a glass of water — I'm parched.

— Who's there?
Arpo.
Arpo who?
Arpo ain't got no 'andle.

— Who's there?
Doctor.
Doctor who?
Doctor Foster — I've just come from Gloucester.

School Reports

'Anna, who was the first woman?'
  'Don't know, Miss.'
  'Come along, come along. It was something to do with an apple . . .'
  'Oh, yes, Miss. Granny Smith!'

'What did Sir think of your homework?'
  'He took it like a lamb.'
  'Really? What did he say?'
  'Baa!'

Tommy was late for school yet again, this time coming out with a spectacularly lurid and transparently false excuse.
  'Now then, Tommy,' said his teacher, 'do you know what happens to children who tell lies?'
  'Yes, Miss' said the impertinent lad. 'They become teachers!'

This year's class outing will be to the seaside!	Hooray!
It will cost £40 . . .	Boo!
. . . by train or £1.50 on the coach!	Hooray!
The headmaster will be coming . . .	Boo!
. . . to see us off!	Hooray!
The weather will be wet and windy . . .	Boo!
. . .in Russia and warm and sunny in Britain!	Hooray!
There will be no swimming . . .	Boo!
. . .until we get there!	Hooray!
Lunch will be boiled fish and cabbage . . .	Boo!
. . . for me and crisps and Coke and Smarties for you!	Hooray!
There will be a visit to the museum . . .	Boo!
. . . or if preferred to the Funfair!	Hooray!
But we must be back by twelve o'clock . . .	Boo!
. . . at midnight!	Hooray!

'Sarah,' said the teacher, 'what is a cannibal?'
  'Dunno, Miss.'
  'Well, if you were to eat your parents, what would you be?'
  'An orphan, Miss.'

'Viola, can you spell "banana" for me?'
'Well, Sir, I know how to start but I don't know when to stop.'

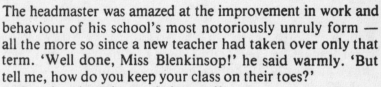 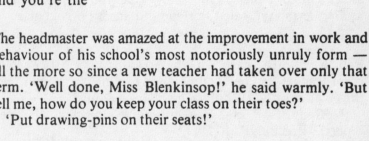

'How old would you say I am, Francis?' the teacher asked.
'Forty, Sir,' said the boy promptly.
'You seem very sure,' said the puzzled teacher. 'What makes you think I am forty?'
'My big brother's twenty, Sir,' replied the boy 'and you're twice as daft as he is!'

'Melanie!' said the teacher sharply, 'you've been doing Rebecca's homework for her again! I recognized your handwriting in her exercisebook.'
'No, I haven't, Miss, declared Melanie. 'It's just that we both use the same pencil!'

'Mum, I don't wanna go to school! I don't wanna go to school!'
'Now, dear, you must go, and for two very good reasons. First, you're fifty-six years of age and second you're the Headmaster!'

The headmaster was amazed at the improvement in work and behaviour of his school's most notoriously unruly form — all the more so since a new teacher had taken over only that term. 'Well done, Miss Blenkinsop!' he said warmly. 'But tell me, how do you keep your class on their toes?'
'Put drawing-pins on their seats!'

'Jarvis — I hope I didn't see you copying just then : . .?'
'I hope you didn't as well!'

'Philip,' asked the chemistry mistress, 'what is HNO_3?'
'Oh, er . . . just a minute, Miss . . . er . . . it's on the tip of my tongue, Miss . . .'
'Well in that case — spit it out. It's nitric acid!'

'Theo, why were you absent from school yesterday?'
'Oh, er, I wasn't well, Miss. Had a bit of a temperature.'
'I see. And do you have a note from your Mother or your Father?'
'No, Miss.'
'I shall expect to see one tomorrow. Is that clear?'
'Yes. Miss.'
Next day Theo handed in the following note: 'Dear Miss, Theo was absent from skool on Toosday on account of a cold. Yours faithfully, My Father.'

'Selena, why are you late this time?'
'Sorry, Sir, but I was in good time walking along the High Street until I saw a road sign that said Go Slow. So I did!'

What must you pay when you go to school?
Attention.

P.E. Teacher: 'Alison, you're hopeless at sports. You'll never come first in anything.'
Alison: 'I'm first every day in the dinner queue, Miss!'

The primary class had been told to draw a scene representing the flight into Egypt. One little tot proudly displayed a drawing of a Jumbo Jet containing the three members of the Holy Family — but also a fourth figure. 'When I said "flight" I didn't quite mean a jet-plane,' said the teacher. 'However, we'll let that pass for now. But who is the fourth person on the plane?' To which the little one replied, 'That's Pontius Pilot!'

Andy came home from his first day at school weeping buckets. 'What's the matter, Andy?' asked his worried parents. 'It's the school dinner,' he sobbed. 'It was awful! I couldn't touch it, and I'm hungry!' 'I'm sure it can't have been that bad,' said his father. 'What was the dinner?' 'Worms and cow-muck!' came the astounding reply. Andy's mother immediately telephoned the school and spoke to the Headmistress. 'Andy's very upset about today's school meal,' she said. 'Can you tell me what it was?' 'Certainly,' said the Head. 'Spaghetti bolognaise!'

Paul was on the carpet in the Headmaster's office. 'Your form teacher has been complaining to me about you,' said the Head sternly. 'What have you been doing?'

'Nothing, Sir,' said Paul miserably, to which the Head replied, 'Precisely!'

In the changing room after a football match the P.E. master asked whether any of the boys had seen his glasses. 'I saw them on the pitch, Sir,' answered Harry.

'Well, why didn't you bring them in?' asked the teacher.

'I thought you didn't want them any more, Sir,' said Harry, 'so I stepped on them!'

'Gary, did your sister help you with this homework?'
'No, Miss. She did it all!'

'Philip, what does it mean when the barometer falls?'
'Er — the nail's come out of the wall, Miss?'

Geography Teacher: 'Monica, where are the Andes?'
Monica: 'At the end of your armies, Sir!'

Stewart owned a very small newt of which he was extremely fond, so much so that he couldn't bear to be parted from it even when going to school. One day his teacher spotted him at his desk gazing intently into a matchbox. 'What have you got there, Stewart?' demanded the teacher. 'It's a newt, Miss' replied the boy. 'Why do you keep it in a matchbox?' asked the teacher, to which Stewart replied, 'Because it's my newt!' (Minute)

'Miss! Miss! cried little Jamie, 'I just banged my fumb on the door!'

'Not "fumb", Jamie,' said the teacher. 'It's *th*umb!'

'Yes, Miss. And I banged my thinger as well!'

'Sir, you know you told us yesterday that a pound of feathers was the same as a pound of lead?'

'Yes. what about it?'

'My Dad said you were wrong. He said I should try tickling your toes with a pound of lead!'

'Our new P.E. master thinks that exercise is so good for you it'll solve all your problems.'

'I know. Doesn't matter what's wrong he reckons that gym'll fix it!'

I won't say our school-dinners are bad but even the dustbins have ulcers!

A girl was sent home by an angry teacher for not attending in school uniform. She returned half an hour later dripping wet. 'What's the meaning of this?' demanded her teacher. 'You told me to wear my school clothes,' said the miserable pupil, 'but they were in the wash!'

'Sir!' said Alexander. 'Empty Coke tins, fish-and-chip paper, plastic bag, used tissues, broken bottles, empty cardboard boxes — '

'Alexander!' snapped the teacher. 'You're talking rubbish again!'

'Now Frank,' said the weary maths master, 'if you had £7 in one pocket and £7 in another pocket, what would you have?'

'Someone else's trousers on!'

History teacher: 'Georgina, in the second World War the Germans conquered Poland, they conquered France, they conquered Belgium, Holland, Denmark and several other countries. But why didn't they conquer Britain?

Georgina: 'Er — 'cos they'd run out of conkers, Sir?'

'Why are you home from school so early, Jackie?'

'I was sent home, Mum, 'cos the boy next to me was smoking.'

'But if *he* was smoking why should *you* be sent home?'

'It was me that set him alight!'

A young shaver called Jimmy Mickey Rigsby was complaining to his mother about his new teacher. 'My name is Jimmy Mickey Rigsby, isn't it, Mum?' 'Yes, of course,' replied his mother soothingly. 'Why do you ask?' 'Well, my teacher says it's too long and just calls me Jimmy Rigsby.' 'What's wrong with that?' 'I don't like having the Mickey taken out of me!'

Teacher: 'Marian, what is the Order of the Bath?'
Marian: 'Well, miss, first there's little Ricky, then my sister Betty, then me.'

Jackie: 'Sir, do hams grow like plants, sir?'
Sir: 'No, of course they don't.'
Jackie: 'Then what's an "ambush", sir?'

The local vicar was paying a visit to the school, and visiting each classroom in turn. At one particular class he entered beaming, greeted the teacher and the children, and then said, 'Well, what shall I talk to you about?'

At which a small voice at the back growled, 'About five minutes!'

Miss: 'Jane, what comes after G?'
Jane: 'Whizz!'
Miss: 'Let's try again. What comes after U?'
Jane: 'The bogeyman!'
Miss: 'Last chance. What comes after T?'
Jane: 'Supper!'

Teacher: 'Stone, give me three reasons why you know the Earth to be round.'
Stone: 'Ma says so, Pa says so, and you say so!'

Teacher: 'You seem to be exceedingly ignorant, Williams. Have you read Dickens?'
Williams: 'No, sir.'
Teacher: 'Have you read Shakespeare?'
Williams: 'No, sir.'
Teacher: 'Well, what *have* you read?'
Williams: 'Er . . . er . . . I've red hair, sir.'

Teacher: 'Miles, what do you call someone who drives an automobile?'
Miles: 'Depends how close he misses you, sir.'

Teacher: 'Mason, what is the outer part of a tree called?'
Mason: 'Don't know, sir.'
Teacher: 'Bark, boy, bark!'
Mason: 'Woof-woof!'

Teacher: 'Where is the River Thames?'
Norman: 'You're the goegraphy master – you tell me!'

Teacher: 'In 1940, what were the Poles doing in Russia?'
Irene: 'Holding up the telegraph wires.'

Miss: 'Why do we put a hyphen in a bird-cage?'
Stella: 'For the parrot to perch on, miss.'

One small boy on his first day in school was being interviewed by the school secretary.

'Father's name?' asked the secretary, filling in a big official form.

'Same as mine,' answered the child, in some bewilderment.

'No, no, no,' said the secretary. 'I mean his Christian name.'

'Oh, I dunno, miss,' said the child.

'Well, what does your mother call him?'

'She doesn't call 'im nothin' – she likes 'im!'

Teacher: 'If eggs were 20p a dozen, how many would you get for 5p?'
Pupil: 'None.'
Teacher: 'None?'
Pupil: 'If I had 5p I'd get a bar of toffee crunch.'

Teacher: 'Why weren't you at school yesterday?'
Sean: 'I was sick.'
Teacher: 'Sick of what?'
Sean: 'Sick of school!'

Teacher: 'Kevin, why are you late yet again?'
Kevin: 'Oh, sir, I stopped two boys fighting.'
Teacher: 'How did you manage that?'
Kevin: 'I licked both of 'em!'

Miss: 'Rosemary, I wish you'd pay a little attention.'
Rosemary: 'I'm paying as little as I can, miss!'

'Raymond, in what battle was Admiral Lord Nelson killed?'
'His last one, sir.'

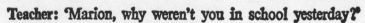

Teacher: 'Marion, why weren't you in school yesterday?'
Marion: 'I had a bad tooth, miss.'
Teacher: 'Oh, I'm sorry to hear that. Is it better now?'
Marion: 'Dunno, miss. I left it with the dentist.'

History master: 'Skinner, when did motor cars first appear on the streets?'
Skinner: 'In the reign of King John, sir.'
History master: 'In the reign of King John? How do you make that out?'
Skinner: 'Well, sir, you told us that King John was always grinding the people down with taxis.'

Judy was spotted by her form mistress with a large bulge in her cheek.

'Judith!' said the mistress sternly. 'What have you got in your mouth? Bring it here!'

'I wish I could, miss,' said poor Judith. 'It's a gumboil.'

'Who spilt that ink on the floor? Come on, own up . . . was it you, Faulkner?'

'I cannot tell a lie, sir. Yes, I done it.'

'Where's your grammar?'

'In bed with 'flu.'

'Maurice, if you bought 30 jam tarts for 20p, what would each one be?'

'Stale . . .'

A headmaster about to cane a particularly naughty boy said to him the time-honoured words, 'Bend down, boy – this is going to hurt me more than it will you.'

To which the lad replied, 'Can I wallop you then, sir?'

'What's your name, boy?'

'Henry.'

'Say "sir".'

'All right, Sir Henry . . .'

'Margaret, you mustn't use "a" before a plural – you say "a" horse, not "a" horses.'

'But, miss, the vicar's always saying "a-men" . . .'

Chemistry master: 'Robinson, give me the name of a liquid that won't freeze.'

Robinson: 'Hot water, sir?'

Teacher: 'Rosemary, what do we get from Germany?'

Rosemary: 'Germs?'

Cookery mistress: 'Gwyneth, how can we prevent food from going bad?'

Gwyneth: 'By eating it, miss.'

'Kevin, why are you always late?'

''Cos you're always ringing the bell before I get here!'

'Boy, why have you got cotton-wool in your ear? Is it infected?'

'No sir, but you said yesterday that everything you told me went in one ear and out of the other, so I'm trying to stop it!'

'Kevin, why are you late?'

'I must have over-washed.'

History mistress: 'Emma, name the Tudor monarchs.'

Emma: 'Yes, miss. Henry VII, Henry VIII, Edward VI, Mary, er . . . er . . .'

History mistress: 'Correct so far, Now who came after Mary?'

Emma: 'Er . . . the little lamb, miss?'

'David, your figures are so bad; that 9 looks like a 7.'

'It is a 7, sir.'

'Then why does it look like a 9?'

Teacher: 'Marcia, where are elephants found?'
Marcia: 'Dunno, miss. But they're so big I shouldn't think they're often lost, are they?'

School inspector: 'Would anyone like to ask me a question?'
Impertinent boy: 'When are you going?'

Teacher: 'Smith, what is moss?'
Smith: 'It's stuff that rolling stones don't gather, sir.'

Teacher: 'Gillian, what kinds of birds do we usually find in captivity?'
Gillian: 'Jail-birds, miss."

Teacher: 'Addison, can you tell me what nationality was Napoleon Bonaparte?'
Saunders: "Corsican!'

'How do you spell wrong?'
   'R-o-n-g.'
   'That's wrong.'
   'That's what you asked for, wasn't it?'

One unfortunate teacher started off a lesson with the following instruction: 'I want you all to give me a list of the lower animals, starting with Georgina Clark . . .'

'Did you hear that the Queen's going to open a tellycost in our school?'
   'What's a tellycost?'
   'About fifty quid . . .'

Teacher: 'Georgina, there was the Ice Age, then the Stone Age, What came next?'
Georgina: 'The saus-age!'

Music master: 'Brian, if "f" means forte, what does "ff" mean?'
Brian: 'Eighty!'

'If a quadruped has four legs and a biped has two legs, what is a zebra?'
   'A stri-ped!'

'Why is it you can never answer any of my questions?'
   'If I could there wouldn't be much point in my coming here!'

The arithmetic teacher had written 10.9 on the blackboard, and had then rubbed out the decimal point to show the effect of multiplying this number by ten.

'Johnson,' he asked, 'where is the decimal point now?'

'On the duster, sir!' came the reply.

And the English master was trying to explain the meaning of the word 'collision' to a class of small boys.

'If two boys ran into each other in the playground,' he said, 'what would the result be?'

'A fight, sir,' came the answer in chorus.

Dad: 'Bert, why are your school reports so bad lately?'

Bert: 'Oh, that's the teacher's fault, Dad.'

Dad: 'What do you mean, it's the teacher's fault? Your exam marks used to be always very good, and you've got the same teacher, haven't you?'

Bert: 'Yes, but I haven't got the brainiest boy in the class sitting next to me. Teacher's moved him!'

Teacher: 'Harrison what does Hastings 1066 mean to you?'

Harrison: 'William the Conqueror's telephone number, sir?'

Little Sammy Smith was absent from school one Wednesday afternoon. In class the following morning, his teacher said to him, 'Sammy Smith, were you playing football again yesterday afternoon?'

'No, sir,' said Sammy, 'and I've got a jar of tiddlers to prove it.'

Long after the rest of the school had gone into their classrooms, Alison was still running around in the playground. Her form mistress came out and said sharply, 'Alison, don't you know the bell has gone?'

'Well, Miss, I didn't take it!'

Dad: 'Well, Stephen, did you get a good place in your exams?'

Stephen: 'Yes, Dad – next to the radiator.'

Teacher: 'Adrian, which is farther away – America or the Moon?'

Jason: 'America – you can see the moon, but you can't see America.'

Art master: 'Patricia, I told the class to draw a horse and cart, but you've only drawn a horse.'

Patricia: 'Yes, sir – the horse will draw the cart.'

Art master: 'Patricia, I told the class to draw a cow eating grass, but you've only drawn a cow.'

Patricia: 'Yes, sir – the cow's eaten all the grass.'

Teacher: 'Doreen, I told you to write out this poem twenty times because your handwriting is so bad, and you've only written it out seventeen times.'
Doreen: 'My arithmetic's bad as well, miss . . .'

Teacher: 'Trevor, what do you know about the Dead Sea?'
Trevor: 'I didn't even know it was ill, sir.'

Teacher: 'Kevin, why are you late for school?'
Kevin: 'Well, sir, I was dreaming about this football match and it went into extra time so I had to stay asleep to see the finish!'

Teacher: 'What are the chief minerals to be found in Cornwall?'
Class: 'Coca Cola and Orangeade!'

Two boys were scrapping in the playground when a monitor came by. He pulled them apart and said, 'You know the school rules – no fighting allowed.'

'But we weren't fighting aloud,' they protested. 'We were fighting quietly!'

Teacher had set his class an essay on 'A Game of Cricket'. After two minutes Simon Steel handed his paper in and was allowed to go home. His essay read: 'Rain stopped play.'

Teacher: 'Sarah, what was the first thing James 1 did on coming to the throne?'
Sarah: 'He sat down, miss.'

'Here, Norman, you'd better keep your eyes open today.'
'Why?'
'If you don't you'll keep banging into things.'

Teacher: 'Barbara, finish off this proverb: one good turn . . .'
Barbara: 'One good turn gives you all the blankets!'

Teacher: 'Huntley, what is the imperative of the verb "to go"?'
Huntley: 'Dunno, sir.'
Teacher: 'Go, Huntley, Go!'
Huntley: 'Thank you very much, sir.'

Teacher: 'Nigel, I have your English exercise book here. It is my duty to inform you that b-r-i-x does not spell "bricks".'
Nigel: 'Oh? What does it spell then, sir?'

Teacher: 'Michael, if the earth is round, why don't we fall off?'
Michael: 'The law of gravity, sir.'
Teacher: 'Correct.'
Victor: 'But, sir, what happened before the law was passed?'

Groaners

How do you make a coat last?
  Make the trousers first.

Why did a one-handed man cross the road?
  To get to the second-hand shop.

How do you start a flea race?
  Say 'one, two, flea – go!'

How do you start a teddy-bear race?
  Say, 'Ready, teddy – go!'

Two elephants fell over a cliff – boom boom!

What would you do with a sick wasp?
  Take it to waspital.

Why are ghosts invisible?
  'Cos they wear see-through clothes.

What did one witch say to another witch?
  'Snap, cackle and pop!'

Where would you find a prehistoric cow?
  In a moo-seum.

What's black when clean and white when dirty?
  A blackboard.

What orders does everybody like to receive?
  Postal orders.

What is always behind time?
  The back of a clock.

What is the opposite of cock-a-doodle-do?
  Cock-a-doodle-don't.

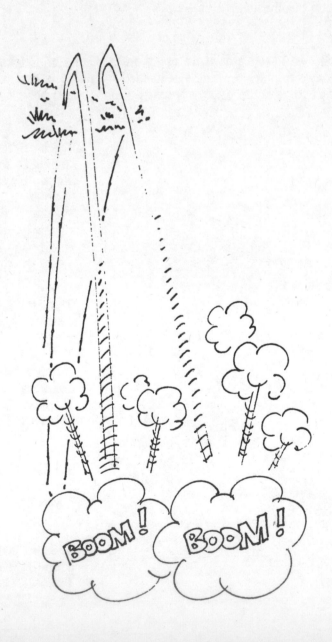

If sixteen boys share a chocolate cake, what is the time?
A quarter to four.

What is a sailor who is married with seven children called?
Daddy . . .

Why did the chicken cross the road?
For fowl [foul] purposes.

When would you be glad to be down and out?
After a bumpy plane trip . . .

When is a window like a star?
When it's a skylight.

What did the toothpaste say to the brush?
Give me a squeeze and I'll meet you outside the tube.

When is a nail like a horse?
When it's driven.

Why are there fouls in football?
Because there are ducks in cricket.

What is the longest word in the English language?
'Smiles' – because there's a mile between its first and last letters.

Where do flies go in winter-time?
To the glassworks to be turned into blue-bottles.

Why did the cow-slip?
'Cos it saw the bull-rush.

Why did the snow-drop?
'Cos it heard the cro-cuss!

What's mad and goes to the moon?
A loony module.

What is the longest night of the year?
A fortnight.

When is a door not a door?
When it's a-jar.

What is it that's yellow and very dangerous?
Shark-infested custard.

What is the biggest moth of all?
A mam-moth.

What are hippies for?
  To keep your leggies up.

Why did Sir Winston Churchill wear, red, white and blue braces?
  To keep his red, white and blue trousers up.

What has four legs and can't walk?
  Two pairs of trousers.

What goes up a drainpipe down, but can't go down a drainpipe up?
  An umbrella.

Why is a blunt axe like coffee?
  Because both have to be ground.

Why do birds in a nest always agree?
  Because they don't want to fall out.

Why does a barber never shave a man with a wooden leg?
  Because he always uses a razor.

What driver can never be arrested for speeding?
  A screwdriver.

Why is honey scarce in Brighton?
  Because there's only one B in Brighton.

Why is a stupid boy like the Amazon jungle?
  They're both dense.

What note do you get if an elephant playing the piano falls down a mine shaft?
  A Flat miner [A flat minor].

Why is a banana skin like a pullover?
  Because it's easy to slip on.

Why is a lazy dog like a hill?
  Because it's a slow pup [slope up].

What has four legs and one foot?
  A bed.

Why is a pig like a bottle of ink?
  Because it keeps going into the pen and then running out.

What did the carpet say to the floor?
  'I've got you covered.'

What did the big chimney say to the little chimney?
  'You're too young to smoke.'

What did the balloon say to the pin?
  'Hi, buster!'

Why is the Isle of Wight a fraud?
    Because it has Freshwater you can't drink, Cowes you can't
    milk, Needles you can't thread and Newport you can't bottle.

What did the necklace say to the hat?
    You go on ahead – I'll hang around.

Who gets the sack as soon as he starts work?
    A postman.

What do cornflakes wear on their feet?
    K-logs [clogs].

What goes zzub-zzub?
    A bee flying backwards.

Why was the ghost arrested?
    Because he hadn't got a haunting licence.

On what side of a school should an elm tree grow?
    On the outside ...

When is it bad luck to have a black cat follow you?
    When you're a mouse.

How do you know when you're in bed with an elephant?
    'Cos he's got 'E' on his pyjamas.

Ten cats were in a boat and one jumped out: how many were left?
    None, because the others were copy-cats.

What is it that goes 99 plonk?
    A centipede with a wooden leg.

What's brown and can see just as well from either end?
    A horse with its eyes shut.

What is it that goes 999 plonk?
    A millipede with a wooden leg.

*If a red house is made of red bricks and a yellow house is made of
yellow bricks, what is a green house made of?*
    Glass ...

What animals need oiling?
    Mice, because they squeak.

How do you stop a dog from barking in the back seat of a car?
    Put him in the front seat.

*What is it that's got meat in it, also bread and tomatoes, an
orange, is tied up in cellophane and flies through belfries?*
    The Lunchpack of Notre Dame.

Why do birds fly south in the winter?
  Because it's too far to walk.

*If a man has ten sons and each son has a sister, how many
children has he altogether?*
  Eleven, because the daughter is each son's sister.

Who is always being let down by his mates?
  A deep-sea diver.

Have you heard the story about the slippery eel?
  You wouldn't grasp it.

Have you heard the story about the peacock?
  'It's a beautiful tale [tail] ...

Have you heard the story about the skyscraper?
  It's a tall story [storey] ...

How can you communicate with a fish?
  Drop him a line.

What's white and goes up?
  A stupid snow-flake.

*Did you hear about the car with the wooden engine and the
wooden wheels?*
  It wooden go.

What flour do elves use?
  Elf-raising flour.

Why did the tortoise beat the hare?
  'Cos nothing goes faster than Shell.

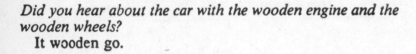

Why did the lobster blush?
  'Cos he saw the salad dressing.

What did Rome-o?
  For what Juli-et.

What is the noisiest of all games?
  Tennis, because you can't play it without raising a racket.

What is it you can put in your right hand but not in your left?
  Your left elbow.

What does an elephant do when it rains?
Gets wet.

Who drives all his customers away?
A taxi-driver.

Why is a guidebook like a pair of handcuffs?
Because it is for tourists [two wrists].

'If a fellow met a fibber in a fallow field' – how many 'f's in that?
None – there are no 'f's in 'that'.

What can you give someone and still keep?
Your word.

Have you heard the story of the church bell?
It hasn't ever been tolled [told] ...

What turns without moving?
Milk – when it turns sour.

What can you touch, see and make but can't hold?
A shadow.

Why are tall people lazier than short people?
Because they're longer in bed.

How do you make a pipe lighter?
Take the tobacco out.

Why do cows wear bells?
Their horns don't work.

What language do they speak in Cuba?
Cubic.

Why is a naughty boy like the letter D?
Both make ma mad.

Why is a mouse like fresh hay?
Because the cattle [cat'll] eat it.

Who is the smallest sailor in the world?
The one who slept on his watch.

Why do people laugh up their sleeves?
Because that's where their funny-bone is.

Do you know what Zulus do with banana skins?
Throw them away, of course ...

Why do we call money 'bread'?
'Cos everybody 'kneads' it.

Why do City businessmen carry umbrellas?
'Cos umbrellas can't walk.

What is the hottest letter of the alphabet?
B, because it makes oil boil.

What did the envelope say to the stamp?
'Stick with me, baby, and we'll go places!'

Why is tennis a noisy game?
'Cos when you play it you have to raise a racket.

What is a happy tin in the United States?
A-merry-can.

Why did the nurse creep into the cupboard?
So as not to wake the sleeping-pills.

What room has no walls, floor, ceiling or windows?
A mushroom.

What is the invention that enables you to see through the thickest walls?
A window.

Why did the man throw his watch out of the window?
To see time fly.

What runs but has no legs?
A tap.

What has a neck but no head?
A bottle.

What has a bottom at the top?
A leg.

What did one eye say to the other eye?
Something's come between us that smells.

Why is Kevin Keegan like a matchstick?
'Cos he strikes from the edge of the box.

Why did the football manager give his team a lighter?
'Cos they kept losing their matches.

What has a bed but does not sleep? What has a mouth but does not speak?
A river.

Why was the little boy glad that everyone called him Cyril?
'Cos that was his name.

Name a shooting star.
Clint Eastwood.

Why do we sing Hymns in church and not Hers?
  Because they all finish with Amen and not Awomen.

What trees do fingers and thumbs grow on?
  Palm trees.

What is worse than a giraffe with a sore neck?
  A centipede with corns.

THROB x 100 !!

Why is a rabbit's nose always shiny?
  'Cos it keeps its powder puff at the wrong end.

Why couldn't the leopard escape from the zoo?
  'Cos he was always spotted.

If there are two tomatoes on a plate, which is the cowboy?
  Neither – they're both redskins.

Can a shoe box?
  No, but a tin can.

Have you ever seen a salad bowl?
  No, but I've seen a square dance.

What coat do you put on only when it's wet?
  A coat of paint.

What nut has no shell?
  A doughnut.

What walks on its head all day?
  A drawing-pin stuck in your shoe.

What did the jack say to the car?
  'Can I give you a lift?'

What's round and bad-tempered?
  A vicious circle.

Where do gnomes live?
  Gnome Sweet Gnome.

What do you do with a sick budgie?
  Give him tweetment.

What is long, has a brown hat and lies in a box?
  A match.

What do lady sheep wear?
  Ewe-niforms.

What is the similarity between soldiers and dentists?
  They both have to drill.

When should you feed tiger's milk to a baby?
  When it's a baby tiger.

What tongue never speaks?
  The tongue in your shoe.

What is a calf after it is one year old?
  A two-year old calf.

Why is a river rich?
  Because it has two banks.

What did one rose say to the other rose?
  Hiya, Bud.

Why is a baby like an old motor-car?
Because both have a rattle.

What does the sea say to the sand?
Nothing – it waves.

What letters are not in the alphabet?
Those that are in the postbox.

What is the hardest thing about learning to ride a bike?
The pavement.

What colours should you paint the sun and the wind?
The sun rose and the wind blew.

If your clock strikes thirteen, what time is it?
Time to get a new clock.

Why did the man comb his hair with his toes?
To make ends meet.

What is the definition of a harp?
A nude piano.

What does a deaf fisherman need?
A herring-aid.

What are hot, greasy and romantic?
Chips that pass in the night.

What did the drunken chicken lay?
Scotch eggs.

Why was the young Scottish owl angry?
Because his mother wouldn't let him hoot at night.

How can you jump off a fifty-foot ladder in complete safety?
You jump off the bottom rung.

If two is company and three is a crowd, what's four and five?
Nine.

Why did the old-aged pensioner put wheels on his rocking-chair?
'Cos he wanted to rock n' roll.

What do cannibals have for lunch?
Baked beings.

What did the pig say when the chef cut off his tail?
'This is the end of me ...'

Why was the cowboy always in trouble?
'Cos he couldn't stop horsing around.

What must you know to be an auctioneer?
Lots.

The Bookworm's Banquet

My Golden Wedding	*by* Annie Versary
The Insurmountable Problem	*by* Major Setback
Crime Does Not Pay	*by* Laura Norder
A Load Of Old Rubbish	*by* Stefan Nonsense
Bilious Attacks	*by* Eva Lott
Tape Recording Made Easy	*by* Cass Ette
Don't Go Without Me	*by* Isa Cummin
Making The Most Of Life	*by* Maxie Mumm
Making The Least Of Life	*by* Minnie Mumm
When Shall We Meet Again?	*by* Miles Apart
The Arctic Ocean	*by* I.C. Waters
Scalp Disorders	*by* Dan Druff
Willie Win	*by* Betty Wont
Return Of The Prodigal	*by* Greta Sonne
A Call For Assistance	*by* Linda Hand
Pain And Sorrow	*by* Ann Guish
Garden Design	*by* Lily Pond
Crossing The Road	*by* Luke About
Sunday Service	*by* Neil Downe
The Laser Weapon	*by* Ray Gunn
Fade Away	*by* Peter Out
Into Battle	*by* Sally Forth
Nappy Making	*by* Terry Towel
Sweet Remembrance	*by* Valentine Card
The Japanese Way Of Death	*by* Harri Kari
Repairing Old Clothes	*by* Fred Bare
Flag Day	*by* Ada Charity
The Lady Artist	*by* Andrew Pictures
The Leaky Tap	*by* Constant Dripping
Summertime	*by* Clement Weather
The Lighthouse	*by* Eddy Stone
Don't Wake The Baby!	*by* Elsie Cries
The Worst Journey In The World	*by* Ellen Back
Knocked For Six	*by* Esau Stars
The Strongman	*by* Everard Muscles
My Happiest Day	*by* Trudy Light
Karate For Beginners	*by* Flora Mugger
Are You A Millionaire?	*by* Jonah Lott
Pig-Breeding	*by* Lena Bacon
Who Killed Cock Robin?	*by* U. Dunnit
Kidnapped	*by* Caesar Quick
The Haunted Room	*by* Hugo First
The Bad Striker	*by* Mr Goal
Making Weatherproof Clothes	*by* Anne O'Rack
Late Again	*by* Misty Buss
Magic For Beginners	*by* Beatrix Ster
English Folk Customs	*by* Morris Dancer

Sport Mad

During a cricket match there was a telephone call in the pavilion for one of the players whose abilities as a batsman were considerably below par. 'He's not here at the moment,' said the captain. 'He's just going in to bat.'

'Oh, all right,' said the caller, 'I'll hang on!'

In the theatre the master of ceremonies was announcing the next act. 'The great Mysto', he declared importantly, 'will now astound you with his amazing magic illusions! He will bring before your eyes all the wonders of the Orient –' At which a voice from the back called out, 'What about Spurs? They could do with some magic as well!'

'May I go swimming, Mummy?'

'No, you may not. There are sharks here.'

'But Daddy's swimming.'

'He's insured.'

At Grotsville United's football ground they always play the National Anthem before each match. It isn't that they are all that patriotic – they just like to make sure the team can stand up ...

'Sorry I missed that open goal, skipper,' said the useless striker. 'I could kick myself, I really could.'

'Don't bother – you'd only miss.'

Did you hear about the boxing referee who used to work at a space rocket launching site? If a fighter was knocked down he'd count 'Ten, nine, eight, seven ...'

'My brother's a professional boxer.'

'Heavyweight?'

'No, featherweight. He tickles his opponents to death.'

'My brother's a professional boxer.'

'Really? What's his name?'

'Rembrandt!'

'Rembrandt?'

'Yes, he's always on the canvas ... mind you, he'd have won his last fight only the referee was standing on his hand.'

As any keen angler knows the best time to fish is at night, so two friends agreed to meet in the village pub and then to go fishing at closing time. Unfortunately they drank rather too much beer, and closing time saw them staggering out with their rods and their reels, very much the worse for wear. But they managed to reach a bridge without mishap, baited their lines, cast into the darkness and sat down to wait for a bite. But their luck was out, hour after hour they sat with their lines remaining motionless, listening to the clock in the village church distantly chiming the night away. By the time dawn was just about to break they were cold, tired, fed up and sober, and had just decided to pack it in and go home – when the 6.30 fast train to London pulled their rods out of their hands ...

'I say, look here!' said an angry member of the grouse-shooting party. 'You nearly shot my wife!'

'I'm terribly sorry,' said the short-sighted offender, 'shall I try again?'

'I say, look here!' said another even angrier member of the party. 'You've just shot my wife!'

'Oh, have I?' said the same offender. 'Here – have a crack at mine!'

'My dog plays chess.'

'Your dog plays chess? He must be very clever!'

'Oh, I don't know. I usually beat him three times out of four.'

'Out!' said the umpire.

'Out?' yelled the outraged batsman, 'what for?'

'For the rest of the afternoon.'

The big-game hunter was showing his friends his hunting trophies. Drawing their attention to a lion-skin rug on the floor he said, 'I shot this fellow in Africa. Didn't want to kill such a magnificent beast, of course, but it was either him or me.'

'Well,' said a guest, 'he certainly makes a better rug than you would!'

Having just swam the Channel, the exhausted swimmer staggered up the beach at Calais. '*Formidable!*' enthused a Frenchman. 'You 'ave performed the great foot!'

'It's feat, actually,' said the English swimmer.

The Frenchman's eyebrows lifted in astonishment. 'So you 'ave swum both ways – *incroyable!*'

'I'm awarding a free kick,' said the football referee firmly.

'Who to?' asked a bewildered player.

'Us,' said the referee.

A layman and a vicar were playing golf one day, and the layman was not having a good game. 'Oh, darn, I've missed!' he said at the first green, missing an easy putt. 'Oh, darn, I've missed again!' he said at the second green as he missed another easy putt. And so it went on – every time he played a bad shot, he would say, 'Oh, darn, I've missed!'

The vicar put up with this for half the round, but then felt he owed it to the dignity of his calling to remonstrate with the layman. 'You really must not keep using such dreadful language, my dear sir,' he said, 'or the Lord may well strike you down!'

And just as the words were out of his mouth there came a jagged flash of lightning – and in a split-second the vicar was burnt to a crisp! Above the rolling thunder-clouds a deep voice was heard to say, 'Oh, darn, I've missed!'

Why was Cinderella kicked out of the soccer team? 'Cos she kept running away from the ball.

'The Manager of Manchester United said I'd be a great footballer if it wasn't for two things.'
'What were they?'
'My feet.'

'Every night of my life I dream about cricket. Always I'm playing an eternal game of cricket. Do you think there's something wrong with me?'
'Don't you even dream about girls?'
'What? And miss my innings?!'

'I went fly-fishing yesterday.'
'Catch anything?'
'Yes. A 3lb bluebottle.'

'Did you go water-skiing on holiday?'
'No. I couldn't find a lake with a slope.'

'Hey, you!' yelled the water-bailiff to the small boy. 'Can't you read that sign? No fishing in this river.'
'I'm not fishing,' came the perky reply. 'I'm just teaching my worm how to swim!'

What football team never meets before a match? Queen's Park Strangers.

'How should I have played that last shot?' the bad golfer asked his partner.
'Under an assumed name.'

Why should a golfer always wear two pairs of trousers? In case he gets a hole in one.

Travellers' Tales

'When we got to Benidorm the hotel was so full I had to sleep on a door across two trestles.'
  'Was it comfortable?'
  'Oh, yes. But a bit draughty round the letter-box.'

A motorist who had the misfortune to run over a woman's dog was extremely apologetic. 'I really am most terribly sorry, madam,' he said. 'I will of course replace your dog.'
  'If you like,' she replied, 'but are you any good at catching rats?'

An extremely rich businessman found himself in a small Lancashire hotel where his wealth and importance seemed to be quite unknown, and to his chagrin he was treated with no more and no less respect than any other guest. Determined to show his worth, at breakfast he said loudly to the waiter, 'Bring me £10 worth of bacon and eggs!' Not a whit abashed, the waiter said, 'Sorry, sir, but we don't serve half-portions!'

Pilot: 'Mayday! Mayday! Starboard engine on fire!'
Ground Control: 'State your height and position.'
Pilot: 'I'm five feet eight and I'm sitting in the cockpit.'

'Last time my wife and I travelled on the ferry from Newhaven to Dieppe we had six meals.'
  'Six meals for that short crossing?'
  'Three down and three up.'

An American visitor to England was wandering round a small county town, and got into conversation with a local. 'What do you do for entertainment round here?' he asked. 'Is there a cinema?'
  'No, no cinema,' said the local.
  'A theatre?'
  'No, no theatre.'
  'A disco?'
  'No, no disco.'
  'So what is there in this town?'
  'Well, we lads like to go to the grocers' shop and watch the bacon slicer.'
  'That's fun, is it?'
  'Well, she's a lovely girl.'

Having asked for shelter for the night at a monastery the traveller was surprised and delighted at being given a magnificent supper of succulent fish and chips. 'That was absolutely superb!' he enthused to the monk who had been serving him. 'That piece of fish was wonderful, and beautifully cooked. And as for the chips — they were the tastiest chips I've ever had in my life. Well done, Brother.' 'Oh, you must thank Brother Ambrose for those,' came the reply. 'I'm the fish friar — he's the chip monk . . .'

A man sat on a train chewing gum and staring vacantly into space, when suddenly an old lady sitting opposite said, 'It's no good you talking to me, young man. I'm stone deaf!'

Fifty Irishmen were travelling on a train. 'Sure and it's too crowded in this compartment,' said the leader. 'The next one's empty — Let's use that one.' So at the next stop the fifty Irishmen alighted — and all promptly went into the empty compartment!

'You deliberately drove into my car!' said the first motorist to the second. 'Why did you do it?'
   'I saw that sticker in your back window,' came the reply. 'It says "Give Blood" so I thought I'd give you some of mine!'

As the bus arrived at the stop, a man in the front of the queue took out his eye, bounced it hard on the pavement, caught it, put it back in his eye and boarded the bus.
   'What did you do that for?' asked the amazed conductor.
   'I just wanted to see,' replied the man, 'if there was any room on top!'

'I told the police that I was not injured, but on removing my hat I found that I had a fractured skull.'

'The pedestrian had no idea which direction to go, so I ran over him.'

'I saw the slow-moving, sad-faced old gentleman as he bounced off the bonnet of my car.'

'The indirect cause of this accident was the little chap in a small car with a moustache.'

'I was thrown from my car as it left the road. I was later found in a ditch by some cows.'

'The telephone pole was approaching fast and I was attempting to swerve out of its path when it struck my front.'

'I was on my way to the doctor when my rear end gave way, causing me to have an accident.'

'I pulled away from the side of the road, glanced at my mother-in-law and drove into the river.'

Whenever there is a road accident each driver involved has to write a report of the occurrence for the insurance company. The following are actual quotations from some of these reports:

'Coming home, I drove into the wrong house and collided with a tree I didn't have.'

'I thought my window was down, but I found it was up when I put my hand through it.'

'I collided with a stationary lorry coming the other way.'

'A van backed through my windscreen into my wife's face.'

'A pedestrian hit me and went under my car.'

'He was all over the road, and I had to swerve a number of times before I hit him.'

'In an attempt to kill a fly I drove into a telephone pole.'

'I had been driving my car for forty years when I fell asleep at the wheel.'

'My car was legally parked as it backed into the other vehicle.'

'An invisible car came out of nowhere, struck my vehicle and vanished.'

'I got a puncture in the rear tyre of my bike yesterday.'
'Hard luck. Did you mend it?'
'No, I just raised the seat.'

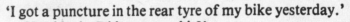

Just as the Jumbo jet was about to take off, a nervous old lady called for an air-hostess. 'I've never been in an aeroplane before,' she said. 'Tell me, my dear, what happens if we run out of fuel?'
'Don't worry, madam,' replied the cheeky young woman. 'We all get out and push!'

A French hitch-hiker in England was delighted when a motorist stopped at his thumbing signal. 'Want a lift, do you?' asked the motorist.
'Oui, oui,' agreed the Frenchman.
'Not in my car you don't!'

A man in the United States decided to make some money by getting himself run over. He stood at a bus stop and stuck his leg out so that when the bus arrived it ran him over. He was in hospital for three months and received $50,000 in compensation. Then he went to France and tried the same trick, this time receiving 200,000 francs in compensation. But when he came to Britain and stood at a bus stop with his leg sticking out he died of pneumonia . . .

2 MILES

On board the liner in mid-Atlantic a nervous passenger was being comforted by a steward. 'There's nothing to worry about, madam,' he said soothingly. 'After all, we're only two miles from land.'

'Only two miles?'

'Yes. Straight down!'

'I hope this plane doesn't travel faster than sound,' said the old lady to the stewardess.

'Why?'

'Because my friend and I want to talk, that's why.'

Charlie always takes his holidays in March. He says he likes to get in early while the sheets are still clean . . .

'I tried surf-riding while I was in Australia.'

'How did you get on?'

'Not very well. I couldn't get the horse near the water.'

It was an extremely rough channel crossing from Weymouth to Jersey, and one wretched green-faced passenger was hugging the rail when a steward approached him.

'Lunch, sir?' asked the tactless steward.

'No, thanks,' groaned the passenger. 'Just throw it overboard and save me the trouble . . .'

A man and his friend were driving through the centre of town, and the driver's handling of the car was decidedly erratic. 'Tell me, Joey,' said his increasingly perturbed friend, 'why do you shut your eyes every time we come to a red light?'

'Why not?' retorted Joey. 'When you've seen one you've seen 'em all . . . !'

The great Explorer claimed to have spent a whole year in the deepest jungles of Central Africa. 'After my supplies ran out,' he declared, 'I lived on nothing but snake and pygmy pie . . .'.

'I flew to Germany last year.'

'So did I.'

'Doesn't it make your arms tired!?'

'I say, cabby! How much to take me to the station?'

'Three quid, sir.'

'And how much for my suitcase?'

'No charge for the suitcase, sir.'

'Very well. Take the case and I'll walk.'

'I've never flown before,' said the nervous old lady to the pilot. 'You will bring me down safely, won't you?'

'All I can say, missus,' said the pilot, 'is that I've never left anyone up there yet!'

Margaret was telling her friend about her holiday abroad. 'When we got to the airport,' she said, 'there was this man outside yelling "It's wrong to fly! It's against nature! If God had meant us to fly he'd have given us wings!"'

'Who was he?' asked her friend.

'The pilot!'

Some people are terrified of flying. Take poor old Royston, who wanted to go to Spain for his summer holiday; nothing would induce him to go on a plane so he had to travel by boat and train. But he was right out of luck – his train crashed. A plane fell on it . . .

The travelling salesman had booked himself in for the night in a small boarding-house, but due to a lengthy business meeting he didn't arrive until after midnight. He could see no signs of life, but not wanting to spend the night on the doorstep he pressed the bell. After an interval an upstairs window opened and an angry woman in dressing-gown and curlers peered out. 'What is it?' she demanded.

'It's Mr Jenkins,' replied the hapless salesman, 'I'm staying here.'

'All right,' came the response. 'Stay there'. And she slammed down the window!

At a small country railway-station the ticket clerk-cum-porter noticed a stranger, who had just alighted from one of the infrequent trains that stopped there, examining a timetable.

'Excuse me, sir' he asked, 'are you lost?'

'Certainly not,' said the traveller, 'I'm here. It's your station that's lost!'

Two friends were having a cup of tea in the buffet at King's Cross station.

'Do you know,' said one, 'I once went from here to Manchester and it didn't cost me a penny!'

'How was that?' asked the second.

'I walked.'

'I think we've just had a puncture.'

'How did that happen?'

'There was a fork in the road!'

Mr and Mrs Thorne had just reached the airport in the nick of time to catch the plane for their fortnight's holiday in Majorca. 'I wish we'd brought the piano with us,' said Mr Thorne.

'What on earth for?' asked his wife.

'I've left the tickets on it.'

'Once when I was shipwrecked,' said the teller of tall stories, 'I lived on a tin of sardines for a week!'

'Really?' yawned a bored listener, 'I'm surprised you didn't fall off.'

The school party was assembled for a day trip to Calais. 'Harris,' said the Headmaster, 'we must all be very careful on the ferry going over to France. If one of the boys falls overboard – what do you do?'

'I shout "boy overboard!", sir.'

'Good. And what do you do if a teacher falls overboard?'

'Er – which one, sir?'

'In China,' said the returned tourist, 'I saw a woman hanging from a tree.'

'Shanghai?'

'No, about six foot off the ground.'

'I come from California.'

'Oh, nice to meet you. I've enjoyed your Syrup of Figs for years.'

'Ah'm frae Glasgae,' said the Scot.

'Are you, now?' replied the Cockney. 'Jus' dahn 'ere ter learn the langwidge, are yer?'

'What do you think of this suit? I had it made in Hong Kong.'

'Very nice. But what's that hump on the back?'

'Oh, that's the tailor. He's still working on it.'

The newly-arrived young Chinese lad from Hong Kong rang his brother who was living in Manchester. The young man was speaking in laborious English when his brother interrupted him, saying, 'Why don't you speak in Chinese?'

'Oh,' said the newcomer, 'I didn't know English telephones could speak Chinese!'

An English tourist in a Cairo bazaar was offered a large skull by a street-trader. 'Dis de skull of great Queen Cleopatra, effendi,' said the Egyptian, 'only one hundred English pounds.'

'No, thank you,' said the Englishman. 'It's far too expensive.'

'How 'bout dis one, effendi?' said the street-trader, producing a small skull.

'Whose skull is that?'

'Dis de skull of great Queen Cleopatra when she was little girl!'

A huge American car screeched to a halt in a sleepy Warwickshire village, and the driver called out to a local inhabitant, 'Say – am I on the right road for Shakespeare's birthplace?'

'Ar, straight on, zur,' said the rustic, 'but no need to hurry. He's dead.'

Desmond was making his very first journey by rail. He sat goggle-eyed in a corner seat watching the landscape flash past, and laughed with glee as another train went whooshing by. His train then stopped at a signal light and another train went rushing by in the opposite direction.

'Oooh, look, Mum!' he cried, 'it came back!'

'When I was on holiday at the seaside last year a crab bit off one of my toes!'

'Which one?'

'I dunno – they all look alike to me.'

A policeman saw a man dressed as a cowboy in the street, complete with huge stetson hat, spurs, and six shooters.

'Excuse me, sir,' said the policeman, 'who are you?'

'My name's Tex, officer,' said the cowboy.

'Tex, eh?' said the policeman, 'Are you from Texas?'

'Nope. Louisiana.'

'Louisiana? So why are you called Tex?'

'Don't want to be called Louise, do I?'

'And on this tour, ladies and gentlemen,' explained the guide, 'we shall be going where the hand of man has never set foot!'

Heavily encumbered with bags and cases, the would-be passenger hurtled across the station concourse, through the barrier and on to the platform – just in time to see his train pulling out. As he stood there, puffing and panting, with sweat streaming down his reddened face, a sympathetic porter said to him, 'Just missed your train, sir?'

'No, you fool,' fumed the man. 'I didn't like the look of it so I chased it out of the station!'

'When you go on a bus, do you prefer riding inside or on the top deck?'

'Well, I prefer on top but I find it very difficult to get the horse up the stairs . . .'

'We've been here four days, Gladys' said the English tourist in Paris, 'and we haven't been to the Louvre yet.'

'I know, dear,' said his wife, 'it must be the change of diet.'

A woman just back from the United States was telling her friends about the trip. 'When my husband first saw the Grand Canyon, his face dropped a mile,' she said.

'Why, was he disappointed with the view?'

'No, he fell over the edge.'

'My wife is like the Mona Lisa.'

'You mean she's beautiful and has an enigmatic smile?'

'No – she's flat as a canvas and ought to be in a museum.'

A new porter in Paris was instructed by the manager that it was important to call the guests by their names, in order to make them feel welcome and that the easiest way to find out their names was to look at their luggage. Armed with this advice, the porter took two guests up to their rooms, put down their bags and said, 'I 'ope you 'ave a 'appy stay 'ere in Paris, Mr and Mrs Genuine Cow'ide.'

A tourist to Ireland was being shown the local beauty spot by a guide. 'Ye see dem mountains in the distance, sorr?'

'Yes,' said the visitor.

'Well, sorr, dem is de highest mountains in de world, sorr. All exceptin' dem in furren parts, dat is.'

'What's Norway like?'
'Sweden without the matches.'

The sweet young lady from Lapland arrived at the English family's house to begin as an *au pair*. 'Now, dear,' said her English hostess, 'I'd like you to make the children's bed in the morning –'

'Oh, excuse me, please, Mrs Benson, but to make beds – I do not know how.'

'Oh,' said Mrs Benson, 'well, never mind. You can make the lunch for me and –'

'Oh, excuse me, please, Mrs Benson, but to cook – I do not know how.'

'I see ... what about cleaning and dusting, then?'

'Cleaning and dusting? I am afraid –'

'You do not know how, yes. Tell me, my dear,' said Mrs Benson through gritted teeth, 'what can you do?'

'I can milk a reindeer.'

'So you're not going to Berlin this year?'

'No, it's Rome we're not going to. It was Berlin we didn't go to last year.'

Two aliens landed from a flying saucer near a small village in Dorset. They walked towards the village, and the first thing they came across was a pillarbox. 'Take me to your leader,' said the first alien.

'It's no use talking to him,' said the other, 'can't you see he's only a child?'

On the doorstep stood a turbanned, brown-skinned figure. 'Who are you?' asked the householder.

'I am your new milkman,' said the caller.

'Oh, yes? Where are you from?'

'Pakistan.'

'Blimey – you've got a big round!'

Did you hear about the Russian company of soldiers answering roll-call? The sergeant sneezed and six soldiers called out, 'Here!'

An English tourist in the west of the United States came across a Red Indian lying down with his ear pressed hard on the trail. 'What are you listening for?' asked the visitor.

'Stage coach pass half hour ago,' said the brave.

'How can you tell?'

'Broke my neck.'

A Yorkshireman on holiday in Spain was taken to see his first bullfight. He watched impassively for a while, and then stood to his feet, yelling, 'Nay, lad! If tha doesn't 'old t'red flag still, 'e'll never run into damn thing!'

The train was crawling slowly across country from Dublin to Ballinasloe, and the English tourist was growing increasingly impatient. Finally he jumped out at one of the many interminable stops, walked along to the engine-driver and said, 'Can't you go any faster, driver?'

'Sure I can at that,' replied the driver, 'but I'm not allowed to leave me train.'

The leader of an Irish expedition to scale Mount Everest had returned, and was giving a press conference in Dublin.

'Did you make it to the summit,' asked a reporter.

'No, not quite,' said the Irish mountaineer. 'We got to within fifty feet of the top, and then we ran out of scaffolding.'

At a diplomatic reception the Mexican general appeared in a magnificent uniform, liberally bespattered with medals and decorations. 'That's most impressive,' said the British ambassador. 'Tell me, general, what did you get all those for?'

'In your money,' replied the Mexican general, 'about £4!'

Commissioned by a zoo to bring them some baboons, the big-game hunter devised a novel scheme to trap them – his only requirements being a sack, a gun, and a particularly vicious and bad-tempered dog.

He tramped into the jungle with his assistant, and after several weeks they finally reached an area where baboons were numerous – though that didn't make them any easier to catch. 'This is what we'll do,' he explained to his baffled assistant. 'I'll climb this tree and shake the branches; if there are any baboons up there they will then fall to the ground – the dog will bite their tails and immobilise them so that you can pick them up quite safely and put them in the sack.'

'But what do I need a gun for?' asked the assistant.

'If I should fall out of the tree by mistake shoot the dog!'

Mr and Mrs Shaw were on safari in darkest Africa. They were walking cautiously through the jungle when suddenly a huge lion sprang out in front of them, seized Mrs Shaw in its jaws and started to drag her off into the bush.

'Shoot!' she screamed to her husband. 'Shoot!'

'I can't!' he yelled back, 'I've run out of film!'

Get This!

What is a buttress?
  A female goat.

What is hail?
  Hard-boiled rain.

What is a vacuum?
  An empty space inhabited by the Pope.

What is a net?
  Holes tied together with string.

What is the equator?
  An imaginary lion running round the earth.

What is a carafe?
  A four-legged animal with a long neck.

What is ice?
  Hard water.

What is an octopus?
  An eight-sided cat.

What is a polygon?
  A dead parrot.

What is a myth?
  A female moth.

What is a water otter?
  A kettle.

What are hydrangeas?
  A Lancashire football team.

What is hypnotism?
  Rheumatism in the hip.

What is the Cheddar Gorge?
  A large cheese sandwich.

What is 'out of bounds'?
  An exhausted kangaroo.

What is a toad stool?
  Toadstools are things that live in damp places, which is why they are shaped like umbrellas.

What is a skeleton?
  Bones with the person off.

What is a posthumous work?
  Something written by someone after they're dead.

Sick Humour

Doctor: 'I'm sorry, Mr Hassleblatt, but I've got bad news. However, I've also got good news. Which would you rather hear first?'
Patient: 'Tell me the bad news first, doctor.'
Doctor: 'The bad news is that we've got to take both your legs off. The good news is that the chap in the next bed wants to buy your slippers.'

Doctor: 'Say one-hundred-and-one.'
Patient: 'Not ninety-nine?'
Doctor: 'Well, everything's going up.'

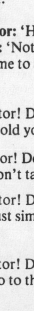
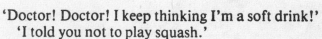

Doctor: 'And how are you now, Mrs Trample?'
Patient: 'Well, doctor, you know you told me to take half a pint of orange juice every night after a hot bath?'
Doctor: 'Yes?'
Patient: 'I managed to drink the orange juice all right but I've had an awful time trying to get the hot bath down.'

'My doctor told me to take two of these pills on an empty stomach.'
   'Did they do any good?'
   'I don't know. They keep rolling off in the night.'

Doctor: 'How is your husband's lumbago?'
Wife: 'Not too good. I rubbed his back with whisky like you told me to and he broke his neck trying to lick it off!'

'Doctor! Doctor! I keep thinking I'm a soft drink!'
   'I told you not to play squash.'

'Doctor! Doctor! Everyone keeps throwing me in the dustbin!'
   'Don't talk rubbish.'

'Doctor! Doctor! I'm boiling!'
   'Just simmer down.'

'Doctor! Doctor! I feel like a snooker ball!'
   'Go to the end of the queue.' (cue)

'Doctor! Doctor! Will this ointment clear up my spots?'
   'I never make rash promises.'

'Doctor! Doctor! I've just swallowed four red snooker balls, three pink snooker balls and two black snooker balls!'
'Eat some greens and you'll soon be all right.'

'Doctor! Doctor! I've just swallowed a roll of film!'
'Let's hope nothing develops.'

'Doctor! Doctor! Can you help me out?'
'Certainly. Which way did you come in?'

'I'm sorry to bother you, doctor, but it's my old Dad. He keeps saying he wants to die.'
'You did the right thing in sending for me.'

'Tell me straight, doctor, is it serious?'
'Well, I wouldn't start watching any new serials if I were you.'

'This is a most unusual complaint, Mrs Quilch. Have you had it before?'
'Yes, doctor.'
'Well, you've got it again!'

A man rushed into the doctor's surgery, jumped on the doctor's back and began shouting 'One! Two! Three! Four.'
'Wait a minute!' yelled the doctor, struggling to free himself. 'What do you think you're doing?'
'Well, doctor,' said the eccentric man, 'they said I could count on you!'

'Doctor! Doctor! I feel like a needle!'
'Yes, I see your point.'

'Doctor, I think I've got flu.'
'Very well. Just put your tongue out and then stick your head out of the window.'
'Will that make me better?'
'No, but I can't stand the woman living opposite...'

'Doctor! Doctor! My sister thinks she's a lift.'
'Tell her to come in.'
'I can't. She doesn't stop at this floor.'

A man went to the dentist, sat in the chair and immediately began shouting and screaming. 'What's all the fuss about?' demanded the dentist. 'I haven't touched your tooth yet.'
'I know,' said the patient, 'but you're — aagh! — standing on my foot!'

'Doctor! Doctor! I feel I'm a goat!'
'Stop acting like a little kid.'

'What seems to be the trouble then, Mr Worryalot?' asked the psychiatrist.

'It's like this doctor,' said the patient. 'I have a huge mansion in the country, two Rolls-Royces, my children go to the most exclusive public schools and my wife is dressed by the finest couturier in Paris.'

'So what's the problem?'

'I only earn £40 a week!'

'I don't think much of that new doctor.'

'Why not?'

'Old Charlie Evans went to see him the other week. He tapped Charlie's knee with that little hammer and his leg fell off!'

'The trouble is,' said the entertainer to the psychiatrist, 'that I can't sing, I can't dance, I can't tell jokes, I can't act, I can't play an instrument or juggle or do magic tricks or do *anything!*'

'Then why don't you give up show-business?'

'I can't — I'm a star!'

'One of my uncles was a doctor, but he gave it up.'

'Why?'

'He just didn't have the patients.'

'Doctor! Doctor! I feel like a racehorse!'

'Take these pills every four furlongs.'

'Doctor! Doctor! I feel like a bee.'

'Buzz off — I'm busy, too!'

'Doctor! Doctor! I'm a burglar!'

'Have you taken anything for it?'

'Doctor! Doctor! I've eaten a pencil! What shall I do?'

'Use a pen.'

'Doctor! Doctor! I keep seeing double.'

'Sit on the couch, please.'

'Which one?'

'Doctor! Doctor! I think I'm a dog.'

'Sit down, please.'

'Oh no — I'm not allowed on the furniture.'

'Doctor! Doctor! I think I'm a telephone.'

'Take these pills and if they don't work give me a ring.'

'Doctor! Doctor! I think I'm shrinking!'

'You'll just have to be a little patient.'

'Doctor, doctor! I feel I want to paint myself gold all over.'
    'You've got a gilt complex.'

'Doctor, doctor! If I take these green pills will I get better?'
    'Well, nobody I've given them to has ever come back.'

'Doctor, doctor! I keep thinking I'm a fridge!'
    'Shut your mouth – you're shining your light right in my eyes.'

'Doctor, doctor! I feel I'm an apple!'
    'Well, come over here – I won't bite you.'

'Doctor, doctor! I keep thinking I'm invisible!'
    'Who's that?'

'Doctor, doctor! I can't sleep!'
    'Sleep on the edge of the bed. You'll soon drop off.'

'Doctor, doctor! I keep thinking I'm a ten pound note!'
    'Well, go shopping. You need the change.'

'Doctor, doctor! I keep thinking I'm a doorknob!'
    'All right, all right! Don't fly off the handle ...'

'Doctor, doctor! I feel like an old sweater!'
    'Well, I'll be darned!'

'Doctor, doctor! I feel like a bar of soap!'
    'That's life, boy ...'

'Doctor, doctor! I feel like a window!'
    'Really? Where's the pain?'

'Doctor, doctor! I feel like a bell.'
    'Take these pills and give me a ring.'

'Doctor, doctor! I feel like a piano.'
    'Wait while I make some notes.'

'Doctor, doctor! I feel like a parrot.'
    'Just perch there a moment.'

'Doctor, doctor! I feel like a strawberry!'
    'You are in a jam, aren't you?'

'Doctor, doctor! I feel like a car!'
    'Just park yourself over there.'

'Doctor, doctor! I keep feeling there are two of me!'
    'Very well, I'll see you one at a time.'

'Doctor, doctor! I keep feeling like a pane of glass.'
    'I though as much – next time don't come in through the window.'

'Doctor, doctor! I feel like a pile of bricks.'
    'You'll find them very hard to swallow.'

'Doctor, doctor! I'm at death's door!'
    'Don't worry – I'll pull you through.'

'Doctor, doctor! I feel I'm a goat.'
'How long have you been like this?'
'Since I was a kid.'

'Doctor, doctor! I keep thinking I'm a bridge!'
'Well, well, well – what's come over you today?'

'Doctor, doctor! I think I've got measles!'
'That's a rash thing to say.'

'Doctor, doctor! I've swallowed a spoon!'
'Lie down and don't stir.'

'Doctor, doctor! Can you give me something for my liver?'
'How about a pound of onions?!'

'Doctor, doctor! What are you writing on my ankle?'
'Just a footnote.'

'Doctor, doctor! Can you give me something for my flat feet?'
'How about a bicycle pump?'

'Doctor, doctor! I can't stop telling lies!'
'I don't believe you.'

'Doctor, everyone thinks I'm a cricket ball.'
'How's that?'
'Oh – not you as well!'

'Doctor, doctor! My family thinks I'm mad!'
'Why is that?'
'I like sausages.'
'There's nothing strange about that. I like sausages too.'
'Really? You must come and see my collection – I've got thousands!'

'Doctor, doctor! I've only got fifty-nine seconds to live.'
'Wait a minute, please ...'

'Doctor, doctor! Everyone keeps ignoring me.'
'Next, please.'

'Doctor, doctor! I feel I'm a pack of cards.'
'All right, I'll deal with you later.'

'Doctor, doctor! I keep thinking I'm a curtain.'
'Pull yourself together.'

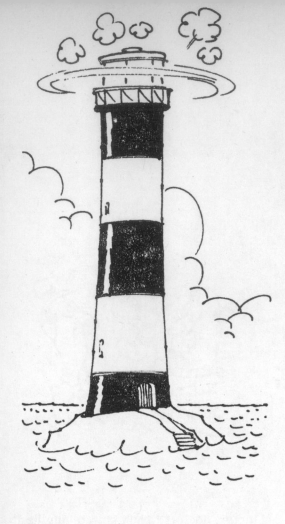

Patient: 'Doctor, I'm afraid my wife mistook that medicine you gave me for furniture polish.'
Doctor: 'So you want me to give you some more?'
Patient: 'No, I want you to come and shake our table.'

Frantic patient: 'Doctor, I've just swallowed a mouth organ!'
Doctor: 'It could be worse – at least you don't play the piano!'

Doctor: 'Well, I've given you a thorough check-up and there's not much wrong with you other than lack of exercise. What you must do is to take a brisk walk every day of not less than three miles.'
Patient: 'Oh, I'll get terribly dizzy if I do that, doctor.'
Doctor: Why on earth should you get dizzy walking?'
Patient: 'I'm a lighthouse-keeper.'

Doctor: 'Well now, is your cough better this morning?'
Patient: 'It should be. I've been practising all night.'

As the doctor approached the schoolboy to give him an injection the boy yelled out loud.
'What's the matter?' said the doctor crossly. 'I haven't touched you yet.'
'You're standing on my foot!' answered the boy.

'My doctor's told me to give up golf.'
'Why – because of your health?'
'No. He looked at my score card.'

Doctor: 'What's your trouble, then?'
Patient: 'Water on the knee.'
Doctor: 'How do you know?'
Patient: 'I dropped a bucketful of it!'

A short-sighted man went to the doctor for advice about his eyesight, and the doctor told him to eat carrots. He came back three months later to complain about the diet.
'Last night, doctor,' he said, 'I went out to my garden. It was very dark and I fell over.'
'Couldn't you see well enough?' asked the doctor.
'Yes, I could see all right. I tripped over my ears.'

Anyone who goes to a psychiatrist wants his head examined . . .

A famous surgeon went on safari to Africa. When he came back his colleagues asked him how he had got on.
'Oh, it was very disappointing ' he said. 'I didn't kill a thing – I'd have been better off staying here in the hospital!'

A doctor had just given a schoolboy a vaccination, and was about to put a bandage on his arm.
'Would you put it on the other arm, please, doctor?' asked the boy.
'What's the point of that?' said the doctor. 'I'll put it over your vaccination so that the other boys will know not to bang into it.'
'You don't know the kids at my school!' said the boy mournfully.

A man had been unfortunate enough to injure his hand at work. As the doctor was examining it he shook his head and said, 'I'm afraid it'll never be right.'

'Why not, doctor?' asked the patient anxiously.

'Because it's your left hand,' replied the daft medico.

The vicar saw one of his older parishioners limping slowly down the street one day and said to him, 'I'm sorry to see you in this state, Mr. Brown. What's the trouble?'

'It's me corns, vicar,' said the old chap.

'What does the doctor say?' asked the kindly vicar.

'Haven't been to a doctor,' said the old fellow stubbornly.

'Well,' said the vicar, 'I should see him if I were you. He'll very likely give you something for them.'

'Why should I?' came the indignant reply. 'They've never done anything for me. Let 'em suffer!'

Doctor: 'You've got quite a nasty chill. You must avoid draughts for a week or two.'
Patient: 'Can I play ludo instead?'

Patient: 'Doctor, I snore so loudly I keep myself awake. What can I do?'
Doctor: 'Sleep in another room.'

Doctor: 'You must take four teaspoonsful of this medicine before every meal.'
Small patient: But we've only got three teaspoons!'

Distraught man: 'Doctor, doctor, my hair's falling out. Can you give me something to keep it in?'
Doctor: 'How about a paper bag?'

Foolish man: 'Doctor, doctor, come quickly! My wife's broken a leg!'
Doctor: 'But I'm a doctor of music.'
Foolish man: 'That's all right – it's the piano leg!'

A boy had the bad luck to break a leg playing football. After his leg had been put in plaster, he asked the doctor, 'When you take the plaster off, will I be able to play the violin?'

'Of course you will,' said the doctor reassuringly.

'That's funny,' said the boy. 'I couldn't before you put it on.'

Mum: 'Jenny, the doctor says you must take one of these pills three times a day.'
Jenny: 'How can I take it more than once?'

Mum: 'Joe, time for your medicine.'
Joe: 'I'll put the bath on.'
Mum: 'Why?'
Joe: 'Because on the bottle it says "to be taken in water".'

A doctor had been attending a rich old man for some time, but it became apparent that the old chap had not long to live. Accordingly, the doctor advised his wealthy patient to put his affairs in order.

'Oh, yes, I've done that,' said the old gentleman. 'I've only got to make my will. And do you know what I'm going to do with all my money? I'm going to leave it to the doctor who saves my life . . .'

Doctor: 'Why didn't you send for me sooner, madam? Your husband is very ill.'
Wife: 'I thought I'd give him a chance to get better first.'

'How are you today?'
 'I'm still having trouble with my breathing, doctor.'
 'Well, I must give you something to stop that.'

Doctor, come quickly!'
 'What's the matter?'
 'We can't get into our house!'
 'That's scarcely my concern, is it?'
 'Yes it is. The baby's swallowed the front door key!'

'Did you take my advice about your insomnia? Did you count sheep?'
 'Yes, I did, doctor. I counted up to 482,354.'
 'And did you fall asleep?'
 'No – it was time to get up!'

A chap at work cut his hand very badly. He was taken to the Casualty Department of the local hospital, where a doctor examined it and said, 'I'll have to put some stitches in that.'
 'Righto, doctor,' said the patient, 'And while you're at it, will you sew this button back on my shirt for me?'

A patient whose doctor advised him to get away to the seaside for a rest and a change came back after a week, and went to report to the doctor.
 'Well, did the rest and the change do you good?' asked the doctor.
 'Not much,' said the disgruntled patient. 'The doorman got my change and the hotel got the rest.'

'Doctor Sawbones speaking.'
 'Oh, doctor, my wife's just dislocated her jaw. Can you come over in, say, three or four weeks' time?'

A plump young woman went to see her doctor.
 'I'm worried about losing my figure, doctor,' she said.
 'You'll just have to diet,' said the doctor unsympathetically.
 'What colour?' asked the woeful patient.

Grab Bag

'I like your Easter tie.'
  'Why do you call it my Easter tie?'
  'It's got egg on it.'

I won't say my sister is a bad driver but my Dad's put a glass floor in the car so whenever she runs anyone over she can see who it is.

Can you spell 'Blind pig'?
Sure – B. L. I. N. D. P. I. G.
No, it's B. L. N. D. P. G. If it had two eyes it wouldn't be blind!

'Why did you put that spider in my bed?'
  ' 'Cos I couldn't find a frog.'

As the housewife opened her door the salesman opened up his case. 'Want any brushes, lady?' he asked.
  'No, thank you.'
  'Dusters?'
  'No, thank you.'
  'Furniture polish? Any cleaning materials at all?'
  'No, thank you.'
  'I thought not,' he replied. 'The woman next door said you never used any . . .!'

'Good morning, sir. I'm from Littlewoods.'
  'Oooo! Have I won the pools?'
  'No – your wife's been arrested for shoplifting.'

My new neighbour's got a glass eye. Mind you, you'd never know unless it came out in the conversation . . .

My Dad's got a new job. He's a test pilot for Kleenex.

'Last week I took the first step towards getting divorced.'
  'Did you see a solicitor?'
  'No, I got married.'

A man whose son had just passed his driving test went home one evening and found that the boy had driven slap into the sitting-room.
  'How on earth did you manage to do that?' he fumed.
  'Quite simple, Dad. I came in through the kitchen and turned left!'

'My grandfather didn't shave till he was thirty years old.'
    'Where was his beard?'
    'Down to his knees!'

Two friends were watching a Clint Eastwood Western film. As Clint rode into town where the baddies were lying in wait, one said 'I bet you £5 he falls off his horse.'
    'Don't be daft,' said the other, 'Clint Eastwood never falls off his horse.'
    'I bet you he does.'
    'All right,' said the second, 'I'll bet you £5 he doesn't!'
    They sat in silence watching the film for a few more minutes; the baddies began shooting, Clint Eastwood's horse reared – and off he fell!
    'There! I told you!' said the first viewer.
    'Oh, all right,' said the second, 'here's your £5.'
    'No, I can't take it,' said his friend. 'I must own up – I've seen this film before.'
    'So have I,' came the reply, 'but I didn't think he'd be such a fool as to fall off again!'

'How old are you?' said one lady to another.
    'I'm thirty-nine,' was the response. 'But I don't look it, do I?'
    'No, but you used to ...'

The dirty old tramp sidled up to a passer-by. 'Got a quid for a bed for the night?' he muttered. 'No,' said the passer-by firmly.
    'Got a fifty pence for a meal?'
    'Certainly not.'
    'Oh ... have you got twenty pence for a cup of tea, then?'
    'No, I have not.'
    'Blimey – you'd better take my mouth-organ. You're worse off than I am!'

Later on the same tramp approached a punk rocker. "Ere, son – I 'aven't 'ad a bite for three days,' he wheezed. So the punk rocker bit him ...

'I'd like some bath salts, please, Mr Chemist.'
    'Certainly, madam. Scented?'
    'No, I'll take them with me. And I'd like a mirror.'
    'Certainly, madam. A hand mirror?'
    'No, I want to see my face.'

The baker was bemoaning the amount of time he had to spend every weekend doing his books. 'How am I going to get through all these accounts?' he wailed to his wife. Back came the unfeeling reply: 'Use your loaf!'

'My husband's a wonderful man. I really think he's one in a million.'
    'Really? I thought he was won in a raffle ...'

'No, I really don't think I want any insurance,' said the house-owner to the salesman.

'Please reconsider, sir. A short time ago one of my clients took out some insurance and the very next day there was a terrible fire at his house – it burned right down! He jumped out of an upstairs window, landed on his car, smashed the roof in and broke both his legs!'

'Yes, well, he was one of the lucky ones.'

Did you hear about the Do-It-Yourself funeral? They just loosen the earth and you sink down by yourself.

'Did you know that in Russia they keep a standing army of two million men?'

'They must be very short of chairs in Russia . . .'

An old lady came across a small boy crying bitterly. 'What's the matter, sonny?' she asked.

'Aaaoowww!' he sobbed. 'It's my birfday, in'it? An' I got a bicycle and some roller skates and I'm 'avin' a party wiv lots of jellies and cakes and ice-creams an' we're 'avin' games and a conjurer –' and again he was overcome with tears.

'That all sounds very nice,' said the old lady. 'Why are you crying then?'

' 'Cos I'm lost, ain't I?!'

'Take the wheel, Harry!' said the nervous lady driver. 'There's a tree coming straight for us!'

'I hate paying my income-tax.'

'You should be a good citizen – why don't you pay with a smile?'

'I'd like to but they insist on money . . .!'

FRANTIC STEER!!

The distinguished old man was being interviewed by a journalist. 'I understand, sir,' said the journalist, 'that you have just celebrated your ninetieth birthday?'

'That is correct – ninety years of age and I haven't an enemy in the world.'

'That's wonderful, sir.'

'Not an enemy in the world. They're all dead!'

Well, sir, I hope to have the privilege of interviewing you on your one hundredth birthday.'

'I don't see why not, young man,' said the eminent personage. 'You look perfectly fit to me!'

'I got thirty Valentine cards last year.'

'Thirty? Wow!'

'But I couldn't afford to post them.'

The after-dinner speaker was droning on and on and on, boring everyone to tears. One of the guests, fighting to keep his drooping eyelids open, turned to the lady on his right and said, 'Can nothing be done to shut him up?'

'If there is I'd like to know,' said the lady, '– I'm his wife and I've been trying to shut him up for twenty years!'

Did you hear about the man who keeps his wife under the bed? He think's she's a little potty!

'We had a wonderful act at the club last week – a man who did farmyard impressions.'
  'What was wonderful about it?'
  'He didn't do the sounds – he did the smells ...'

A man walked into a theatrical agent's office and asked if he could do an audition. 'All right,' said the agent, 'what sort of an act do you do?'
  'I do bird impressions,' said the man.
  'No, I don't want that,' said the agent, 'I've got three bird impressionists on my books already.'
  'Oh, all right,' said the man, and flew out of the window.

'Tell me conductor,' said the old lady passenger, 'does this bus stop at the river?'
  'There'll be an awful splash if it doesn't, ma,' said the cheeky conductor.

'Tell me, conductor, do you stop at the Ritz Hotel?'
  'What – on my salary? You must be joking!'

Mr Jones met a neighbour carrying a front street door. 'Why are you carrying that, Tom?' asked Mr Jones.
  'I've lost my key,' replied Tom.
  'Oh,' said Mr Jones, 'so how will you get in?'
  'It's all right – I've left the window open.'

The removal man was struggling to get a large wardrobe up the stairs.
  'Why don't you get Charlie to help you?' asked the foreman, to which the removal man answered, 'Charlie's inside carrying the clothes.'

'How long will the next bus be, Inspector?'
  'About eight metres, sir.'

'I'm not at all satisfied with the evidence against you,' said the magistrate to the prisoner in the dock, 'so I shall find you not guilty. You are discharged.'
  'Oh, good,' said the prisoner, 'does that mean I can keep the money?'

'The acoustics in this hall are marvellous, aren't they?'
  'Pardon?'

Mr Donovan had spent the evening visiting his old friend Mr Moore, but when the time came for him to leave there was a sudden thunderstorm and the rain began to fall in torrents.
  'You'd better stay the night,' said Mr Moore.
  'Thanks, I will,' said Mr Donovan, 'I'll just pop home for my pyjamas.'

'I had a puncture yesterday.'
'Oh, bad luck. Did you drive over a nail?'
'No, a milk bottle.'
'A milk bottle? Didn't you see it in the road, then?'
'No, the silly woman had it hidden under her coat.'

The two little boys met while paddling in the sea at Brighton during their summer holidays.
'Cor!' said the first, 'your feet ain't 'alf dirty!'
'Yes,' agreed the second, 'we didn't come 'ere last year!'

'Vincent, why have you got a sausage stuck behind your ear?'
'Eh? Oh, blimey – I must have eaten my pencil for lunch!'

At a restaurant which prided itself on its wide selection of dishes, a customer was inspecting the menu. 'You'll find, sir,' said the waiter proudly, 'that everything is on the menu. Absolutely everything!'
'Yes, so I see,' said the customer tartly, 'so take it away and bring me a clean one!'

'Have you got holes in your socks?'
'Certainly not.'
'Then how do you get your feet in?'

An Egyptian lady was speaking to a friend on the telephone. 'Come and spend the evening with me,' she said, 'and if I'm in the bath when you arrive – just Toot 'n' Come In.'

'I went to my doctor to see if he could help me give up smoking.'
'What did he say?'
'He suggested that every time I felt like a smoke I should reach for a bar of chocolate.'
'Did that do any good?'
'No – I can't get the chocolate to light.'

The householder, answering a thunderous knock on the door, opened it to discover a total stranger standing there.
'Who are you?' he asked.
'Police!' came the reply.
'Police? But you're not wearing a uniform.'
'That's right. I'm CID.'
'Oh, I see. Well, come in, Sid.'

It so happened that Tony's brother and girlfriend had their birthdays on the same day; for his brother he bought a shot-gun and for his girlfriend a bottle of very expensive perfume, for which he wrote a note saying 'Use this on yourself and think of me'. Unfortunately Tony put the note in with the wrong present ...

Foreign Phrases

Sic transit gloria mundi My big sister was ill on the bus going back to school after the weekend.

Pas de deux Father of twins.

Coq au vin A chicken on a lorry.

The meanest man in Britain went to the dentist with toothache.

'I'm afraid they'll all have to come out', said the dentist gravely.

'How much will that cost?' asked the man.

'Two pounds.'

'Here's fifty pence. Just slacken them a bit.'

Teacher: 'Today we are going to study "Macbeth" by Shakespeare.'

Boastful pupil: 'My Dad had dinner with Shakespeare last night.'

Teacher: 'But he's been dead for over 300 years!'

Pupil: 'Oh, really. Dad said he was a bit quiet.'

Mike: 'My brother's a puppeteer.'

John: 'How did he get a job like that?'

Mike: 'Oh, he pulled a few strings.'

Sadie: 'I think my brother must be mad.'

Sarah: 'What makes you say that?'

Sadie: 'He thinks he's a dog.'

Sarah: 'How long has this been going on?'

Sadie: 'Ever since he was a puppy.'

A motorist was driving along the motorway when, to his amazement, he was overtaken by a cyclist.

He increased his speed to 80 miles per hour, but once again the cyclist passed him, pedalling furiously. Eventually, the driver could stand it no longer and stopped.

'Thank heavens you've stopped', said the cyclist. 'I had my braces caught in your back bumper.'

Boy: 'A bottle of lemonade, please.'

Café owner: 'How would you like to get one free?'

Boy: How?

Café owner: 'We're giving one away with every 50p bag of crisps.'

Boy: 'Have some nougat'.

Snooty brother: 'NougaR. The T is silent.

Boy: 'Not the way you drink yours.'

Tommy: 'I had a rotten holiday this year!'

Fred: 'Why's that, then?'

Tommy: 'The weather was lousy. We went to the zoo, but all we saw was the keeper building an ark.'

Jack: 'Mum's just had a letter from my brother in Australia.'

Mark: 'How's he doing.'

Jack: 'As big a flop as ever. He tried to go surf riding but he couldn't get the horse into the water.'

Alfie: 'That's a fierce looking alsatian you've got there. Bet he's a good watchdog.'
Tom: 'All he watches is television.'

Colin: 'My Dad's a big game hunter in Scotland.' He shoots lions.'
Jerry: 'But there aren't any lions in Scotland.'
Colin: 'Not now there aren't. He shot 'em all.'

Foreign tourist (to man carrying violin case): 'Excuse me. How do I get to the Albert Hall?'
Violinist: 'Practice.'

Another violinist was convinced he could use his art in music to tame wild animals. So, violin in hand, he travelled to the heart of the African jungle to prove it.

He had no sooner begun to play than the jungle clearing was filled with animals of all kinds gathering to hear him play. Birds, lions, hippos, elephants – all stood round entranced by his beautiful music.

Just then a crocodile crept out of the nearby river and into the clearing, and – snap! – gobbled up the violinist.

The other animals were extremely irate.

'What on earth did you do that for?' they demanded. 'We were enjoying that.'

'Eh?' said the crocodile, cupping its hand to its ear.

Wanted for theft: Man with one eye called Jones.

The unluckiest man in the world: the deep sea diver coming up who met his ship going down.

Teacher: 'Late again. What's the excuse this time?'
Pupil: 'Sorry, miss. There was a notice on the bus saying "Dogs must be carried" and I couldn't find one anywhere.'

A distraught patient rang his doctor at 2 o'clock in the morning.

'I'm very sorry to disturb you at this time of the morning, doctor,' he apologized.

'Oh, that's all right', replied the doctor. 'I had to get up anyway to answer the phone.'

Insurance man (to prospective client): 'What do you keep in the wall safe?'
Client: 'The wall.'
Insurance man: 'And suppose you have a fire.'
Client: 'We'll put that in there too.'

Pete: 'I haven't slept a wink for the past two nights.'
Jimmy: 'Why's that?'
Pete: 'Granny broke her leg. The doctor put it in plaster and told her she shouldn't walk upstairs. You should hear the row when she climbs up the drainpipe.'

Barber: 'How do you want your hair cut, sonny Jim?'
Small customer: 'Like Daddy's – with a hole in the top.'

Proverb: A pen can be driven but a pencil does best when it's lead.

Vicar (to new chorister): 'And what might your name be, little man?'
Chorister: 'It might be Cedric – but it ain't.'

Wanted: Camera stand for photographer with three legs.
   Young assistant to club manager.

'I say, you've got your hat on back to front.'
   'Mind your own business. How do you know which way I'm going?'

If a prehistoric monster took an exam, he'd pass with extinction.

Has it struck you that no matter how short girls' skirts get, they'll always be above two feet?

Do you know the story of the three wells? No? Well, well well ...

Do you know the story of the three eggs? No? Two [too] bad ...

Do you know the story of the empty glass? No? There's nothing in it ...

A wife woke her husband up one night and whispered urgently, 'Alf! Alf! I was woken up by noises downstairs. I went down and there's a burglar in the kitchen eating my fresh-baked apple pie. Ring 999!'
   'Who shall I ask for?' said Alf sleepily. 'Police or ambulance?'

'Stop the bus. An old lady's just fallen off!'
   'It's all right, sir, she's paid her fare.'

An old lady caught two little boys with a packet of cigarettes, and decided to frighten them into giving up cigarettes for life.
   'Now listen to me,' she said sternly, 'do you know where little boys go when they smoke?'
   'Yes, lady,' said the elder of the boys, 'be'ind the church.'

Witness: '. . . he was as drunk as a judge.'
Judge: 'Don't you mean "as drunk as a lord"?'
Witness: 'Yes, my lord . . .'

A man asked his boss for a rise in salary. The boss said, 'What do you mean? Give you a rise? You don't work here at all. Listen: there are 365 days in the year — 366 this year, because it's a Leap Year. The working day is 8 hours — that's one third of a day, so over the year that's 122 days. The office is shut on Sundays so that's 52 off, making 70 days. Then you have two weeks' holiday — take off 14 days which leaves 56. There are four Bank Holidays which leaves 52. Then the office is closed on Saturdays, isn't it? Well, there are 52 Saturdays in the year — so you don't do anything here at all. Yet you're asking me for a rise!'

As the strong-man said on his way to the beach: 'I'm mussel-bound!'

Did you hear about the baby boy whose father was called Ferdinand and whose mother was called Liza? They christened him Ferdilizer.

A town-dweller was visiting the country and was praising the cleanliness of the air.

'So healthy to breathe!' he exclaimed. 'No pollution like the city.'

'Ar,' replied a local, 'Oi can't understand whoi they don't build they owd cities in the country!'

'Why are you crying, sonny?'

'My brother's lost his school cap.'

'But why should that make *you* cry?'

'I was wearing it when he lost it.'

Notice (in a barber's shop window): Hair cut for 40p. Children for 20p.

Do you know the story of the three deer? No? Dear, dear, dear . . . .

Cheeky boy (in shop): 'Have you got any ice-cream left, mister?'

Shop-keeper: 'Yes.'

Cheeky boy: 'Well, you shouldn't make so much.'

Did you hear about the cannibal on a diet? Now he only eats pygmies.

Do you like Shanklin? I don't know — I've never Shankled.

Do you like Kipling? I don't know — I've never Kippled.

LUNCH

Jeff came in to tea groaning and holding his stomach.

'Are you in pain?' his Mum asked anxiously.

'No, the pain's in me!' replied Jeff.

As a large, impressive funeral was passing, a man on the pavement watching it go by asked a small boy, 'Who's died?'

'Chap in the coffin,' said the boy.

Cheeky boy (in another shop): 'Have you got any broken biscuits?'
Shop-keeper: 'Yes.'
Cheeky boy: 'Well, you shouldn't be so clumsy.'

A little boy went into a sweet-shop and asked for a pennyworth of bullseyes. The jar containing the bullseyes was kept on the very top shelf, so the shop-keeper had to get a little ladder, climb up, get the jar, climb down, measure out a pennyworth, then climb back up the ladder to replace the jar.

Just as he had descended the ladder, another boy came into the shop and also asked for a pennyworth of bullseyes. Again the shop-keeper had to go up the ladder, down the ladder, measure out a pennyworth, and then go up and down the ladder again.

In came a third boy – he also wanted a pennyworth of bullseyes. And a fourth. By this time the shop-keeper was getting exhausted, so when the fifth boy came in while he was at the top of the ladder, he said, 'I suppose you want a pennyworth of bullseyes, too?'

'No, I don't,' said the boy.

So the shop-keeper put the jar on the shelf and came down again.

'What *do* you want then, sonny?' he asked, panting hard.

'A ha'pennyworth of bulleyes,' said the lad.

'Who was that at the door?'
  'A chap with a drum.'
  'Tell him to beat it.'

Mean man: 'How much for a haircut?'
Barber: 'Forty pence.'
Mean man: 'How much for a shave?'
Barber: 'Thirty pence.'
Mean man: 'Right – shave my head.'

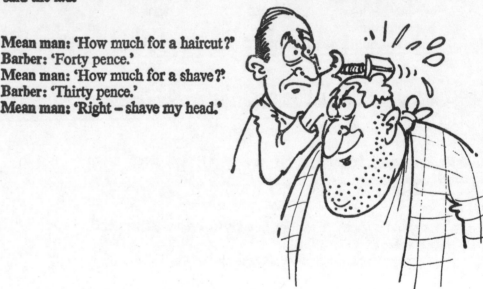

'Who was that at the door?'
  'The Invisible Man.'
  'Tell him I can't see him.'

'Who was that at the door?'
  'A man with a wooden leg.'
  'Tell him to hop it.'

'Who was that at the door?'
  'A man with a trumpet.'
  'Tell him to blow.'

'My friend fell from a window twenty storeys up yesterday.'
  'Was he badly hurt?'
  'No – he fell inside.'

'Who was that at the door?'
  'A woman with a pram.'
  'Tell her to push off.'

Fat man on bus (to schoolboy): 'Who don't you be a gentleman and give a lady your seat?'
'Who was that at the door?'
  'A man selling bee-hives.'
  'Tell him to buzz off.'
Schoolboy: 'Why don't *you* be a gentleman and give two ladies your seat?'

If you're good in this life you will merit everlasting bliss – if not you'll merit an everlasting blister.

Two Irishmen were arranging to meet. 'If oi get there first Oi'll put a chalk cross on the wall, Paddy.'

'Roight ye are, Mick,' said Paddy. 'And if Oi get there first Oi'll rub it off.'

This story is about a man from one of the remotest parts of England where there is still no electricity or gas. For the first time in his life he left his village and went to visit London. When he returned, his friends asked him how he had enjoyed himself.

'Well, the trouble was I couldn't sleep,' he told them.

'Why was that then, Harry?'

'The light was on in my bedroom all the time.'

'Why didn't you blow it out, then?'

'I tried to — but it were inside a little glass bottle.'

A country lad on one of his rare visits to the market town saw a music stool in the window of a shop. He went in, bought it and took it home. Two weeks later he was back at the shop in a furious rage.

'Oi bin sittin' on this dratted stool for two weeks,' he told the manager, 'an Oi ain't got a note out of it yet!'

Fred: 'Are you trying to make a fool out of me?'

Jack: 'Oh no, I never interfere with nature.'

Why is it that no matter who the buyer is, coal always gets delivered to the cellar [seller].

Larry: 'What's the greatest race on earth?'

Mike: 'The Derby?'

Larry: 'No.'

Mike: 'The Grand National?'

Larry: 'No.'

Mike: 'I give up. What *is* the greatest race in the world?'

Larry (laughing): 'The human race!'

Mike: 'I don't know why you're laughing. You're not in it!'

Boy (at dentist's): 'Oh, I wish we were born without teeth.'

Dentist: 'We usually are!'

A boastful American from Texas was being shown the sights of London by a taxi-driver.

'What's that building there?' asked the Texan.

'That's the Tower of London, sir,' replied the taxi-driver.

'Say, we can put up buildings like that in two weeks,' drawled the Texan.

A little while later he said, 'And what's that building we're passing now?'

'That's Buckingham Palace, sir, where the Queen lives.'

'Is that so?' said the Texan, 'Do you know back in Texas we could put up a place like that in a week?'

A few minutes later they were passing Westminster Abbey. The American again asked, 'Hey, cabby, what's that building over there?'

'I'm afraid I don't know, sir,' replied the taxi-driver. 'It wasn't there this morning!'

Chris: 'Hello, Colin. I like your tie. I bet I know where you got it.'
Colin: All right, then, smartie. Where?'
Chris: 'Round your neck!'
Colin: 'Never mind my, tie. I was in the supermarket this morning with Mum and there was a man with no trousers on.'
Chris: 'Was he arrested?'
Colin: 'No – he was wearing a kilt!'
Chris: 'Very funny – ha, ha! My Mum took me to the panto last night.'
Colin: 'Cor, did she? Did you like it?'
Chris: 'No, I cried.'
Colin: 'Why, was it sad?'
Chris: 'Dunno – we couldn't get in!'
Colin: 'My Mum took me to the cemetery this afternoon.'
Chris: 'Oh – anyone dead?'
Colin: 'Yes – all of 'em!'

An angel in heaven was welcoming a new arrival. 'How did you get here?' he asked.
And the new angel replied, "flu . . .'

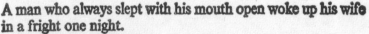

A man who always slept with his mouth open woke up his wife in a fright one night.
'What is it?' she said.
'I've just swallowed a mouse!' cried the husband. 'What shall I do?'
'Don't worry,' said his wife, 'I'll tie a piece of cheese to your nose, then the mouse will come out.'
So she did just this and went back to sleep. But an hour later her husband was waking her up again, even more panic-stricken.
'What is it this time?' she demanded.
'I've just swallowed the cat!'

Extract from a reply to an advertisement: 'I am replying to your advertisement for an organist and chorus master, either lady or gentleman. I have been both for many years . . .'

The proud owner of an impressive new clock was showing it off to a friend.
'This clock,' he said, 'will go for fourteen days without winding.'
'Really?' replied his friend. 'And how long will it go if you do wind it?'

Mum: 'You can't come in unless your feet are clean.'
Small boy: 'They are clean, Mum. It's only my shoes that are dirty.'

Charlie: 'I bet I know where you're going tonight.'
Sadie: 'All right, then, clever dick. Where am I going tonight?'
Charlie: 'To sleep.'

A man who moved into a new house called it 'Simla'. A friend visted him and asked, 'Why do you call your house Simla. Were you in India?'
'No,' the owner replied, 'it's just that it's *sim'lar* to all the other houses in the street!'

A passer-by saw a small boy reaching up and trying to ring a door-bell. He stopped and rang the bell for the boy.

'Thanks, mister,' said the rascal, 'now we'd both better run for it!'

Crafty boy (in shop): 'How much for these toy soldiers?'
Shop-keeper: 'Fifteen pence for two. Tenpence for one.'
Crafty boy: 'Here's fivepence – I'll have the other one.'

Haughty woman: 'Little girl, I'm looking for a small brown dog with one eye.'
Saucy girl: 'If he's only small you'd better use two eyes!'

So you want to play the banjo? Why pick on that . . . ?

Wanted: Strong lad for bottling.
        Cottage for family with good drainage.
        Room for gent. with south view and good ventilation.
        Woman to wash and iron and milk three cows.
        Mattress by a gentleman stuffed with horsehair.

A man stood up in a crowded restaurant and shouted, 'Anybody lost a roll of five pound notes with a rubber band round them?'

There was a rush of people claiming to be the loser. The first to arrive was an old tramp.

'Here you are,' said the man, 'I've found your rubber band!'

Romance gone wrong
'Your teeth are like the stars . they come out at night!'
'Your cheeks are like peaches . . . football peetches!'
'Your ears are like petals . . . bicycles petals!'

Two boys went fishing one summer's morning and trespassed on to the Squire's land. The gamekeeper spotted them and came running up.

'Didn't you see that notice?' he roared.

'Yes,' said the quick-witted boy of the two, 'but it said "Private" at the top so I didn't like to read any further.'

A city boy was taken to the country and saw a horse for the first time. 'Where's his rockers?' he demanded.

Vicar: 'How old are you, Mark?'
Mark: 'Nine, vicar.'
Vicar: 'And what are you going to be?'
Mark: 'Ten, vicar.'

Jenny: 'I haven't slept for days.'
Sarah: 'Why not?'
Jenny: 'I sleep at night.'

And the Banns Played On

'I could marry anyone I please.'
    'So why don't you?'
    'I haven't pleased anyone yet.'

'I want to get married, vicar.'
    'So you want me to put the banns up?'
    'No, we thought we'd just have a concertina after tea.'

To everyone's astonishment the middle-aged spinster announced her engagement.
    'But I thought you said all men were stupid,' said one of her friends, 'and that you'd never marry?'
    'Yes, I did,' she replied, 'but then I found one who asked me.'

George had reached the age of forty-six, and not only was he still unmarried but he had never even had a girlfriend. 'Come along now, George,' said his father. 'It's high time you got yourself a wife and settled down. Why, at your age I'd been married twenty years.'
    'But that was to Mum,' said his son. 'You can't expect me to marry a stranger!'

Harry was madly in love with Betty, but couldn't pluck up enough courage to pop the question face to face. Finally he decided to ask her on the telephone. 'Darling!' he blurted out, 'will you marry me?'
    'Of course, I will, you silly boy,' she replied, 'who is it speaking?'

Poor old Steve sent his photograph off to a Lonely Hearts Club. They sent it back saying they weren't that lonely ...

'I think my wife is trying to tell me something,' said the unfortunate husband, '– she keeps wrapping my sandwiches in a road map!'

Young Andrew was being interviewed by his girlfriend's father. 'So,' said that august personage, 'you want to be my son-in-law, do you?'
    'Not particularly,' said Andrew tactlessly, 'but if I want to marry your daughter I haven't much choice, have I?'

Jim and Mike were in the pub, mulling over Mike's problems. 'Alice and I want to get married,' said Mike, 'but we can't find anywhere to live.'

'Why don't you live with Alice's parents?' suggested Jim.

'We can't do that,' said Mike, 'they're still living with *their* parents!'

Freddie had persuaded Amanda to marry him, and was formally asking her father for his permission. 'Sir,' he said, 'I would like to have your daughter for my wife.'

'Why can't she get one of her own?' said Amanda's father, disconcertingly.

'How's your new wife's cooking then, Barry?'

'Not up to much. She can't even boil the washing-up water without burning it!'

On their first evening in their new home the bride went in to the kitchen to fix drinks. Five minutes later she came back into the living-room in tears.

'What's the matter, my angel?' asked her husband anxiously.

'Oh, Derek!' she sobbed, 'I put the ice-cubes in hot water to wash them and now they've disappeared!'

'After we'd been married two years there was the patter of tiny feet around the house.'

'You had a baby?'

'No – mice.'

'Why aren't you married?'

'I was born that way.'

Mrs Jones and her little daughter Karen were outside the church watching all the comings and goings of a wedding. After the photographs had been taken, everyone had driven off to the reception and all the excitement was over Karen said to her mother 'Why did the bride change her mind, Mummy?'

'How do you mean, change her mind?' asked Mrs Jones.

'Well,' said the moppet, 'she went into the church with one man and came out with another!'

'When I grow up,' confided little Amy to her uncle, 'I'm going to marry the boy next door.'

'Why is that?'

''Cos I'm not allowed to cross the road.'

Mr and Mrs Harris were celebrating their Silver Anniversary with a big party, at which the centre of attraction was a huge cake. 'This cake was made by my wife's fair hands,' said Mr Harris proudly. 'Every year on our anniversary she makes a cake, and I like to think of them as milestones on our journey through life ...'

'Today is my twenty-fifth wedding anniversary.'

'Congratulations.'

'Yes, I've been married twenty-five times.'

Two women were talking at a party, and one said. 'Look at that awful-looking man over there...isn't he hideous? I think he must be the most unattractive man I've ever seen in my life!'

'That happens to be my husband!' said the second icily.

'Oh dear,' said the first, covered in confusion, 'I'm so sorry.'

To which the unfortunate wife replied. '*You're* sorry ...?'

'Do you think, Professor, that my wife should take up the piano as a career?'

'No, I think she should put down the lid as a favour.'

'How old is your wife?'

'She's approaching thirty.'

'From which direction?'

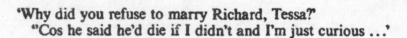

'I thought you were going to marry Eddie? You sad it was love at first sight.'

'It was – it was the second and third sights that put me off him.'

'It's odd how many girls nowadays don't want to get married,' said Bob disconsolately.

'What makes you say that?' asked his friend.

'Cos I've asked them.'

'Why did you refuse to marry Richard, Tessa?'

"Cos he said he'd die if I didn't and I'm just curious ...'

'The man I marry,' said the romantically-minded girl, 'must be as noble as King Arthur, as brave as Hercules, as wise as Solomon, and as handsome as Apollo!'

'How fortunate we met.'

'Why does your husband always call you his Fair Lady when you're a brunette?'

'He's a bus conductor.'

'My wife's an angel – she's never got anything to wear, she's always up in the air and forever harping on about something ...'

'My Peter keeps telling everyone he's going to marry the most beautiful girl in the world.'

'What a shame! And after all the time you've been engaged!'

'But she's so young to get married,' sobbed Diana's mother. 'Only seventeen!'

'Try not to cry about it,' said her husband soothingly. 'Think of it not as losing a daughter but as gaining a bathroom.'

'Will you be my wife one day?'

'Not for one hour, creep.'

The Same Only Different

What's the difference between

— *a bottle of medicine and a doormat?*
One is shaken up and taken and the other is taken up and shaken.

— *a tube and a crazy Dutchman?*
One is a hollow cylinder and the other is a silly Hollander.

— *a sick horse and a dead bee?*
One is a seedy beast and the other is a bee deceased.

— *a married man and a bachelor?*
One kisses the missus and the other misses the kisses.

— *a railway shed and a tree?*
One leaves its shed and the other sheds its leaves.

— *a spendthrift and a pillow?*
One is hard up and the other is soft down.

— *a barber in ancient Rome and an excited circus owner?*
One is a shaving Roman and the other is a raving showman.

— *a watchmaker and a sailor?*
One sees over watches and the other watches over seas.

— *a lighthouse keeper, a thief and a pot of glue?*
One watches over seas, one seizes watches. And the pot of glue? Ah, that's where you get stuck.

— *an angler and a dunce?*
An angler baits his hooks and a dunce hates his books.

— *electricity and lightning?*
You don't have to pay for lightning . . .

— *a nail and a bad boxer?*
One is knocked in and the other is knocked out.

What's the difference between...

—*the Prince of Wales and a tennis ball?*
One is heir to the throne and the other is thrown into the air.

—*seasickness and an auction?*
One is the effects of a sail and the other is the sale of effects.

—*a cat and a comma?*
A cat has claws at the end of its paws and a comma has a pause at the end of its clause.

—*a farmer and a dressmaker?*
One gathers what he sows and the other sews what she gathers.

—*a stubborn donkey and a postage stamp?*
One you lick with a stick and the other you stick with a lick.

—*an orchestral conductor and an oven?*
One makes the beat and the other bakes the meat.

—*a country bumpkin and a welsh rabbit?*
One is easy to cheat and the other is cheesy to eat.

—*a flea-bitten dog and a bored guest?*
One is going to itch and the other is itching to go.

—*a good darts player and a violin-case?*
One finds the middle and the other minds the fiddle.

—*a girl and a postage stamp?*
One is a female and the other is a mail fee.

—*a satirist and a clock-maker?*
One takes the mick and the other makes the tick.

—*a sick cow and an angry crowd?*
One moos badly and the other boos madly.

WELSH RABBIT

—*a hill and a pill?*
One goes up and the other goes down.

—*an oak tree and a tight shoe?*
One makes acorns and the other makes corns ache.

—*a young lady and a fresh loaf?*
One is a well-bred maid and the other is a well-made bread.

—*a coyote and a flea?*
One howls on the prairie and the other prowls on the hairy.

—*a hungry man and a greedy man?*
One longs to eat and the other eats too long.

—*a gutter and a bad fielder?*
One catches drops and the other drops catches.

114

Our Dumb Friends

SOME ADDER!!

Rabbits can multiply – but only a snake can be an adder.

I call my dog Camera because he's always snapping.

A huge lion was roaring through the jungle when he suddenly saw a tiny mouse in his way. He stopped and snarled at it menacingly.

'You're very small,' he growled fiercely.

'Well, I've been ill,' replied the mouse piteously.

Did you hear about the boy who does bird impressions? He eats worms ...

What does a cat have that no other animal has? Kittens ...

City boy (visiting country for the first time): 'That farmer's a magician.'

Country boy: 'What – old Farmer Giles? How do you know?'

City boy: 'He told me he was going to turn his cow into a field.'

A cat must have three tails. You don't believe me? Listen: any cat has more tail than no cat, right? And no cat has two tails, right? So any cat must have three tails!

'Dad, what has a green and yellow striped body, six hairy legs and great big eyes on stalks?'

'I don't know. Why?'

'One's just crawled up your trouser leg!'

A man was boasting about the number of fish he had caught in a lake.

'Mind you,' he said, 'they were biting easily. Why, I had to hide behind a tree to bait my hook!'

'Dad, what would happen if I stole that pony?'

'You'd go to prison, my lad.'

'Oh. You wouldn't forget to feed him while I was away, would you?'

The owner of a donkey-cart called the vet to a country lane.
'What's the matter?' asked the vet.
'I don't know,' was the reply, 'he just won't move.'
'I'll soon fix that,' said the vet. 'I'll give him some of my special medicine.'

About three seconds after the donkey had taken the medicine he went galloping off up the lane with his cart rattling behind him.
'Fantastic!' exclaimed his owner. 'What do I owe you?'
'That'll be 50p, please,' said the vet.
'Well, you'd better give me £1's worth or I'll never catch him!'

Smart Alec: 'How far can a dog chase a rabbit into a wood?'
Innocent friend: 'I suppose it depends on how big the wood is.'
Smart Alec: 'Oh, no it doesn't. A dog can only chase a rabbit halfway into a wood. After that, he's chasing it *out*!'

A small girl was telling her friend all about her first visit to the zoo. 'And I saw the elephants,' she said, 'and what do you think they were doing? Picking up peanuts with their vacuum cleaners!'

Donald: 'Mum, do you water a horse when he's thirsty?
Mum: 'That's right, Donald.'
Donald: 'Then I'm going to milk the cat!'

Why does an ostrich have such a long neck?
Because its head is so far from its body.

What did the lion say when it saw two hunters in a jeep?
'Meals on Wheels...'

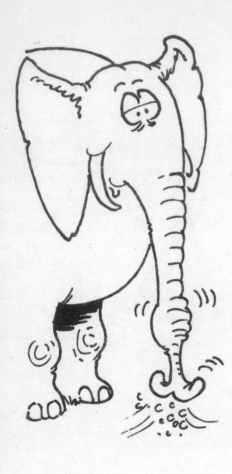

'I've lost my dog.'
'Why not put an ad. in the paper?'
'Don't be daft – he can't read.'

A little fledgling fell out of its nest and went crashing through the branches of the elm tree towards the ground.
'Are you all right?' called out an owl as the chick went hurtling past his perch.'
'So far!' said the little bird.

A farmer was showing a schoolboy round his farm when they came to a field where the farmer's sheep were grazing.
'How many sheep do you reckon there are?' asked the farmer proudly.
'Seven hundred and sixty-four,' replied the boy after a few seconds.
The farmer gaped. 'That's exactly right, boy. How did you count them so quickly?'
'Simple,' said the boy genius. 'I just counted the legs and divided by four!'

Man at auction: 'I say, I've bid a great deal of money for this parrot. Are you sure he talks?'
Auctioneer: ''Course I'm sure. He's been bidding against you!'

First farmer: 'Is that new scarecrow of yourn any good, Giles?'
Second farmer: 'Good? I'll say so. The crows are so scared they're bringing back the seeds they took last week!'

'Why did the mother kangaroo scold her children?'
'I don't know. Why?'
'Because they ate biscuits in bed!'

First cat: 'How did you get on in the milk-drinking competition?'
Second cat: 'Oh, I won by six laps!'

A city boy was staying for the first time on a farm. The morning after he arrived, he asked the farmer if there was anything he could do to help, since he knew that there was always a lot of work to do on a farm.

'That's very thoughtful of you, my boy,' said the farmer. 'Yes, would you go and harness up the old cart-horse for me?'

So off went the lad, full of enthusiasm. But being a city lad he tried to put a harness on the farmer's prize bull! When the farmer eventually arrived, the poor boy exclaimed, 'Oh, farmer, I've tried so hard to get the harness on him – but his ears are too stiff!'

'If a horse's head is pointing north, where would its tail be pointing?'
'To the south.'
'No – to the ground!'

'Are we poisonous?' the baby snake asked his Mummy.
'Yes, dear,' she replied. 'Why do you ask?'
''Cos I've just bitten my tongue!'

A country visitor saw a sign *Chickens For Sale*. He followed the signpost and found himself at a little country cottage. He knocked on the door and an old lady answered.

'How much are your chickens?' he asked.
'They're £3 each,' was the reply.
'Did you raise them yourself?' asked the visitor.
'Oh yes,' she said. 'Yesterday they were only £2 each.'

Do you know why giraffes are nosey?
Because they're always looking over walls to see what giraffe-ter [you're after].

How can you tell a weasel from a stoat?
A weasel's weasily wecognised – but a stoat's stoatally different...

What do you get if you cross an elephant with a mouse?
Great big holes in the skirting board.

What do you get if you cross a lion with a parrot?
I don't know: but if he says 'Pretty Polly' – *smile*!

An absent-minded farmer once fed his broody hen on sawdust. She eventually laid ten eggs. When they hatched nine chicks had a wooden leg and the tenth was a woodpecker.

'Have you ever seen a dog make a rabbit hutch?'
'No, but I've seen a fox make a chicken run.'

Over the public address system came the following announcement: 'Here is the result of today's sheepdog trials. All the sheepdogs have been found not guilty.'

'Why do you call your dog Mechanic?'
'Because every time I throw something at him he makes a bolt for the door!'

The new kitten sitting by the fireside began to purr in the cosy warmth. This unexpected reaction threw little Peter into a panic. 'Mum,' he called, 'the kitten's starting to boil!'

'Would you like to play with our new dog?'
'He looks very fierce. Does he bite?'
'That's what I want to find out.'

'What's your new dog's name?'
'Dunno – he won't tell me.'

Old lady: 'Little boy, don't pull faces at that poor bull-dog.'
Little boy: 'Well, he started it!'

A man went into a pet shop to buy a parrot. He was shown an especially fine one which he liked the look of, but he was puzzled by the two strings which were tied to its feet.
'What are they for?' he asked the pet shop manager.
'Ah, well, sir,' came the reply, 'that's a very unusual feature of this particular parrot. You see, he's a trained parrot, sir – used to be in a circus. If you pull the string on his left foot he says "Hello!", and if you pull the string on his right foot he says "Goodbye!"'
'And what happens if I pull both the strings at the same time?'
'I fall off me perch, you fool!' screeched the parrot.

'Have you ever seen a man-eating tiger?'
'No, but in the caff next door I once saw a man eating chicken!'

'My cat took first prize at the Bird Show.'
'Your cat took first prize at the *Bird* Show? How did he manage that?'
'He ate the prize canary . . .'

A mean horseman went into a saddler's shop and asked for one spur.
'One spur?' asked the saddler. 'Surely you mean a pair of spurs, sir?'
'No, just one,' replied the horseman. 'If I can get one side of the horse to go, the other side is bound to come with it!'

All the animals in the jungle decided to form themselves into football teams and play a knock-out competition. Over a period of several months dozens and dozens of teams played each other, until the great day dawned for the final match to decide the champion animal team. It was a fast and furious match, with thousands of animals from miles and miles around cheering and shouting with excitement.

The score was six-all, and there were just five minutes left for play when Alexander the Ant went scorching down the middle. It looked as though he was just about to score when Elias the Elephant, on the defending side, squashed Alexander flat as a pancake! The referee – Claud the Camel – blew his whistle and came running over.

'You've killed him!' he said to Elias the Elephant. 'That means a penalty – and I'll have to send you off.'

'But I didn't mean to kill him, ref!' pleaded the distraught Elias. 'I only meant to trip him!'

'My dog's got no nose.'
'Poor thing! How does he smell?'
'Terrible!'

'My dog can jump ten feet.'
'That's nothing – my dog can jump as high as our house.'
'I don't believe it!'
'It's true. Mind you, our house can't jump very high.'

'Who went into a lion's den and came out alive?'
'Daniel.'
'Who went into a tiger's den and came out alive?'
'I don't know.'
'The tiger!'

'Do you sell cat's meat?'
'Only if they're accompanied by a human being.'

'I've lost my Budgie. What shall I do?'
'Notify the Flying Squad!'

A little boy was paying his first visit to the country, and his Dad was taking him round a farmyard showing him the various animals.
'And that's a Jersey,' he explained.
'Is it, Dad?' asked the lad. 'I thought it was a cow.'

Mum: 'Louisa, have you changed the water in the goldfish bowl?'
Louisa: 'No, Mum – they haven't drunk the last lot yet.'

'We've got a new watch-dog.'
'Is he a good watch-dog?'
'I'll say! The other day he stopped a dirty old tramp eating a steak and kidney pie my Mum had left on the kitchen table.'
'Go on!'
'He did. He ate it himself!'

Heard of Elephants

Did you hear about the elephant who was always drunk?
   He kept seeing pink people.

What do you get when you cross an elephant with a truck?
   A three-ton pick-up.

Why can't you put an elephant in a sandwich?
   'Cos it's too heavy to lift.

How can you tell if an elephant's been in your bed?
   'Cos it'll be full of peanut shells.

How can you tell if an elephant's been in the fridge?
   'Cos there'll be giant footprints in the butter.

What do elephants have that no other animal has?
   Baby elephants.

How do you know when there's an elephant in your custard?
   When it's *ever* so lumpy.

Why did the elephant cross the road?
   'Cos it was the chicken's day off.

How do you know when an elephant is hiding under your bed?
   'Cos when you wake up your nose is squashed against the ceiling.

What do you do when an elephant sits on your hanky?
   Wait for him to get up.

How does an elephant go up a tree?
   It stands on an acorn and waits for it to grow.

Why do elephants paint their feet yellow?
   So they can hide upside down in a bowl of custard ...
you've never found an elephant in your custard, have you?
No? Works well, then, doesn't it?

Why did the elephant sit on the tomato?
  He wanted to play squash.

Why do elephants have trunks?
  They'd look silly with suitcases, wouldn't they?

If you see an elephant sitting on a chair – what time is it?
  Time to get a new chair.

'How big is an elephant?'
  'What kind of elephant.'
  'A big one.'
  'How big?'

What do you do if an elephant sneezes?
  Get out of the way!

How does an elephant come down a tree?
  It stands on a leaf and waits for autumn.

Why are elephants bad dancers?
  'Cos they have two left feet.

What do elephants do in the back of a Mini?
  Play squash.

What are the largest ants in the world?
  Eleph-ants.

Everyone knows an elephant never forgets – but then what does he have to remember?

How do you get four elephants in a Mini?
  Two in the back and two in the front.

How do you get a rhinoceros in a Mini?
  Chuck one of the elephants out.

When do elephants have sixteen feet?
  When there are four of them.

How do you get down off an elephant?
  You can't – you get it off a swan.

Why can't an elephant ride a bike?
  'Cos he hasn't a thumb to ring the bell.

What do you get if a herd of elephants tramples Batman and Robin?
  Flatman and Ribbon.

Who is Tarzan's favourite singer?
  Harry Elefante.

Why is an elephant large, grey, hairy and wrinkled?
  'Cos if he was small, white, hairless and smooth he'd be an aspirin.

How do you stop an elephant passing through the eye of a needle?
  Tie a knot in his tail.

Why don't elephants eat Penguins?
'Cos they can't get the wrappers off.

What did the elephant say when the crocodile bit off his trunk?
'I thuppothe you think thad's fuddy...'

What's big and red and hides its face in the corner?
An embarrassed elephant.

Why did the elephant cross the road?
To pick up the squashed chicken.

Why do elephants wear sandals?
To stop their feet sinking in the sand.

Why do ostriches bury their heads in the sand?
To see all the elephants who aren't wearing their sandals.

How do you get an elephant in a matchbox?
Take out the matches first.

Why did the elephant take two trunks on holiday?
One to drink through and the other to swim in.

What do you do with a blue elephant?
Cheer him up.

If you shoot a white elephant with a white gun, what do you shoot a pink elephant with?
No, not a pink gun — you paint the elephant white then shoot it with a white gun...

What's grey and wrinkled and lights up?
An electric elephant.

What's the best way to raise an elephant?
Put her on a fork-lift truck.

What happened to Ray when he was stepped on by an elephant?
He became an X-Ray.

Is it difficult to bury a dead elephant?
Yes, it's a huge undertaking.

When do elephants paint their toe-nails red?
When they want to hide in strawberry jam.

How do you get an elephant into a telephone box?
Open the door.

What did the grape say when an elephant stepped on it?
Not much — it just gave a little w(h)ine.

Law and Disorder

The police patrol-car driver was astounded to see, as he overtook a fast-moving car, that the woman at the wheel was knitting. He wound down his window and yelled, 'Pull over!' 'No,' she called back. 'A pair of socks!'

Seeing a woman standing helplessly by her car in a remote part of the countryside, the kindly policeman alighted from his bicycle and asked what was the matter. 'Oh, thank you, officer,' she said. 'I've had a flat tyre. I've managed to change the wheel, but now I can't lower the jack.' 'Very good, madam,' said the policeman. 'I'll see what I can do.' 'Please lower the car gently,' said the woman. 'My husband's asleep in the back seat!'

The policeman had brought a suspect in to the station and was smugly reporting his triumph to the sergeant.

'Good work, Plod,' said the sergeant. 'Has he got a record?'

'Oh, yes, Sarge,' said P.C. Plod. 'He's got three Adam Ants and a pile of Cliff Richard's . . .'

'I'll have to report you, sir,' said the traffic cop to the speeding driver. 'You were doing eighty-five miles an hour.' 'Nonsense, officer,' declared the driver. 'I've only been in the car for ten minutes!'

'Why were you speeding, madam?' asked the traffic cop.

'Well, officer,' came the reply, 'my brakes are bad and I wanted to get home before I had an accident.'

'Last year I opened a jeweller's shop.'

'Any good?'

'No. He caught me at it.'

The only way a constable could quieten a rowdy drunk was to clonk him on the head with his truncheon. 'What was that?' said the drunk. 'It's just struck one,' said the policeman. 'Blimey!' said the drunk. 'It's a good thing I wasn't here an hour ago!'

'Stick 'em down!' snarled the fierce highwayman.
'Eh?' said the startled passenger.
'I said stick 'em down!'
'Don't you mean stick 'em up?'
'Oh — no wonder I'm losing money!'

Do you know what happened to the crook who stole the calendar? He get twelve months . . .

The criminal mastermind found one of his gang sawing the legs off his bed. 'What are you doing that for?' demanded the crook boss.
'Only doing what you ordered,' said the stupid thug. 'You told me to lie low for a bit!'

Why did the police go to the chippy?
'Cos they'd had a report of fish being battered.'

Why did the peanut complain to the police?
'Cos he'd been assaulted.

'No trouble with the football fans this week, Sarge.'
'Why's that, constable?'
'United are playing away!'

'Now as I understand it, sir,' said the policeman to the motorist, 'you were driving this vehicle when the accident occurred. Can you tell me what happened?'
'I'm afraid not, constable,' replied the motorist. 'I had my eyes shut!'

A crook dashed into a Chinese restaurant, brandished a sawn-off shot-gun under the manager's nose and said, 'I want everything you've got in the till!' To which the manager inscrutably replied, 'To take away?'

A jeweller standing behind the counter of his shop was astounded to see a man come hurtling head-first through the window. 'What on earth are you up to?' he demanded. 'I'm terribly sorry,' said the man. 'I forgot to let go of the brick!'

Two petty crooks had been sent by the Big Boss to steal a van-load of goods from a bathroom suppliers. One stayed in the van as look-out and the other went into the storeroom. Fifteen minutes went by, then half an hour, then an hour — and no sign of him. The look-out crook finally grew impatient and went to look for his partner in crime. Inside the store the two came face to face.
'Where have you been?' demanded the worried look-out.
'The boss told me to take a bath,' came the reply, 'but I can't find the soap and towel!'

A murderer sitting in the electric chair was about to be executed. 'Have you any last request?' asked the prison chaplain.

'Yes,' replied the wretched killer. 'Will you hold my hand?'

What do policemen in Hawaii say when they come across something suspicious? 'Aloha, aloha, aloha! What's going' on 'ere, then?!'

Policeman: 'Why are you driving with a bucket of water on the passenger seat?'
Motorist: 'So's I can dip my headlights!'

At three o'clock in the morning a policeman came across a suspicious character skulking down a side street carrying two suitcases. 'What's in the suitcase?' he demanded, pointing to one. 'That's sugar for my tea!' said the man. 'And what's in that suitcase?' asked the policeman, pointing to the other. 'That's sugar for my coffee!' replied the man, whereupon the policeman hit him on the head with his truncheon. 'What's that for?' said the man, rubbing his skull. 'That's a lump for your cocoa!'

'Last week in my self-service store a man served himself to three tins of peaches, the till and a pair of trousers!'
   'Didn't you chase after him?'
   'No — they were my trousers!'

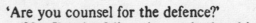

What do you get if you dial 666? Three policemen standing on their heads.

'Are you counsel for the defence?'
   'No. I'm the feller what stole the chickens.'

MURPHY → ← GEORGE

Three men were in the dock, and the judge, who had a terrible squint, said to the first, 'How do you plead?'
   'Not guilty,' said the second.
   'I'm not talking to you,' snapped the judge.
   'I didn't say a word,' said the third.

'I see the police in Liverpool are looking for a man with one eye called Murphy.'
   'What's his other eye called?'

'I see the police in Manchester are looking for a man with a deaf-aid.'
   'Why don't they use glasses?'

'What did your father say when you were sent to gaol?'
   'Hello, son.'

'What is your occupation?' asked the magistrate.
  'I'm a locksmith, your honour.'
  'And what were you doing in the jeweller's shop at three in the morning when the police officers entered?'
  'Making a bolt for the door!'

'I knew a man who married his sister.'
  'That's against the law!'
  'No, it isn't. He was a parson.'

'I'll have to lock you up for the night.'
  'Lock me up? What's the charge?'
  'No charge. It's on Her Majesty.'

A man travelling at 130 miles per hour on the M1 was stopped by traffic police.
  'Sorry, officer,' said the driver, 'was I driving too fast?'
  'No, sir. You were flying too low.'

A policeman was escorting a prisoner to gaol when his hat blew off. 'Shall I run and get it for you?' asked the prisoner obligingly.
  'You must think I'm daft,' said the constable. 'You stand here and I'll get it.'

'What makes you think the prisoner was drunk?' asked the magistrate.
  'Well, your honour,' replied the arresting officer, 'I saw him lift up a manhole cover and walk away with it, and when I asked him what it was for he said, "I want to listen to it on my record-player"!'

'Why do you like being a policeman?'
  'Because in my job the customer is never right!'

'Guilty or not guilty of begging?' asked the beak.
  'Nearly guilty,' said the beggar.
  'What do you mean, "nearly" guilty?' asked the puzzled magistrate.
  'Well, your honour, I asked the lady for fifty pence but I didn't get it.'

A country policeman cycling down the lane was astonished to see a hiker walking along bent under the weight of a large wooden sign which read: *To Plymouth*.
  'Why are you carrying that?' asked the limb of the law.
  'I'm walking to Plymouth,' explained the hiker, 'and I don't want to lose my way!'

'It's a pity you've gone on hunger strike,' said the convict's wife on visiting day.
  'Why?'
  'I've put a file in your cake.'

'You say you have only one brother?' queried the not very alert magistrate. 'But your sister has testified that she has two ...'

The agitated woman had rung 999.
    'Police, fire or ambulance?' asked the operator.
    'I want a vet!' demanded the panic-stricken woman.
    'A vet?' said the emergency service operator in surprise.
'What for?'
    'To open my bulldog's jaws.'
    'But why did you ring 999?'
    'There's a burglar in them.'

'Why did you steal that budgie?'
    'For a lark, your honour.'

At the police station the drunk was asked his name by the station sergeant.
    'John Smith,' was the reply.
    'Come along now,' said the station sergeant wearily, 'you can do better than that.'
    'Oh, all right,' said the drunk, 'I'm the Prince of Wales.'
    'That's better,' said the policeman, 'you can't fool me with that John Smith stuff!'

The constable was calling up his station on his pocket radio. 'I'm outside the Plaza Cinema in the High Street,' he reported. 'A man has been robbed – I've got one of them.'
    'Which one?'
    'The one that was robbed.'

'You say your brother hit you over the head with a shovel?'
    'That's right – and I want him arrested.'
    'When was this, sir?'
    'Last night.'
    'You don't show any marks of having been hit with a shovel?'
    'You should see the shovel!'

'So, it took six policemen to lock you up, I understand?' said the magistrate to the burly prisoner.
    'That it did, your honour,' he admitted, 'but it would only take one to let me out!'

'Why have you painted your car red on one side and blue on the other?'
    'So that if I bang into anyone the witnesses will have a marvellous time in court contradicting each other!'

'I was thrown in prison once, you know,' said the teller of tall stories. 'They put me in a cell with my hands tied behind my back. So I put my big toe in the keyhole and gave a mighty jerk. And *snap!*'
    'You broke the lock?'
    'No, I broke my big toe.'

'Prisoner at the bar, you have pleaded not guilty although no fewer than six people claim to have seen you in the act of stealing the diamonds!'
    'That's nothing; I can produce millions who didn't!'

The Happiest Days of Your Life

A hillbilly dragged his protesting son to a new school that had just opened in a nearby township.

On arrival at the school, the hillbilly Dad asked the teacher, 'What kind of larnin' are yew a-teachifyin'?'

The teacher replied, 'Well, all the usual subjects. Reading, writing, arithmetic –'

The earnest Dad interrupted him, 'What's this here arith . . . arith . . . what you said?'

'Arithmetic, sir,' repeated the teacher. 'I shall be giving a full course of geometry, algebra, trigonometry –'

'Triggernomoetry!' cried the hillbilly. 'Dang me! That's just what my boy needs – he's the worsest shot in the family!'

Teacher: '. . . and as you know, heat causes expansion and cold contraction. Elliot, can you give me an example?'
Elliot: 'Yes, sir. In summer when it's hot the days are longer than in the winter when it's cold.'

Teacher: 'Anyone here quick at picking up music?'
Terence and Tony: 'I am, sir!'
Teacher: 'Right, you two. Move that piano!'

Teacher: 'Archie, if you were in a sailing boat a mile from the harbour's mouth and a storm blew up, what would you do?'
Archie: 'Throw the anchor out, sir.'
Teacher: 'And supposing another storm blew up then what would you do?'
Archie: 'Throw out another anchor, sir.'
Teacher: '. . . er . . . I see. And supposing yet another storm blew up?'
Archie: 'I'd throw out yet another anchor, sir.'
Teacher: 'Just a minute – where are you getting all these anchors from?'
Archie: 'The same place as you're getting all the storms from, sir.'

A keen young teacher wanted to introduce her class to the glories of classical music, so she arranged an outing to an afternoon concert at the Albert Hall. To make the occasion even more memorable, she treated everyone to lemonade, cakes, chocs and ices. Just as the party was getting back into their coach, she said to little Sally, 'Have you enjoyed yourself today?'

'Oh, yes, miss!' said Sally. 'It was lovely. All except the music, that is.'

'The handicraft teacher doesn't like what I'm making.'
'Oh? What are you making, then?'
'Mistakes.'

Cookery mistress: 'Helen, what are the best things to put in a fruit cake?'
Helen: 'Teeth!'

One day, Helen went home and said to her mother, 'Mum, I'm not to go to cookery classes any more.' Naturally her mum asked her why.
'Because I burnt something.' said Helen,
'And what did you burn?' said Mum.
'The cookery classroom.'

Teacher: 'Kevin, why are you late this time?'
Kevin: 'Please sir, I bruised two fingers knocking in a nail at home.'
Teacher: 'I don't see any bandage.'
Kevin: 'Oh, they weren't *my* fingers!'

Teacher: 'Gregory, you've put two "t's" in "rabbit" – there should be only one.'
Gregory: 'Oh. Which "t" should I have left out, sir?'

'I'm our school champion in the 100 metre sprint.'
'Are you really? What do you do it in?'
'Oh, the usual white singlet, shorts and running shoes!'
'Ha, ha! I bet I could beat you if you give me a yard start.'
'OK, you're on. Where?'
'Up a ladder.'

New teacher: 'Doreen, I understand that English grammar is your favourite subject. What tense have I just spoken in?'
Doreen: 'Pre-tence, miss.'

Teacher: 'Matthew, what is the climate of New Zealand?'
Matthew: 'Very cold, sir.'
Teacher: 'Wrong.'
Matthew: 'But, sir! When they send us meat it always arrives frozen!'

'Teacher likes me better than you.'
'How do you know?'
'She puts more kisses in my book than in yours.'

Teacher: 'Fiona, give me a sentence containing the word "gruesome".'
Fiona: 'Er – er – my dad didn't shave for a week and grew some whiskers.'

Vicar: 'To do anything in life you must start at the bottom and work up.'
Small choirboy: 'What about swimming, Vicar?'

Teacher: 'Spell the word "needle", Kenneth.'
Kenneth: 'N-e-i-'
Teacher: 'No, Kenneth, there's no "i" in needle.'
Kenneth: 'Then it's a rotten needle, miss!'

The school inspector asked the class to tell him a number. 'Twenty-seven,' called out one pupil, and the inspector wrote down 72 on the blackboard. No-one said anything, so again he asked the class for a number. 'Twenty-four,' came a voice, and again the inspector wrote on the blackboard – 42. And again no-one said a word. 'Can I have another number, please?' asked the inspector. 'Thirty-three,' shouted someone, and a quiet voice at the back added, 'Let's see 'im muck abaht wiv' '*at* one!'

Teacher: 'Carol, what is "can't" short for?'
Carol: 'Cannot.'
Teacher: 'And what is "don't" short for?'
Carol: 'Doughnut!'

Jeremy was sprawling half out of his desk and chewing gum in a very slovenly manner, causing his teacher to say, 'Jeremy – take that gum out of your mouth and put your feet in!'

Teacher: 'Why is it said that lightning never strikes the same place twice?'
Roy: 'Because after it's struck once the same place ain't there any more!'

Teacher: 'Why was the period between 500 AD and 4200 AD known as the Dark Ages?'
Heather: 'Because those were the days of the (k)nights.'

Mum: 'Hello, Jack. Learn anything new in school today?'
Jack: 'Yeah, how to get out of class by stuffing red ink up my nose.'

Teacher: 'Ivor, where is Felixstowe?'
Ivor: 'On the end of Felix foot!'

Teacher: 'What is "love", Derek?'
Derek: 'Well, miss, I *like* my Mum and Dad but I *love* bubble-gum.'

Teacher: 'Who can tell me something of importance that didn't exist one hundred years ago?'
Smallest girl in class: 'Me!'

Teacher: 'Where are you from, Andy?'
Andy: 'Scotland, miss.'
Teacher: 'What part?'
Andy: 'All of me, miss.'

Teacher: 'What is a Red Indian's wife called?'
A girl: 'A squaw, miss.'
Teacher: 'Quite right. And what are Red Indian babies called?'
A boy: 'Squawkers?'

Teacher: 'Tommy Russell, you're late again.'
Tommy: 'Sorry, sir. It's my bus – it's always coming late.'
Teacher: 'Well, if it's late again tomorrow, catch an earlier one.'

Teacher: 'Alan, give me a sentence starting with "I".'
Alan: 'I is –'
Teacher: 'No, Alan. You must always say "I am".'
Alan: 'Oh, right. "I am the ninth letter of the alphabet".'

Alfred: 'Sir, should someone be punished for something they haven't done?'
Teacher: 'No, of course not.'
Alfred: 'Good, 'cos I haven't done my homework.'

Teacher: 'Harris, when is the best time to gather fruit?'
Harris: 'When the vicar's dog's tied up, sir!'

A boring teacher was droning on one hot summer's afternoon, when he spotted what looked like one of his class reading under the desk.
   'Lambert!' he snapped. 'What are you doing? Learning something?'
   'Oh, no, sir,' said Lambert, all innocence. 'I'm listening to you, sir.'

Teacher: 'Albert, who were the Phoenicians?'
Albert: 'The people who invented Phoenician [Venetian] blinds.'

When one teacher told his class to write the longest sentence they could compose, a bright spark wrote: 'Imprisonment for Life'!

Teacher: 'Ford, you're late for school again. What is it this time?'
Ford: 'I sprained my ankle, sir.'
Teacher: 'That's a lame excuse.'

Teacher: 'Jill, what do you know about Good Friday?'
Jill: 'He did the housework for Robinson Crusoe.'

131

Teacher: 'What is the plural of mouse?'
Infant: 'Mice.'
Teacher: 'And what is the plural of baby?'
Infant: 'Twins.'

Teacher: 'Find Australia on the map for me, Johnny.'
Johnny: 'It's there, sir.'
Teacher: 'That's right. Now, Sammy, who discovered Australia?'
Sammy: 'Johnny, sir.'

Crazy teacher: 'Spell the word "receive" for me, Jackson.'
Jackson: 'Yes, sir. Er . . . r-e-c-e-e-v-e.'
Crazy teacher: 'No Jackson. It's r-e-c-e-i-v-e. The "i" is moist as in "onion".'

Teacher: 'Now, Harrison, if your father borrows £10 from me and pays me back at £1 a month, at the end of six months how much will he owe me?'
Harrison: '£10, sir.'
Teacher: 'I'm afraid you don't know much about arithmetic, Harrison.'
Harrison: 'I'm afraid you don't know much about my father, sir.'

Teacher: 'Now, Jonathan, if I gave you three rabbits and then the next day I gave you five rabbits, how many rabbits would you have?'
Jonathan: 'Nine, sir.'
Teacher: 'Nine?'
Jonathan: 'I've got one already, sir.'

Teacher: 'Why are you standing on your head, Jackson?'
Jackson: 'Just turning things over in my mind, sir . . .'

Teacher: Martin, I've taught you everything I know and you're *still* ignorant!'

Teacher: 'Williams, your writing has improved.'
Williams: 'Thank you, sir.'
Teacher: 'Now I've discovered what an atrocious speller you are!'

Teacher: 'Smith, now that you've kindly consented to come to school, what would you like to do?'
Smith: 'Go home.'

A stern school inspector was putting one class through their paces.

'You, boy,' he roared, pointing at one nervous child. 'Who signed Magna Carta?'

'Please, sir, it wasn't me!' came the agonised answer.

A little girl was playing in the park, when a kindly old lady started talking to her.

'And do you go to school!' she asked.

'No,' was the sulky answer, 'I'm sent!'

Two friends were talking in break-time.

'Would you like to hear a poem?' asked one.

'OK – as long as it rhymes,' said the other. 'I only like poetry if it rhymes.'

'Oh, you'll like this one. Here goes:

"A silly little girl whose name was Nellie,
Fell into the water right up to her knees."

'But that didn't rhyme,' came the complaint.

'No,' said the poet. 'The water wasn't deep enough.'

Teacher: 'Jane, what's five and three?'
Jane: 'Don't know, miss.'
Teacher: 'You silly girl – it's eight, of course.'
Jane: 'But miss, you said yesterday that four and four was eight!'

Teacher: 'Ralph, what are two and two?'
Ralph: 'Four.'
Teacher: 'That's good.'
Ralph: 'Good? It's perfect!'

Teacher: 'How old would a person be who was born in 1935?'
Pupil: 'Er . . . er . . . man or woman?'

Teacher: 'Fiona, what do we get from whales?'
Fiona: 'Coal, miss.'
Teacher: 'No, no. I mean whales in the sea.'
Fiona: 'Oh. Sea-coal, miss.'

A truant officer caught a boy up a tree in the park during school time.

'When are you coming down?' he called.

'When you go away!' was the saucy answer.

Teacher: 'Jones, you should have been in the classroom at nine o'clock.'
Jones: 'Why – did I miss something good?'

Teacher: 'Martha, what does the word "trickle" mean?'
Martha: 'To run slowly.'
Teacher: 'Quite right. And what does the word "anecdote" mean?'
Martha: 'A short, funny tale.'
Teacher: 'Right again. Now, can you give me a sentence with both of those words in it?'
Martha: 'Er – our dog trickled down the street wagging his anecdote!'

'Johnny, I've had a letter from your Headmaster. It seems you're very careless in your appearance.'

'Am I, Dad?'

'Yes. You haven't appeared in school since last term!'

'Now my motto in life', said the school chaplain, 'is work hard, play hard and pray hard. How about you, Harriet?'

'My motto is let bygones be bygones.'

'That's good. Why did you choose that?'

'Then I wouldn't have to have any history lessons!'

The three chums were walking home from school. 'What shall we do this afternoon?' said one. 'I know,' said the second, 'let's spin a coin. If it comes down heads let's go skating, and if it comes down tails let's go swimming.'

'And if it comes down on its edge,' said the third, 'let's stay in and do our homework!'

Have you noticed, kids, how if you pass your exams everyone says you get your brains from your parents, but if you fail your exams everyone says you're stupid ...?

Anthony Brown had been fooling around in class, so his teacher told him to stay in and write out a sentence containing not less than fifty words. Tony thought for a few minutes, and then submitted the following sentence, after which he was allowed to go home – for his ingenuity as much as for his skill at composition!

This was his sentence:

'Mrs Smith wanted to call her cat in for the night, so she went to the front door, opened it and called: "Here, pussy pussy!"'

Teacher: 'Charles, what did Sir Walter Raleigh say as he dropped his cloak before Queen Elizabeth the First?'
Charles: 'Step on it, kid!'

Young Timmy was on the carpet in the Headmaster's study. 'I'm getting rather tired of seeing you here,' said the Head, 'What is it this time?'

'Nothing, sir,' said the indignant young scholar, 'I was only doing what Mr Jackson told me.'

'Really?' said the Headmaster with a sigh, 'Are you sure you weren't being insolent again?'

'No, sir. Mr Jackson got all upset with me over my homework and said 'What do you think I am?' So I told him!'

Norman left school with regret. He was sorry he'd ever had to go.

'How did you get on with your cookery exam, Sharon?'

'Well, Mum, I got eight out of ten for de-frosting.'

'You really must pay more attention, Jenny,' complained the long-suffering form-mistress, 'After all – what are you in school for?'

'Er – to learn, miss?'

'Yes. Anything else?'

'Er – to play sports?'

'Yes. And why else are you here?'

'Er – because they came and got me, miss.'

Teacher (to unruly class): 'Now this afternoon I want to tell you all about a hippopotamus. Please pay attention, all of you! If you don't look at me you'll never know what a hippopotamus is like!'

Teacher: 'Today I'm going to instruct you on Mount Everest.'
Johnny: 'Will we be back in time for "Coronation Street", sir?'

Teacher: 'Shirley, what is the Dog Star?'
Shirley: 'Rin-Tin-Tin, miss.'

Teacher: 'Victor, if I say "I have went", that is wrong, isn't it?'
Victor: 'Yes, sir, 'cos you *ain't* went – you're still 'ere!'

Teacher: 'Alexandra, will you correct the following sentence, please: "the bull and the cow is in the field".'
Alexandra: 'That should be "the cow and the bull is in the field", miss. Ladies should always go before gentlemen.'

Teacher: 'Simon, where is Leeds?'
Simon: 'Top of the First Division, sir!'

Teacher: 'Daphne, name the four seasons.'
Daphne: 'Salt, mustard, pepper and vinegar.'

Nathan: 'Hey, George – I'm leaving school on Friday!'
George: 'Cor! Are you? Why?'
Nathan: 'To have my tea.'

Teacher: 'Doris, what's the opposite of misery?'
Doris: 'Happiness, miss.'
Teacher: 'Correct. And what's the opposite of sadness?'
Doris: 'Gladness.'
Teacher: 'Correct. And the opposite of woe?'
Doris: 'Gee-up!'

The teacher was warning the class about the dangers of going out in cold weather insufficiently clad. 'There was once a boy', he said, 'who was so keen to go out and play with his sledge that he didn't put a coat or scarf on; he caught a chill, the chill led to pneumonia and he died!'

The teacher paused to allow the moral of this story to sink in, when a small voice said, 'What happened to the sledge . . .?'

'What would you like to be when you grow up, Tommy?'

'I'd like to be a teacher, sir.'

'Would you, indeed? And why would you like to be a teacher?'

''Cos I wouldn't have to do any more learning – I'd know everything by then!'

'Tracey, can you count up to ten?'

'Yes, miss.' *(Counting on her fingers held at waist level)* 'One, two, three, four, five, six, seven, eight, nine, ten.'

'Very good, Tracey. Can you count any higher?'

'Yes, miss.' *(Counting again on her fingers from one to ten but this time with her hands above her head!)*

'Helen, if I had £1,000 in my right hand and £2,000 in my left hand, what would I have?'

'Riches, miss.'

'Alfred, if I had 20 marbles in my right trousers pocket, 20 marbles in my left trousers pocket, 40 marbles in my right hip pocket and 40 marbles in my left hip pocket – what would I have?'

'Heavy trousers, sir!'

'What is the most popular answer to school teachers' questions?'

'I don't know.'

'Correct.'

'Come along, Daphne, do your homework.'

'Oh, Dad . . .!'

'Do it now, please. Homework never killed anyone so far as I know.'

'So why should I be the first?'

Why did the teacher have to wear sun-glasses? Because his pupils were so bright.

'Any complaints?' asked the teacher during school dinner.

'Yes, sir,' said one bold lad, 'these peas are awfully hard, sir.'

The master dipped a spoon into the peas on the boy's plate and tasted them.

'They seem soft enough to me,' he declared.

'Yes, they are *now*,' agreed the boy, 'I've been chewing them for the last half hour!'

'Simon, if I had eight apples in my right hand and ten apples in my left hand, what would I have?'

'Huge hands, sir.'

'Julian, why are you late?'

'Sorry, sir. I overslept, sir.'

'You mean you sleep at home as well?!'

'Christopher, give me a sentence with the word "fascinate" in it.'

'Yes, sir. Er – if I have a shirt with ten buttons and two of them fall off, I can only fasten eight!'

'Christina, give me a sentence containing the word "centimetre"!'

'Yes, miss. Last summer, when my Gran was coming to stay with us, I was sent-to-meet-'er.'

'Harold,' asked the maths teacher, 'which would you prefer: eight ice-creams or eighty ice-creams?'

'Eight, sir,' replied Harold.

'Eight?' sneered the teacher, 'don't you know the difference between eight and eighty?'

'Yes, sir,' replied Harold calmly, 'but I don't like ice-cream.'

School meals are not generally popular with those that have to eat them – and sometimes with good reason. 'What kind of pie do you call this?' asked one schoolboy indignantly.

'What's it taste of?' asked the cook.

'Glue!'

'Then it's apple pie – the plum pie tastes of soap.'

When the Headmaster retired from Cokeville High School the sixth form gave him an Illuminated Address. They burned his house down.

'What would you like to do when you leave school, Jacquie?' asked the careers mistress.

'I'd like to be a Lollipop Lady,' said Jacquie, 'at Brands Hatch!'

'What did your Mother do yesterday morning, Vicky?'

'She done her shopping, miss.'

'Done her shopping, Vicky? Where's your grammar?'

'She done her shopping as well, miss.'

'Why aren't you writing, George?'

'I ain't got no pencil, sir.'

'You ain't got no pencil? You have no pencil, you mean.'

'Sir?'

'I have no pencil, he has no pencil, she has no pencil, we have no pencils.'

'Blimey – who's stolen all the pencils!?'

'There's something I can do that nobody else in my school can do. Not even the teachers!'

'What's that?'

'Read my handwriting!'

'Do you obtain good O Level results?' asked the father of a prospective pupil.

'Oh indeed we do,' said the Headmaster of the expensive public school. 'We guarantee satisfaction – or we return the boy ...'

'I think I'd like to join the Royal Air Force,' said the lad to the careers master.

'You like flying, do you?'

'Yes, sir. As long as I can keep one foot on the ground.'

'How are you doing in school?'

'I'm doing well in everything except lessons.'

'I thought I told you to stand at the end of the line!' said the teacher crossly at morning assembly.

'I did, sir,' said the new boy miserably, 'but there was someone there already!'

'You're looking well, young Hubert,' said the visitor heartily.

'Yes, I am, aren't I?' agreed the boy. 'Especially as I've just had angina, arteriosclerosis, tuberculosis, pneumonia and phthisis, aphasia, hypertrophic cirrhosis, and eczema!'

'That's terrible!' exclaimed the visitor in concern, 'to have had all those things at your tender age.'

'Yes,' the lad agreed. 'It was the hardest spelling test I've ever had!'

'Any complaints?'

'Yes, sir. This.'

'Tastes all right to me. That's excellent tea.'

'But it isn't tea, sir. It's stew.'

'And very good stew it is, too ...'

Why did Ken take his bike to school?

'Cos he wanted to drive his teacher up the wall!

Why did Ken take his ladder to school?

'Cos he wanted to go to High School!

The pretty young lady teacher entered the Sixth Form unexpectedly early one morning and saw written in large letters on the blackboard: Lenny David Is The Best Kisser In The Sixth Form.

'Lenny!' she snapped, 'did you write this?'

'Yes, miss, I did,' he admitted sheepishly.

'Stay in after school.'

'Yes, miss.'

The next morning Lenny's friends asked him how long he had had to stay in and what kind of punishment he had received.

'I'm saying nothing, fellers,' he said smugly, 'but I'll tell you this – it certainly pays to advertise!'

LENNY DAVID IS THE BEST KISSER IN THE SIXTH FORM

'Kenneth, name ten things with milk in them.'

'Yes, sir. Milk-shake, tea, coffee, cocoa, and – er – six cows.'

Ian, who was renowned for his insolence, was taken by the scruff of his neck by the sports master to the Head's study.

'What is it this time?' sighed the Headmaster.

'He called me a stupid, boring old twit!' declared the aggrieved sports master.

'Now, Headmaster, how would you like to be called a stupid, boring old twit – supposing you weren't one?!'

'It's no good, sir,' said the hopeless pupil to his English teacher, 'I try to learn, but everything you say goes in both ears and out the other.'

'Goes in both ears and out the other?' queried the puzzled teacher, 'but you only have two ears, boy.'

'You see, sir? I'm no good at maths, either!'

'How are you getting on with your exams?'

'Not bad. The questions are easy enough – it's the answers I have difficulty with!'

'Can you count up to ten, Prunella?'

'Yes, miss. One, two, three, four, five, six, seven, eight, nine, ten.'

'Very good. Now, can you go on from there?'

'Yes, miss. Jack, Queen, King!'

Brian Backchat was living up to his reputation as the most argumentative boy in the school. Furious at being contradicted yet again, his teacher yelled at him,

'That's enough from you! Who's the teacher here – you or me?'

'You, sir.'

'Then why are you talking like an idiot?!'

'Sharon, name two pronouns.'

'Who, me?'

'Correct.'

Boy: 'I'd like to follow the medical profession, sir.'
Careers master: 'So you want to be a doctor?'
Boy: 'No, an undertaker.'

'Mum! I've got a prize for being the school swot!'

'That's wonderful.'

'I've killed more flies than anybody else in the whole school!'

Acting Stupid

'Did you see that open-air show in the park last week?'
   'Yes, I did. Terrible! It was so bad that half an hour after it started four trees got up and walked out!'

'I've been in films, you know,' boasted the small-time actor to the wide-eyed young girl.
   'Have you really?' she breathed admiringly.
   'Oh yes. Did you see *Star Wars*?'
   'Yes, I did indeed.'
   'So did I – jolly good film, wasn't it ...?'

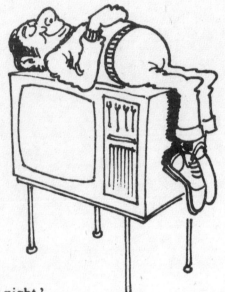

'Did you see *Lassie Come Home*?'
   'Yes.'
   'I played the lead.'
   'What other films have you been in?'
   'Unfortunately my best film wasn't released.'
   'Oh, why not?'
   'It escaped.'

'So you do bird impressions, eh?' said the theatrical agent.
   'That's right, sir.'
   'What kind of bird impressions?'
   'I eat worms.'

'I was on the telly last night.'
   'Were you?'
   'Yes. When I'm drunk I'll sleep anywhere.'

The effect of TV commercials on young viewers can be gauged from this version of part of the Lord's Prayer, as rendered by a small boy: 'Give us this day our oven-fresh, slow-baked, vitamin-enriched, protein-packed, nourishing, delicious, wholemeal daily bread!'

'What sort of an act do you do?'
   'I bend over backwards and pick up a handkerchief with my teeth.'
   'Anything else?'
   'Then I bend over backwards and pick up my teeth.'

'What sort of an act do you do?'
   'I catch razor-sharp butcher's cleavers in my teeth!'
   'In your teeth?!'
   'Sure – I suppose you think I'm smiling ...'

'Did they laugh at your jokes?' the comedian's wife asked.

'Laugh? I thought they'd never start.'

'What was your dressing-room like?'

'Quite nice but rather small. Every time I stood up I kept hitting my head on this chain ...'

'I finished a film last week.'

'Did you?'

'Yes, I should have it back from the chemist tomorrow.'

The conceited comedian sought out the stage-manager, saying petulantly, 'I've just seen the running order of the show. You can't put an artiste of my reputation on after the performing monkeys!'

'Yes, you're right,' mused the stage-manager, 'your acts are rather similar ...'

'I used to be in show business. I had a very spectacular act.'

'What did you do?'

'I used to dive into a wet sponge from a height of fifty feet. But then I broke my neck.'

'Did you miss the sponge?'

'No. Some idiot squeezed it dry.'

'I had a nasty shock while I was doing my act last night,' said the comedian to a pal.

'What happened?'

'There was this chap in the front row – I thought he was laughing from ear to ear, but then just as I was finishing I saw he'd cut his throat!'

Did you hear about the actor who was so keen to get the part of Long John Silver that he had his leg cut off? He still didn't get the job – it was the wrong one.

Did you hear about the teenage-boy who ran away with a circus? The police made him bring it back.

'I'm desperate to get a job as an actress.'

'Why don't you break your leg?'

'Break my leg?'

'Sure – then you'd be in a cast for months!'

'Why did John Travolta break his leg?'

'Why?'

''Cos he slipped on Grease.'

'I was once in a play called *Breakfast In Bed*.'

'Did you have a big role?'

'No, just toast and marmalade.'

'Oh dear,' said the singer as he was about to go on stage, 'I've got a frog in my throat.'

'Then I should let the frog sing,' said a rival vocalist, 'It's got a better voice than you!'

Hey Riddle Diddle

What is it that men do standing up, ladies do sitting down, and dogs on three legs?
Shake hands.

What happens if pigs fly?
Bacon goes up.

What did the crook get who stole the calendar?
Twelve months.

If an apple a day keeps the doctor away, what does a clove of garlic do?
Keeps *everyone* away!

What would you call five bottles of fizzy lemonade?
A pop group.

What do you take off last when you get into bed?
Your feet off the floor.

What should you do for a starving cannibal?
Give him a hand.

What did one tomato say to the other?
'You go on ahead and I'll ketchup.'

What happened to the man who listened to a match?
He burnt his ear.

Why are Frenchmen cannibals?
'Cos they like eating Froggies' legs.

Why did the school-leaver not want to work in the fabrics firm?
'Cos she was too young to dye.

Why was Christopher Columbus a crook?
'Cos he double-crossed the Atlantic.

Who were the first gamblers?
Adam and Eve, 'cos they had a pair 'o dice (Paradise).

What nut sounds like a sneeze?
A cashoo!

What happened when the axe fell on the car?
There was an axe-i-dent.

What did the pilot say as he left the pub?
Must fly now!

Why was the crab arrested?
'Cos he was always pinching things.

142

When does a horse have six legs?
  When it's got a rider on its back.

Why does a horse have six legs?
  'Cos it has forelegs in front and two behind.

How do you keep an idiot waiting?
  I'll tell you later ...

Why should you never gossip in fields?
  'Cos corn has ears, potatoes have eyes and beanstalk.

What is cowhide most used for?
  Holding cows together.

What has one hundred limbs but cannot walk?
  A tree.

What do we do with trees after we chop them down?
  Chop them up.

What tools do we use in arithmetic?
  Multipliers.

What water won't freeze?
  Boiling water.

Why are cooks cruel?
  'Cos they beat eggs and batter fish.

What occurs once in every minute, twice in every moment, but not once in a thousand years?
  The letter M.

What wears a coat all winter and pants in the summer?
  A dog.

What's shut when it's open and open when it's shut?
  A level-crossing.

What training do you need to be a rubbish collector?
  None, you pick it up as you go along.

What gets wetter as it dries?
  A towel.

When is a black dog not a black dog?
  When it's a greyhound.

Why did Kojak throw away the keys?
  'Cos he didn't have any locks.

What does the winner of a running-race always lose?
  His breath.

Why do white sheep eat more grass than black sheep?
  'Cos there are more of them.

What would you see at a chicken show?
Hentertainment.

How do you stop a cockerel crowing on Sunday?
Cook him on Saturday.

Why do idiots eat biscuits?
Because they're crackers.

What is striped and goes round and round?
A zebra in a revolving door.

What is green and hairy and goes up and down?
A gooseberry in a lift.

Where was King Solomon's Temple?
On his forehead.

What do you call an American drawing?
A Yankee Doodle.

What party game did Jekyll like best?
Hyde and Seek.

What's tall and smells nice?   *What's stupid and yellow?*
A giraff-odil.   Thick custard.

What dance do ducks prefer?
A quackstep.

Why do bears wear fur coats?
They'd look silly in plastic macs.

What happened to the man who couldn't tell porridge from putty?
All his windows fell out.

If all the cars in Britain were pink, what would you have?
A car-nation.

What is brown, has four feet, a hump and is found in Alaska?
A lost camel.

Where did the policeman live?
Nine nine nine Let's-Be Avenue.

Why is there no tug-o'-war match between England and France?
'Cos no-one can find a rope twenty-six miles long!

Did you hear about the little boy called Nicholas?
He was called Nicholas because he never wore any.

What goes black and white and black and white and black and white and black and white ...?
A penguin rolling down a hill.

Where are whales weighed?
At a whale weigh station.

144

What is grey and has four legs and a trunk?
   A mouse going on holiday.

Did you hear about the Irish dog which sat down to gnaw a bone?
   When it got up it only had three legs ...

If a flea and a fly pass each other, what time is it?
   Fly past flea.

Why did the man take a pencil to bed?
   To draw the curtains ... I'd tell you another joke about a pencil but it hasn't any point.

What happened when a man bought a paper shop?
   It blew away.

What time did the Chinaman go to the dentist?
   Two-thirty. (Tooth hurtee)

Why did the burglar take a shower?
   He wanted to make a clean getaway.

What's big and yellow and eats rocks?
   A big yellow rock eater.

What did the Father Phone say to the Son Phone?
   You're too young to be engaged.

NEWS FLASH:
   1,000 MATTRESSES STOLEN. POLICE ARE SPRINGING INTO ACTION!

HOLE FOUND IN WALL OF NUDIST COLONY. POLICE ARE LOOKING INTO IT!

What did Dick Turpin say at the end of his ride to York?
   Whoooaaaa!

Who has the biggest boots in the British Army?
   The soldier with the biggest feet.

Why doesn't the sea ever fall into space?
   It's tide.

What is a waste of energy?
   Telling a hair-raising story to a bald man!

What did Mrs Spider say when Mr Spider broke her new web?
   Darn it!

What do you call a bald-headed smiler?
  Yul Grynner.

What do Frenchmen eat for breakfast?
  Huit heures bix.

What kind of meringues repeat?
  Boo-meringues.

What has four legs, a tail, whiskers, and flies?
  A dead cat.

What wobbles when it flies?
  A jellycopter.

What did the mayonnaise say to the fridge?
  'Close the door – I'm dressing.'

What are spiders' webs good for?
  Spiders.

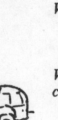

What's blue and yellow and has a wing span of 14 metres?
  A two and a half ton budgie.

Have you heard the joke about the butter?
  I'd better not tell you – you might spread it around.

What is the largest mouse in the world?
  A hippopota-mouse.

What do you call an Eskimo wearing five balaclavas and a crash helmet?
  Anything you like – he can't hear a thing.

What do cannibals eat for breakfast?
  Buttered host.

What do you call a constipated budgie?
  Chirrup of figs.

What do you call an astronaut's watch?
  A luna-tick.

When does an astronaut have his midday meal?
  At launch time.

What did the policeman say to the three-headed man?
  ''Allo, 'allo, 'allo!'

What did the German say to the broken clock?
  'Ve haff vays off makink you tock!'

If a buttercup is yellow, what colour is a hiccup?
  Burple.

What do you give a pig with a sore nose?
  Oinkment.

What lies at the bottom of the sea and shivers?
  A nervous wreck.

What do you get if you run over a canary with a lawn-mower?
Shredded tweet.

What was the police dog's telephone number?
Canine, Canine, Canine.

What do you get if you pour boiling water down a rabbit hole?
Hot Cross Bunnies.

What do you call a foreign body in a chip pan?
An Unidentified Frying Object.

When is it bad luck to be followed by a black cat?
When you're a mouse.

What is the opposite of minimum?
Minidad.

How did the exhausted sparrow land safely?
By sparrowchute.

What is hairy and coughs?
A coconut with a cold.

What cake wanted to rule the world?
Attila the Bun.

What game do horses like?
Stable-tennis.

Which King of England invented the fireplace?
Alfred the Grate.

What do you get if a cat swallows a ball of wool?
Mittens.

What lives under the sea and carries 64 people?
An octobus.

Where does a general keep his armies?
Up his sleevies.

What was purple and wanted to rule the world?
Alexander the Grape.

What did the German policeman say to his chest?
'You're under a-vest!'

Why is there always a wall round a gravevard?
'Cos people are dying to get in.

If a man was born in Australia, worked in America and died in Europe, what is he?
Dead.

How did Noah see to the animals in the Ark?
By flood-lighting.

What swings through trees and is very dangerous?
A chimpanzee with a machine-gun.

What's green and holds up a stage coach?
Dick Gherkin.

What did the rock pool say to another rock pool?
  'Show us your mussels.'

What is yellow, has twenty-two legs and goes crunch?
  A Chinese football team.

Who invented gunpowder?
  A lady who wanted guns to look pretty.

Who was the first underwater spy?
  James Pond.

What do you get when you eat foam?
  Soft in the head.

What do you call an Eskimo's house which has no lavatory?
  An ig.

What travels 100 miles per hour underground?
  A mole on a motor-bike.

How do you milk a mouse?
  You can't – the bucket won't fit under it.

What is the worst kind of weather for rats and mice?
  When it's raining cats and dogs.

What's worse than raining cats and dogs?
  Hailing taxis.

What do you get when you jump in the Red Sea?
  Wet.

What do you call a cat who swallowed a duck?
  A duck-filled fatty puss.

What's black and white and red all over?
  A sun-burnt penguin.

Did you hear about the Irish caterpillar?
  It turned into a frog.

What noise does a cat make on the motorway?
  MAAAIIIOWWWW!

Why did Tiny Tim throw the butter out of the window?
  'Cos he wanted to see a butterfly.

Why did the surveyor take his ruler to bed?
  'Cos he wanted to see how long he would sleep.

Why do cows have horns?
  'Cos their bells don't work.

Where do gnomes do their shopping?
  At the British Gnome Stores.

Have you heard the joke about the dustcart?
  It's a load of rubbish.

What goes in black and comes out white?
A miller's boot.

Why is the sand wet?
Because the seaweed.

Why did the Red Indian put a bucket over his head?
'Cos he wanted to be a pailface.

How do frogs and rabbits make beer?
Dunno, but they start with hops.

What's seven feet high, green and sits in the corner?
The Incredible Sulk.

What is yellow and has twenty-two legs?
Banana United.

When is the best time to go to bed?
When the bed won't come to you.

Why did Nelson wear a three-cornered hat?
To keep his three-cornered head warm.

What's brown and white and yellow and goes at 125 miles per hour?
A train-driver's egg sandwich.

What was Nelson's baby brother called?
Half-Nelson.

What goes in pink and comes out blue?
A swimmer on a cold day.

What's the best way to catch a squirrel?
Hang upside down from a tree and look like a nut.

What insect is musical?
A humbug.

HUUUUUUMMMMMMMM

What is a cloak?
The mating call of a Chinese frog.

What goes dot-dot-croak, croak-dot-croak, dot-croak-dot-croak?
Morse toad.

What are frogs' favourite tales?
Croak and dagger stories.

Did you hear the joke about the field of corn that was 100 feet high?
You wouldn't like it – it's a very tall story.

In a fight between a hedgehog and a fox, who won?
The hedgehog won on points.

What did the Daddy Hedgehog say to his son as he was about to spank him?
'This is going to hurt me far more than it will you ...'

Which member of Robin Hood's band was Welsh?
Rhyl Scarlet.

What is a common illness in China?
Kung Flu.

Where do they go dancing in California?
San Frandisco.

What do spacemen play in their spare time?
Astronaughts and crosses.

What do jelly babies wear on their feet?
Gum boots.

What did the spider say to the beetle?
'Stop bugging me.'

What did the puddle say to the rain?
'Drop in sometime.'

What did the tie say to the hat?
'You go on ahead and I'll hang around.'

What do you call a baby whale?
A little squirt.

What did the invisible man say to his girlfriend?
'Baby, you're outta sight!'

Why does Batman search for worms?
To feed his Robin.

What did the picture say to the wall?
'I've got you covered.'

What do ducks like on television?
Duckumentaries.

What did the cork say to the bottle?
'If you don't behave I'll plug you.'

What famous detective liked to take bubble baths?
Sherlock Foams.

What was Noah's profession?
He was an Ark-itect.

What goes A B C D E F G H I J K L M N O P Q R S T U V W
X Y Z slurp?
A man eating alphabet soup.

What did Cinderella say when the chemist mislaid her
photographs?
'Some day my prints will come.'

What do you do if you split your sides laughing?
Run till you get a stitch.

What is the best thing to take into the desert?
A thirst-aid kit.

Where will you always find diamonds?
In a pack of cards.

What do you call someone who has a dictionary in their
Wellies?
Smarty-boots.

How does an octopus go into battle?
  Fully-armed.

What has one horn and gives milk?
  A milk delivery van.

Why did the tap run?
  'Cos it saw the kitchen sink.

Where do tadpoles change into frogs?
  In the croakroom.

What did the plug say to the wall?
  'Socket to me, baby!'

How do you make a thin guinea-pig fat?
  Throw him off a cliff and he'll come down 'plump!'

What is woolly, covered in chocolate and goes round the sun?
  A Mars Baaaa!

How do you make a cigarette lighter?
  Take the tobacco out.

Why did the owl make everyone laugh?
  'Cos he was a hoot!

Do you know the joke about the rope?
  Aw, skip it ...

Do you know the joke about the two-ton doughnut?
  It takes some swallowing.

Do you know the joke about the bed?
  It hasn't been made yet.

Do you know the joke about the dirty window?
  You wouldn't see through it.

Do you know the joke about the umbrella?
  It'd be over your head.

Do you know how to make a bandstand?
  Take away their chairs.

What did the blackbird say to the scarecrow?
  'I'll knock the stuffing out of you.'

How would you avoid starvation on a desert island?
  By eating the sand-which is there.

What did the strawberry say to the second strawberry?
  'However did we get into this jam?'

What did the saucer say to the cup?
  'None of your lip.'

Why does the giraffe have a long neck?
'Cos he can't stand the smell of his feet.

What do mermaids eat for breakfast?
Merma-lade on toast.

What goes cluck-cluck bang? *What goes tick-tick woof-woof?*
A chicken in a minefield.　**A watchdog.**

What goes ha-ha-ha clonk?　*What dog has no tail?*
A man laughing his head off.　A hotdog.

What is red, has bumps and a horse and lives on the prairie?
The Lone Raspberry.

What is pretty, has big teeth and flies?
A killer butterfly.

What did the Pink Panther say when he stepped on the ant?
(Sing 'Ping Panther tune') 'Dead-ant, dead-ant, dead-ant-
dead-ant-dead-ant ...'

What did the Lone Ranger say when he went to the refuse tip?
'To-de-dump, to-de-dump, to-de-dump-dump-dump ...'

Where do cows go on holiday?
Moo York.

What did Batman's mother say when she wanted to call him for lunch?
(Sing) 'Dinner-dinner-dinner-dinner, dinner-dinner-
dinner-dinner, BATMAN!'

What does a ball do when it stops rolling?
Looks round.

Which chestnut invaded Britain?
William the Conker.

What happened when the glow-worm got tramped on?
He was de-lighted.

Why did the biscuit cry?
'Cos his mother was a wafer so long.

What did one Egyptian say to the other Egyptian?
'I can't remember your name but your fez is familiar.'

What do you get if you dial 4978344672355746392837462?
A blister on your finger.

What's yellow on the inside and green on the outside?
A banana disguised as a cucumber.

Where does a dog go when he loses his tail?
To a re-tailer.

Situations Vacant

At a business conference a self-made millionaire approached the managing director of a rival company and said, 'I started my business life working for you.'

'Really, Sir Henry?' said the managing director. 'I'm afraid I don't recall . . .'

'Yes, indeed,' said the millionaire smugly. 'Thirty years ago I started as an office boy for your company. Do you remember giving me a message to deliver to the despatch department?'

'Oh, yes, Sir Henry,' said the managing director. 'Now I remember. Any reply?'

'My brother's got a good job.'
  'What's that?'
  'Test pilot for Kleenex.'

Who earns a living by driving customers away?
  A taxi-driver.

'I'm the boss and you're nothing! What are you?'
  'Nothing.'
  'And what am I?'
  'Boss over nothing.'
  'Pshaw! You're next to an idiot.'
  'Very well. I'll move.'

'My grandfather was a ship's carpenter. He was a champion poopdeck maker. He made five hundred poopdecks and then he died.'
  'Why?'
  'He was all pooped out.'

'Are you still working in that florist's?'
  'No, I got the sack.'
  'Why?'
  'I had to put the cards into the floral tributes and I got two of them mixed up. The flowers going to a wedding I thought were going to a funeral, so I put in a card which read 'With Deepest Sympathy' . . . and the flowers going to the funeral had a wedding card in them.'
  'What did it say?'
  'Hope You'll Be Happy In Your New Home!'

'Did you hear about old Harry? He's become a big-time operator.'
　'Really? What does he do?'
　'Winds up Big Ben.'

'This loaf is nice and warm!'
　'It should be — the cat's been sitting on it all day!'

'Mr Butcher, have you got a sheep's head?'
　'No, madam, it's just the way I part my hair.'

'Two pounds of cats' meat, please.'
　'Certainly, sir. Shall I wrap it or will you eat it here?'

'I say, waiter! Are you in the Union?'
　'Yes, sir. I'm the chop steward.'

What job has plenty of openings?
　A doorman.

Why did the lazy man get a job in a bakery?
　'Cos he wanted a good loaf.

'Late again, Slattery? Why don't you get an alarm clock?'
　'I did, sir, but it keeps going off while I'm asleep!'

'Boss, there's a man here to see you.'
　'Tell him to take a chair.'
　'Why, is he buying old furniture?'

'Is it difficult to be a coroner?'
　'Oh, yes. You have to take a stiff exam.'

'Why do you want to be an astronomer?'
　'I should think it's a heavenly job!'

'I want a hair-cut, please.'
　'Certainly, sir. Which one?'

'How's the trampoline-selling business?'
　'Oh, up and down.'

A worker on a building site rushed up to the foreman. 'Gaffer! Gaffer!' he cried. 'Someone's just dropped a trowel from the top of the scaffolding and sliced my ear off!' Immediately the foreman organized a search party to find the ear in the hope that surgeons might be able to sew it on again. 'Here it is!' cried one of the searchers, waving an ear. 'No, that's not it,' said the injured workman. 'Mine had a pencil behind it!'

Did you hear about the worker in a banana-packing firm?
He got the sack for throwing the bent ones away . . .

A boy went into a pet-shop and said to the man behind the counter, 'Have you got any parrot-seed?'
'Oh, you've got a parrot, have you?' said the man.
'No,' said the boy, 'but I'd like to grow one!'

'What would you like?' asked the man in the chip shop.
'Shark and chips,' replied the customer. 'And make it snappy!'

A diner in a restaurant was handed the menu by the waiter who, the diner was disconcerted to observe, stood by the table scratching his bottom. 'I say, waiter,' said the customer icily, 'have you got an itchy bottom?'
'No, sir,' replied the waiter. 'Only what's on the menu!'

Boss: 'What's your name?'
New Boy: ''Erbert 'Arris.'
Boss: 'Say "sir" when you address me.'
New Boy: 'All right. Sir 'Erbert 'Arris.'

Did you hear about the really high-powered business tycoon? He had a tall secretary for taking dictation in longhand, a small secretary for taking dictation in shorthand, and a tiny secretary for taking footnotes!

'Don't you like being a lamplighter?'
'No, it gets on my wick.'

'Don't you like being a telegraph linesman?'
'No, it's driving me up the pole.'

'Your reference is excellent. Apparently your last employer considered you a real live-wire salesman. What were you selling?'
'Live wires.'

'I thought, Jessop, that you wanted yesterday afternoon off because you were seeing your dentist?'
'That's right, sir.'
'So how come I saw you coming out of United's ground at the end of the game with a friend?'
'That was my dentist.'

'Why did you leave your last job, Miss Lovejoy?'
'The boss kept kissing me.'
'Oh, indeed? Then I can understand why you wanted to quit.'
'Yes. I can't stand beards.'

'There's only one honest way to make money.'
'What's that?'
'I thought you wouldn't know it!'

Sally had applied for a book-keeping job, and was being tested on her ability with figures. 'Tell me,' said the manager, 'if you were to buy something for £8.73 and sell if for £9.42, would you make a profit or a loss?'

Sally screwed up her forehead in concentration, doodled on her notepad, and then said, 'Well, I'd make a profit on the pounds and a loss on the pence!'

The young lad had applied for a job, and was asked his full name.

'Aloysius Montmorency Geoghan,' he replied.

'How do you spell that?' asked the manager.

'Er – sir – er – can't you just put it down without spelling it?'

'Did your previous employer give you a reference?'

'Yes, but I left it at home.'

'What does it say?'

'Er, well, it says I was one of the best employees he had ever turned out ...'

'Miss Gimlet,' said the shop manager, 'you really must be more polite to our customers. This morning old Mrs Scatter came to me with a very serious complaint.'

'Why?' asked Miss Gimlet pertly, 'are you a doctor?'

'If you're going to work here, young man,' said the boss, 'one thing you must learn is that we are very keen on cleanliness in this firm. Did you wipe your feet on the mat as you came in?'

'Oh, yessir.'

'And another thing we are very keen on is truthfulness: there is no mat.'

'How's that new boy getting on, Jarman?' asked the squire.

'I've found something suited to 'im at last, squire,' said the head gardener.

'Good. What's that?'

'Chasing snails off the paths!'

The works manager discovered four of his men hidden in a corner of the warehouse playing cards. 'Come along now, men, come along!' he said shortly. 'Haven't you anything else to do?'

'Oh yes, guv,' said one of the slackers. 'There's always darts.'

'Why did you leave your last employment?'

'The boss accused me of stealing a five pound note.'

'But why didn't you make him prove it?'

'He did.'

'Miss Cosgrove,' said the boss to his secretary, 'I have to reply to someone whose christian name is Shirley. Do you think that is a man or a woman?'

'It could be either, sir.'

'Yes ... how can I start the letter then? I can't put Dear Sir or Dear Madam if I don't know, can I?'

'How about starting it, "Dear Shir ...?!"'

'What did his lordship say when you smashed up his Rolls-Royce?'
 'Dunno. I never caught 'is last words.'

The flighty young girl was being interviewed for a job.
 'You are not married, are you?' asked the boss.
 'No, but I've had several near Mrs.'

Chief clerk: 'Miss Robbins, who put those hideous flowers on my desk?'
Secretary: 'I did, Mr Rumball.'
Chief clerk: 'And who told you to do that?'
Secretary: 'The manager's wife, Mr Rumball.'
Chief clerk: 'Don't they look nice?'

A bricklayer was continually being harried by his foreman to work faster. 'Let up on us a bit, guv,' the brickie finally protested. 'Rome wasn't built in a day, you know.'
 'Maybe not,' said the foreman, 'but I wasn't on that site.'

'I need a smart boy,' said the boss to the young applicant. 'Someone quick to take notice.'
 'Oh, I can do that, sir. I had it twice last week!'

'I've come in answer to your advert for a handyman.'
 'And are you handy?'
 'Couldn't be handier. I live next door.'

The manager of a shop observed one of his customers in a furious argument with a junior assistant. As he hurried over the customer finally yelled, '... and I shall never come into this place again!' And he stalked out, slamming the door behind him. 'Hicks,' said the shop manager severely, 'how many more times must I tell you: the customer is always right!'
 'As you wish, sir,' said the junior. 'He was saying you were a lop-eared, bald-headed, brainless twit!'

'Sir, there's a debt collector in the outer office.'
 'Tell him he can take that pile on my desk.'

The apprentice electrician was on his first job. 'Take hold of those two wires, Alec,' said his master, 'and rub them together.' Alec did as he was bid, and his master said, 'D'you feel anything?'
 'No,' said Alec.
 'That's good – so don't touch those other two wires or you'll get a nasty shock!'

'You play fair with me and I'll play fair with you,' said the boss to the new worker. 'Just remember: you can't do too much for a good employer.'

'Don't worry, I won't.'

'I just want you to remember one thing, Boyce,' said the managing director to the new sales manager. 'If at first you don't succeed – you're fired!'

'Come on, slowcoach,' said the foreman to a tardy workman. 'The hooter's gone.'

'Well, don't look at me, guv. I didn't take it!'

There had been an explosion in the gunpowder factory, and the management were holding an enquiry into the cause of the accident. 'Now, Parsley,' said the chairman of the board, 'You were on the spot. Exactly what happened?'

'It was like this, sir,' explained Parsley, 'Old Charlie Higgins was in the mixing-room, and I saw him – absent-minded, like – take out a box of matches to light up a fag.'

'He struck a match in the mixing-room?' said the chairman in horror. 'How long had Higgins worked for us?'

'About twenty years, sir.'

'Twenty years, and he struck a match in the mixing-room? I'd have thought that would be the last thing he'd do.'

'It was, sir.'

'You're asking a lot of money for an unskilled man,' said the foreman to a job applicant, 'and you've no experience of our kind of work at all, have you?'

'No, well,' explained the hopeful one, 'I fink I oughter 'ave more money 'cos it's so much 'arder when you don't know nuffink abaht it, ain't it?'

The butcher's boy had been dismissed for insolence, and vowed vengeance on his ex-employer. The following Saturday morning, when the shop was packed with people buying their weekend joints, he marched in, elbowed his way to the counter and slapped down one very, very dead cat. 'There you are, guv!' he called out cheerily, 'that makes up the dozen you ordered!'

'I've worked here for three years now, sir, and during most of that time I've been doing the work of three men. So what about a rise in salary?'

'I can't see my way to giving you a rise, Phillips,' said the skinflint boss, 'but I'll tell you what I'll do. I'll sack the other two men!'

Master Carpenter: Son, you're certainly hammering those nails in like lightning!
Apprentice: 'You mean I'm fast?'
Master Carpenter: 'No – you never strike in the same place twice!'

Worker: 'I bet the boss was furious when you told him I'd be leaving next week.'
Foreman: 'Yes, he was. He thought it was this week.'

'Here you are, Davidson,' said the boss to a notoriously lazy employee. 'Here's your pay for forty hours' slacking!'
  'Be fair, guv,' said the indolent one. 'Forty-one hours!'

'Why did you leave your last job?'
  'Something the boss said.'
  'Was he abusive?'
  'Not exactly.'
  'What did he say, then?'
  'You're fired!'

The pert young copy-typist arrived at the office late as usual. 'Mary!' called the supervisor, 'don't you know what time we start work here?'
  'No,' said the saucy miss, 'you're always at it by the time I arrive!'

'I was a waiter at the Hotel Splendiferous for three months, but I had to leave on account of the head waiter's nerves.'
  'His nerves?'
  'He couldn't stand the sound of breaking crockery.'

'Witherspoon, I gave you half a day off because you said you had to tend your prize garden, and now I have been informed that you do not have a garden. What have you to say for yourself?'
  'Well, sir, if you've been told there is no garden someone must have pushed it off the window-ledge!'

An apprentice blacksmith was told by his master to make a hammer. The lad had not the slightest idea how to begin, so he thought he'd be crafty and nip out and buy one. He duly showed the new hammer to his master who said, 'That's excellent boy! Now make fifty more just like it!'

A youth had applied for a job at a poulterer's and fishmonger's.
  'I can only offer you £25 a week,' said the manager. 'Can you fillet a fish?'
  'Yes,' said the lad.
  'Can you dress a bird?'
  'What – on £25 a week?'

'The first thing you can do,' said the boss to the new office boy, 'is to look up a telephone number for me. I want to call Mr Henry T. Zachary – got it?'
  'Henry T. Zachary, sir,' said the lad, reaching for the directory. 'Righto, sir.'
  Half an hour later the manager called the boy into his office. 'Come on,' he said, 'how are you doing with that number?'
  'It's coming along, sir,' replied the keen youngster. 'I'm up to the M's already!'

The chief clerk answered the telephone, and an aged quavery voice said, 'Oh, excuse me, but would it be possible to speak to Darren, the messenger boy?'

'Who is it speaking?' asked the chief clerk.

'This is his grandfather.'

'I'm afraid Darren isn't here. He's gone to your funeral!'

'Why do you want next Wednesday off, Carstairs?'

'I'm getting married, sir.'

'Getting married?! Great Scott, what feeble-minded girl would want to marry you?'

'Your daughter, sir.'

'Mossop! Why are you late this morning?'

'I got married, sir.'

'Very well, but see that it doesn't happen again.'

'Brendan,' scolded his mother, 'you've been at that job five years and you're still the office junior. When are you going to get ahead?'

'I've already got one, Mum.'

'May I have an hour off to get my hair cut, sir?'

'Certainly not. Have it cut in your own time.'

'But it grows in office hours, sir.'

'It doesn't do all its growing during office hours, boy.'

'I'm not having it all off!'

The beautiful film star was giving her chauffeur/handyman a severe ticking off. 'Harry,' she said firmly, 'I must ask you not to come into my bathroom or my bedroom without knocking. Is that quite clear?'

'Don't worry, miss,' responded the aggrieved servant, 'I allus looks through the key'ole fust, an' if you got nuffink on I don't come in!'

'How many people work in this office?'

'About half of them, sir.'

'Rachel, this tea you've made tastes like dishwater!'

'Does it, sir? How can you tell . . .?'

'Very well, my boy,' said the manager, 'I'll take you on. I take it you're not afraid of early hours?'

'Oh, no, sir,' said the teenage applicant, 'you can't close too early for me!'

'Doreen!' said the boss crossly, 'I can never find what I want in these files. What system do you use?'

'The Biblical system, sir.'

'The Biblical system? What's that?'

' "Seek and ye shall find"!'

Happy Families

An auntie who very rarely came visiting was very touched by the attention paid to her by the son of the house.

'You've been very nice to me this afternoon, Johnny,' she said. 'I do believe that you don't want me to go.'

'You're right, I don't, Auntie. Dad says he's going to give me a good hiding as soon as you've gone.'

'Come here, you greedy wretch. I'll teach you to eat all your sister's birthday chocs.'

'It's all right, Dad, I know how.'

Mum: 'Nicholas, don't be mean. Let your little brother play with your marbles if he wants to.'
Nicholas: 'Oh, Mum! He wants to keep them.'
Mum: 'I'm sure he doesn't.'
Nicholas: 'Well, he's swallowed two already!

Mum: 'Susan, just look at the mess you're in! What *have* you been doing?'
Susan: 'I fell in a puddle, Mum.'
Mum: 'In your new dress?'
Susan: 'Well, I didn't have time to change.'

Dad (to daughter): 'Well, Anne, I suppose that boyfriend of yours will be coming round after supper?'
Small brother: 'That's all he *does* come round for!'

'I had a funny dream last night, Mum.'
'Did you?'
'I dreamed I was awake, but when I woke up I found I was asleep!'

Prunella: 'Mum, Simon's broken my doll.'
Mum: 'How did he do that?'
Prunella: 'I hit him on the head with it.'

'Why are your class marks always so low?'
'Because I sit in the last desk at the back, Dad.'
'What difference does that make?'
'Well, there are so many of us in the class that when it's my turn for marks there aren't many left.'

'Mum, will you wash my face?'

'Why can't you wash it yourself?'

''Cos that'll mean getting my hands wet, and they don't need washing!'

'So you are distantly related to the family next door, are you?'

'Yes – their dog is our dog's brother.'

A rather stern aunt had been staying with Sharon's parents, and one day she said to the little girl, 'Well, Sharon, I'm going tomorrow. Are you sorry?'

'Oh, yes, Auntie,' replied Sharon. I thought you were going today.'

'No, Billy, you can't play with the hammer. You'll hurt your fingers.'

'No I won't, Dad. Sis is going to hold the nails for me.'

'Joyce, how many more times must I tell you to come away from that cake tin?'

'No more, Mum. It's empty!'

'Eve, do you know a girl called Clare Cook?'

'Yes, Mum. She sleeps next to me in geography class.

'Dad, are caterpillars good to eat?'

'No, son. Why?'

''Cos you've just eaten one on your lettuce.'

'Tell me, Jason, do you like going to school?'

'Yes, Uncle Harry, I like *going* to school – it's when I get there that I don't enjoy myself much.'

'What's your father's walk in life?'

'He's a bit bandy – why?'

'Dad, the boy next door said I look just like you.'

'Did he now? And what did you say?'

'Nothing. He's bigger than me.'

A scoutmaster asked one of his troop what good deed he had done for the day.

'Well, Skip,' said the scout. 'Mum only had one dose of castor oil left, so I let my baby brother have it.'

Yet another bad school report was received by an irate father.

'Stevie, I'm not at all pleased with your report this term,' he said furiously.

'I told Sir you wouldn't be,' said Stevie, 'but he insisted on sending it just the same.'

'Mum, how do you spell "high"?'
'H-I-G-H. Why, what is your composition about?'
'High-enas.'

'My dad hasn't done a day's work since 1968.'
'Why not?'
'He's a night-watchman.'

'Mum, do you think the baby would like some blotting-paper to eat?'
'No, dear, I don't think he would. Why?'
'He's just swallowed a bottle of ink . . .'

'Barbara, what are you doing out there in the rain?'
'Getting wet!'

'Vicar told us that in the Bible it says we're made of dust'
'That's right'
'So when I go swimming why don't I get muddy?'

Dad: 'My word, I slept like a log last night'
Ken: 'I know you did, Dad I heard you sawing it.'

'Jeremy, I want you to wash before your music mistress arrives.'
'I have, Mum.'
'Did you wash your ears?'
'Well . . . I washed the one next to her.'

'Dad, if I plant this pip in the garden, will it grow into an orange tree?'
'It might do, son, yes'
'That's funny – it's a lemon pip.'

'What happened to all those mince pies? I told you you couldn't have one and now there's only one left.'
'That's the one I haven't had, Mum.'

Paul's teacher had had enough of his larks and impertinenence in the schoolroom, so he wrote a letter of complaint to Paul's father.
'Paul,' roared Dad, 'come here! What's all this about? Your teacher says he finds it impossible to teach you anything!'
'I told you he was no good,' said Paul.

'Now, little man, what are you going to give your sister for Christmas?'
'Well, last Christmas I gave her measles . . .'

Jimmy was caught by his mother in the pantry. 'And what do you think you're up to?' she asked furiously.
'I'm up to my seventh jam tart,' said Jimmy, 'but they're only little 'uns, Mum!'

Mum: 'Maria, was that the step-ladder I heard falling over?'
Maria: 'Yes, Mum.'
Mum: 'Has your dad fallen down?'
Maria: 'No, mum, he's still hanging on the curtain-rail.'

A small boy had the misfortune to have the meanest dad in Britain. One rainy day, the little lad came in shivering with the wet and the cold, and said, 'Dad, my boots let the water in.'

'So what?' said his flinty-hearted parent. 'They let it out again, don't they?'

A little girl from a very poor family went into the local baker's shop. 'Me Mum wants a large loaf, please,' she said, putting down her pennies. 'And would you please cut it in slices with a jammy knife?'

'Is this your brother?'
  'Yes, vicar.'
  'He's very small, isn't he?'
  'Well, he's only my half-brother ...'

'Who broke the window?'
  'It was Andrew, Dad. He ducked when I threw a stone at him.'

'Dad, I don't want to go to Australia!'
  'Shut up and keep digging ...'

Grandma: 'Sylvester, I wouldn't slide down the banisters like that if I were you.'
Sylvester: Why, how would you slide down them then, Grandma?'

'Mum, if someone broke your best vase what would you do?'
  'I'd spank him and send him to bed without any supper!'
  'Well, you'd better get the slipper. Dad's just broken it!'

A nine-year-old was grubbing about in the garden, when his mum came out and asked him what he was doing.
  'I'm collecting slugs, Mum,' was the happy answer.
  'Oh,' said his mum unenthusiastically. 'And what are you going to do with them?'
  'Press them!'

Mum: 'Horace, why are you crying?'
Horace: 'I've hurt my finger, Mum.'
Mum: 'When did you do that?'
Horace: 'Half an hour ago.'
Mum: 'I didn't hear you crying then.'
Horace: 'No, I thought you were out.'

'Mervyn, your great-grandfather is one hundred years old today! Isn't that wonderful?'
  'Huh! It's taken him long enough to do it ...'

'My dad's a sorter in the House of Commons.'
  'What sort of sorter?'
  'A sorter window-cleaner.'

Dad: 'Gary, how was your first day at school?'
Gary: 'OK, Dad, but I haven't got my present yet.'
Dad: 'What present is that?'
Gary: 'Well, Miss said to me "Gary, sit there for the present".
P'raps I'll get it tomorrow.'

Grandma: 'You've left all your crusts, Mary. When I was your
age I ate every one.'
Mary: 'Do you still like crusts, Grandma?'
Grandma: 'Yes, I do.'
Mary: 'Well, you can have mine.'

Benjamin, go and kiss your auntie goodbye.'
   'Why, I ain't done nuffink!'

'Will you have some blancmange to finish up with?'
   'No, I'll have another bun to go on with!'

Pa was taking Danny round the museum where they came
across a magnificent stuffed lion in a glass case.
   'Pa,' asked the puzzled Danny, 'how did they shoot the lion
without breaking the glass?'

'How did your exams go?'
   'I nearly got 10 in every subject.'
   'How do you mean – nearly 10?'
   'Well, I got the noughts . . .'

'Dad, a man called while you were out.'
   'Did he have a bill?'
   'No, just an ordinary nose like everyone else.'

A visitor to Geoffrey's house remarked at tea-time on the
friendliness of Geoff's dog.
   'He's wagging his tail at me and sitting up all the time!' said
the visitor, pleased.
   'I'm not surprised,' said Geoffrey. 'You're eating off his plate.'

'You've been fighting again – you've lost two of your front
teeth!'
   'I haven't lost them, Mum. I've got 'em in my pocke..'

'Ma, Ma! Dad's fallen over the cliff!'
   'My goodness! Is he hurt?'
   'I dunno – he hadn't stopped falling when I left!'

Midge was scribbling industriously over some paper with a
pencil when her mother asked what she was drawing.
   'I'm not drawing, Mum,' she said indignantly. 'I'm writing
a letter to Jenny.'
   'But you can't write,' Mum pointed out.
   'That's all right,' said Midge. 'Jenny can't read.'

'Dad, would you like to save some money?'
   'I certainly would, son. Any suggestions?'
   'Sure. Why not buy me a bike, then I won't wear my shoes out
so fast.'

A child one Christmas time asked for some paper and crayons in order to draw a crib. Eventually the artistic masterpiece was displayed for parental approval. The manger, the shepherds, Jesus and the Holy Family were duly admired.

'But what's that in the corner?' asked Mother.

'Oh, that's their telly,' replied the tot.

That was kind of you to let your sister have first go with your skates.'

'I'm waiting to see if the ice is thick enough . . .'

Mum: 'How was your first day at school?'

Johnny: 'It was all right, except for some bloke called Sir who kept spoiling the fun.'

'What did you learn in school today, son?'

'I learned that those sums you did for me were wrong!'

'Rebecca, you've been a long time putting salt in the saltcellar'

'Well, Mum, you can't get much at a time through that little hole in the top'

'You wicked little imp! If you're not good, I shall fetch a policeman!'

'If you do, Mum, I'll tell him we haven't got a telly licence.'

Mum: 'Come on, Mike. Time waits for no man, you know.'

Mike: 'Yes it does, Mum.'

Mum: 'What do you mean?'

Mike: 'Well, when Dad and me was walking back from church last Sunday and we passed the pub on the corner, he said to me: "Wait here – I'll just stop a few minutes".'

'What would you like?'

'Cake.'

'Cake what?'

'Cake first.'

'Jimmy, what did I say I'd do if I caught you smoking cigarettes again?

'That's funny, Dad – I can't remember, either.'

'Julia, this report is most disappointing. I promised you a bicycle if you passed your exams. What have you been doing with yourself?'

'Learning to ride a bike.'

'Do you look in the mirror after you've washed?'

'No, I look in the towel!'

'Dad, I bet there's something I can do that you can't do.'

'What's that, son?'

'Grow up!'

Dad was furious about Sonny's school report. 'I've never read anything like it!' he roared. 'It says here that you're nothing but a little terror! What does this mean?'

'It means, Dad,' said the object of the report, 'that I'm the son of a big terror.'

'Geoffrey, pick up your feet when you walk!'
'Why, Mum? I've only got to put them down again.'

'My brother's in hospital.'
'What's wrong with him?'
'He's got spotted fever.'
'Cripes! Is it serious?'
'No – it was spotted in time.'

Mum: 'Jimmy, where are you off to now?'
Jimmy: 'I'm going to join the Army.'
Mum: 'But legally you're only an infant.'
Jimmy: 'That's all right. I'm going to join the infantry.'

Teddy came thundering down the stairs, much to his father's annoyance.

'Teddy,' he called, 'how many more times have I got to tell you to come down those stairs quietly! Now, go back upstairs and come down like a civilised human being.'

There was a silence, and Teddy reappeared in the front room.

'That's better,' said his father. 'Now in future will you always come down the stairs like that.'

'Suits me,' said Teddy. 'I slid down the bannisters.'

Luke: 'Mum, am I made of sage and parsley and breadcrumbs?'
Mum: 'Of course not. Why do you ask?'
Luke: 'Because that big boy from the corner said he's going to knock the stuffing out of me tomorrow.'

The Jones family were just about to leave on their annual holiday. 'Have you packed everything?' Mrs Jones asked her small son.

'Yes, Mum,' he answered.

'Are you sure?' she said suspiciously. 'Have you packed your soap?'

'Soap?' he said in dismay. 'I thought this was supposed to be a holday!'

'Giles, we're having very important guests for lunch today so clean yourself up and make yourself presentable, please.'

'Why – they're not going to eat me, are they?'

'Now then, Deirdre, eat up all your greens like a good girl. They're good for the complexion, you know.'
'But I don't want to have a green complexion!'

Teacher: 'What's this a picture of?'
Class: 'Don't know, miss.'
Teacher: 'It's a kangaroo.'
Class: 'What's a kangaroo, miss?'
Teacher: 'A kangaroo is a native of Australia.'
Smallest boy: 'Cor – my big sister's married one of them!'

'Was that you singing as I came in, Sis?'

'Yes, I'm just killing time before my singing lesson.'

'Well, you're sure using the right weapon!'

'But don't you think my voice has improved?'

'Yes – but it's not cured yet.'

A little boy was taken to a seance by his mum. The medium asked him who he would like to speak to.

'My Grandad,' he said.

The medium went into a trance and soon a spooky voice could be heard speaking softly in the darkened room.

'This is your Grandad speaking to you Timmy,' said the voice. 'What is it you wish to ask me?'

'What are you doing in Heaven, Grandad?' asked the little boy. 'You're not even dead yet!'

Julie was saying her bedtime prayers. 'Please God,' she said, 'make Naples the capital of Italy. Make Naples the capital of Italy –'

Her mother interrupted and said, 'Julie, why do you want God to make Naples the capital of Italy?'

And Julie replied, 'Because that's what I put in my geography exam!'

A certain little boy had been spanked by his father one morning. When his dad came in from the office that evening, the boy called out sulkily, 'Mum! Your husband's just come home.'

Did you hear about the little boy who was named after his father? They called him Dad.

Another little boy's father worked away from home a good deal. In fact he saw his father so rarely that he called him 'Uncle Dad'.

'Grandad, Mary Brown's mum says you're not fit to live with pigs.'

'Did she now? And what did you say?'

'Oh, I stuck up for you – I said you were!'

One little boy had a very strange granny. In the winter, no matter how cold it was, she would go out and get the coal in her nightie. His Dad bought her a shovel, but grannie said her nightie held more . . .

When a Very Important Person came to the house, little Penny was allowed to take him a glass of sherry. She handed it to him and then stood there staring.

'What is it, Penny?' he asked.

'I want to see you do your trick,' she replied.

'What trick is that?' asked the guest.

'Well, Dad says you drink like a fish.'

Little George was crying one day, and his dad asked him why.
  'I've lost 5p,' sobbed George.
  'Never mind,' said his dad kindly. 'Here's another 5p for you.'
  At which Georgie howled louder than ever.
  'Now what is it?' asked his dad.
  'I wish I'd said I'd lost 10p!'

Extract from a letter written by a fond mum to her son: *Your Auntie Betty's just had her teeth out and a new fireplace put in. Well, I must write quickly now because my pen's running out . . .*

Mum: 'I've just looked in the mirror, and I've got two grey hairs!'
Emma: 'Why's that, Mummy?'
Mum (seizing the chance): 'Because you're such a bad girl to me, I expect.'
Emma: 'Gosh, Mum, you must have been awful to Grandma!'

Mum: 'Teddy, you are a naughty boy! When Billy threw stones at you why didn't you come and tell me instead of throwing stones back at him?'
Teddy: 'Come off it, Ma. You know you can't throw for toffee!'

Mum: 'Sue, why did you drop the baby?'
Sue: 'Well, Mrs. Jones said he was bonny bouncing baby, so I wanted to see if he did!'

Rebecca: 'Mum, did baby brother come from Heaven?'
Mum: 'That's right, dear.'
Rebecca: 'I don't blame the angels for chucking him out!'

Johnny: 'Dad, the vicar says we're all here to help others.'
Dad: 'That's right, Johnny.'
Johnny: 'So what are the others for?'

'Mum! There's a man at the door collecting for the Old Folks' Home. Shall I give him Grandma?'

Mum: 'If you've finished your dinner, Jimmy, say Grace.'
Jim: 'All right, Mum. Thanks for my dinner, Lord.'
Mum: 'That wasn't much of a Grace.'
Jim: 'It wasn't much of a dinner.'

Auntie: 'Do you always say your prayers, Sally?'
Sally: 'Oh, yes, Auntie, every night. I always ask God to make my baby brother a good boy – but he hasn't done it yet.'

Sammy: 'Were you in Noah's ark, grandpa?'
Grandpa: 'Er – no, Sammy, I wasn't.'
Sammy: 'Then why weren't you drowned?'

Jane: 'Did you know, Mum, that the wireless was invented by Marconi?'
Ignorant Mum: 'Not Marconi, Jane, that's rude. You should say Mrs. Coni.'

Dad: 'Harry, how did your clothes get all torn?'
Harry: 'I tried to stop a boy getting bashed up.'
Dad: 'Oh? Who?'
Harry: 'Me.'

Mum: 'Jimmy, you always want your own way.'
Jimmy: 'Well, if it's mine, why not give it to me?'

Old lady: 'And what is your new brother's name?'
Little girl: 'I don't know. He can't talk yet.'

Terry: 'Mum, can I have 10p for an old man crying outside in the street?'
Mum: 'Yes, of course. What's he crying about?'
Terry: 'Toffee apples – 10p each.'

Dad: 'Jimmy, who gave you that black eye?'
Jimmy: 'Nobody gave it to me, dad. I had to fight for it!'

Sister: 'Boo-hoo! I made a lovely steak and kidney pie and the cat's eaten it.'
Brother: 'Never mind, Sis. Mum'll buy us another cat.'

A boy from a coastal resort had learned to swim in the sea. One day his father took him to a public swimming bath for the first time.

After he had been in the pool for a few minutes, the lad called his father over and whispered: 'Dad, I've swallowed some. Will they mind?'

Tony: 'Yah – you're a baby! You're afraid to go upstairs in the dark by yourself!'
Terry: 'I'm not afraid.'
Tony: 'Yes, you are. 'Fraidy cat!'
Terry: 'I'm not afraid – you come up with me and see!'

Two brothers had had a fight and were sent to bed without supper. After lying in silence in their beds for ten minutes, the bigger brother wanted to make up, so he whsipered, 'Pete, are you awake?'

'I'm not telling you,' was the sulky reply.

'No, you can't have any more cakes. It's bad for you to go to bed on a full stomach.'
'Oh, Mum . . . I can lie on my side, can't I?'

Dad: 'Now, son, if you're a good boy I'll give you a nice new shining 5p piece.'
Son: 'Couldn't you make it a dirty old 10p piece...?'

A mother heard her daughter giggling and whispering with her friends in the bedroom, so she called upstairs, 'What are you doing, children?'
'We're playing at church,' came the answer.
'Well, you shouldn't giggle and whisper in church, should you?'
'Oh, we're the choirboys.'

Jimmy (boasting): My dad once faced a snarling tiger in the jungle and didn't turn a hair.'
Johnny: 'I'm not surprised – your dad's bald!'

Bus conductor: 'Pass farther down the car, please. Pass farther down the car.'
Small boy: 'That's not father, it's granddad.'

Mum: 'Sue, there were two chocolate cakes in the larder yesterday and now there's only one. Why?'
Sue: 'I don't know. It must have been so dark I didn't see the other one.'

Mum: 'Jackie, go outside and play with your whistle. Your father can't read his paper.'
Jackie: 'Cor, I'm only eight and I can read it!'

Helen: 'Mum, do you know what I'm going to give you for your birthday?'
Mum: 'No, dear, what?'
Helen: 'A nice teapot.'
Mum: 'But I've got a nice teapot.'
Helen: 'No you haven't. I've just dropped it!'

Grandma: 'Come on, Lucy, I'll give you a penny for a kiss.'
Lucy: 'I get more than that for taking my castor oil!'

Little girl, having been sent to get the morning milk in: 'Mum, the milkman's been and gone and not come!'

Little Sally: 'Mum, does God go to the bathroom?'
Mum: 'No, dear. Why do you ask?'
Little Sally: 'Well, this morning I heard Dad knock on the bathroom door and say, "Oh, God, are you still in there?"'

A little girl was being driven very erratically in a car by her grandma. 'Don't go round corners so fast, Gran,' she pleaded.

'Do as I do, dear,' said the sweet old lady, 'and close your eyes!'

'My big sister can play the piano by ear.'

'That's nothing. My big brother can fiddle with his whiskers!'

Trevor came rushing in to his dad.

'Dad,' he puffed, 'is it true that an apple a day keeps the doctor away?'

'That's what they say,' said his dad.

'Well, give us an apple – quick. I've just broken the doctor's window!'

A woman with a baby in her arms was sitting in the waiting-room at a railway station, sobbing bitterly. Up came a porter and asked her what the trouble was.

'Oh, dear me,' she cried, 'some people were in here, and they were so rude to me about my son! I'm all upset – they said he was so ugly.'

'There, there, now luv,' said the porter soothingly. 'Don't worry about it. I tell you what – how about a nice cup of tea?'

'You're very kind,' she said, wiping her eyes, 'that would be very nice.'

'And while I'm at it,' he said, 'how about a banana for your monkey?'

Little Johnny was playing in the garden and squinting ferociously in the sunlight. His mother came out and said, 'Why don't you move out of the sun?'

'Why should I?' demanded Johnny. 'I was here first!'

'Mum, you know that vase that's been handed down from generation to generation?'

'Yes.'

'Well, this generation's dropped it.'

One very stormy night, Mum went upstairs to little Johnny's bedroom in case he was frightened by all the thunder and lightning.

'Are you all right, Johnny?' she asked softly.

'Yes, Mum,' said Johnny. 'Is that Dad mucking about with the telly again?'

'My Grandad was still alive at the age of 102!'

'That's nothing. My Grandad is still alive at 133!'

'What? A hundred and thirty-three?'

'Yes – 133 Acacia Avenue!'

Jeremy was showing his sister photographs of his holiday. When they came to one of him sitting on the back of a donkey on the sands, she exclaimed, 'Oh, that's nice. But who's that sitting on your back?'

Visitor: 'You're very quiet, Jennifer.'
Jennifer: 'Well, Mum gave me 10p not to say anything about your red nose.'

'Mum, can I have two pieces of cake, please?'
  'Certainly – take this piece and cut it in two!'

'Here you are, Uncle, here's some wool from my needlework classes.'
  'Thank you, my dear, but what would I want with wool?'
  'I don't know, but Dad says you're always wool-gathering.'

'Dad, when I get old will the calves of my legs be cows . . .?'

'Why are you looking at the mirror with your eyes shut?'
  'I want to see what I look like when I'm asleep.'

'Don't eat the biscuits so fast – they'll keep.'
  'I know but I want to eat as many as I can before I lose my appetite.'

'You youngsters are soft and lazy today. When I was your age I got up at six o'clock every morning and walked five or six miles before breakfast. I used to think nothing of it.'
  'I don't blame you, Grandpa. I wouldn't think much of it myself.'

'Your sister's cooking Sunday lunch for us.'
  'Ugh! I suppose that means Enthusiasm Soup again.'
  'Enthusiasm Soup? What's that?'
  'She puts everything she's got into it!'

After a visit to the circus, Geoff and Don were discussing the thrills and marvels they had seen.
  'I didn't think much of the knife-thrower, did you?' said Geoff.
  'I thought he was super!' enthused Don.
  'Well, I didn't,' said Geoff. 'He kept chucking those knives at that soppy girl and didn't hit her once!'

'Stuart, you're taking a long time over that letter to Grandma.'
  'Well, she can't see very well, Mum, so I'm having to write slowly.'

'Frankie, have you got your shoes on yet?'
  'Yes, Mum – all except one!'

Mum: Mary, how are you getting on with your catechism lessons?'
Mary: 'They're very hard, Mum. I wish I could have started with kitty-chism lessons first.'

Little girl: 'Mummy, why do you feed baby brother with a spoon?'
Mummy: 'Because he's still learning to eat.'
Little girl: 'Then why not give him an L-plate?'

Len: 'Do you know, my dad's a magician.'
Tom: 'Is he really?'
Len: 'Yeah. One wave of his magic slipper and I disappear!'

A schoolboy went home with a pain in his stomach. 'Well, sit down and eat your tea,' said his mother. 'Your stomach's hurting because it's empty. It'll be all right when you've got something in it.'

Shortly afterwards Dad came in from the office, complaining of a headache.

'That's because it's empty,' said his bright son. 'You'd be all right if you had something in it.'

'How did you get on with your arithmetic exam?'
'I only got one sum wrong.'
'That's very good. How many were there?'
'Twelve.'
'Twelve! So you got eleven of the sums right?'
'No – they were the ones I couldn't do!'

'Mum, I caught a trout two feet long!'
'Did you? Where is it, then?'
'Well, I remembered our frying-pan is only about nine inches across, so I threw it back!'

'Oh, you're such a pest in the holidays. I'll be glad when you're back at school!'
'I'll be there longer this term, Mum.'
'Why, has term-time been extended, then?'
'No, but I'll be taller, won't I?'

Sister: 'You're stoopid! You don't know nuffink!'
Brother: 'Oh, yes I do! It's what Dad gimme for weedin' the garden last Sat'dy.'

'My dad bought my mum a mink outfit for her birthday.'
'Cor, did he?'
'Yeah. Two steel traps and a shotgun.'

'My Uncle Ben and Aunt Flo haven't had a row for five years.'
'That's wonderful.'
'Not really. Uncle Ben lives in China.'

Big sister: 'Here, Johnny, try one of my cakes.'
Small brother (biting into one): 'Ugh! It's horrible!'
Big sister: 'The trouble with you is you've no taste. It distinctly says in my cook book that this recipe is delicious.'

A naughty boy was caught up a tree scrumping. 'Come down this minute!' shouted the furious owner. 'Or I'll tell your father!'

'You can tell him now,' replied the boy. 'He's up here with me.'

Big sister had been taking singing lessons, and was demonstrating her vocal prowess to her unenthusiastic little brother.

'What would you like me to sing for you next?' she asked brightly.

'Do you know "Loch Lomond"?' he asked.

'Yes,' she replied.

'Well, go and jump in it!'

Dad was in a terrible temper over his son's latest school report.

'It says here that you came bottom in a class of twenty,' he raged. 'That's dreadful!'

'It might be worse, Dad,' said the unrepentant boy. 'There might have been more kids in the class!'

Two boys were boasting about their respective dads.

'My dad's got so many gold teeth he has to sleep with his head in a safe,' said one.

'That's nothing,' said the other. 'My dad rides around all day with his pockets full of money.'

'What does he do, then?'

'He's a bus conductor.'

'My brother's one of the biggest stick-up men in town.'

'Gosh, is he really?'

'Yes, he's a six foot six bill-poster.'

Dotty Aunt Muriel received a letter one morning, and upon reading it burst into floods of tears.

'What's the matter?' asked her companion.

'Oh dear,' sobbed Auntie, 'it's my favourite nephew. He's got three feet.'

'Three feet?' exclaimed her friend. 'Surely that's not possible?'

'Well,' said auntie, 'his mother's just written to tell me he's grown another foot!'

Little Susie was staying with her grandmother in the country for a few days.

'Would you like to see the cuckoo come out of the cuckoo clock?' asked her grandmother.

'I'd rather see Grandpa come out of the grandfather clock,' said Susie.

Grandpa: 'Why are you crying, Robin?'

Robin: ''Cos Dad won't play Cowboys and Indians with me.'

Grandpa: 'Never mind, I'll play Cowboys and Indians with you.'

Robin: 'That's no good – you've been scalped already.'

'Come on, Charles, I'll take you to the zoo.'

'If the zoo wants me, let 'em come and get me!'

175

'You've got your socks on inside out.'
    'I know, Mum, but there are holes on the other side.'

'Dad, is an ox a sort of a male cow?'
    'Sort of, yes.'
    'And "equine" means something to do with horses, doesn't it?'
    'That's right.'
    'So what's an equinox?'

'Grandpa, can you make a noise like a frog?'
    'I don't think I've ever tried, me lad. Why?'
    ''Cos Dad says we'll get £10,000 when you croak.'

At the seaside, mum waxed all lyrical at the beauty of the sunset over the sea.
    'Doesn't the sun look wonderful setting on to the horizon?' she breathed.
    'Yes,' said young Sammy, 'and there won't half be a fizz when it touches the water!'

'Dad, what are all those holes in the new garden shed?'
    'They're knot-holes.'
    'What do you mean "they're not holes"? I can put my finger into them.'

Kindly old lady: 'I suppose your new baby sister is a lovely pink and white?'
Nasty child: 'No, she's an 'orrible yeller.'

'Eat your dinner.'
    'I'm waiting for the mustard to cool off.'

Grandma: 'I'll take your baby brother for a walk in his pram, shall I?'
Little girl: 'That's not much of a walk, Grandma.'

'How did your mum know you hadn't washed your face?'
    'I forgot to wet the soap.'

Tasmin: 'Mum, can I play the piano?'
Mum: 'Not till you've washed your hands. They're filthy.'
Tasmin: 'Oh, Mum – I'll only play on the black notes.'

Mum: 'I thought you were going to see your dentist this afternoon?'
Dad: 'That's right.'
Mum: 'Then how is it that when I was on the bus going to do my shopping I saw you going into the football ground with a short, fat man?'
Dad: 'That's my dentist!'

Verse and Worse

She stood on the bridge at midnight,
Her lips were all a-quiver;
She gave a cough, her leg fell off
And floated down the river!

There was a young lady from Jarrow
Whose mouth was exceedingly narrow;
She ate with a spoon
By the light of the moon,
But all she could eat was a marrow!

A charming young singer named Hannah,
Got caught in a flood in Savannah;
As she floated away,
Her sister – they say;
Accompanied her on the Piannah!

There was a young man from Dumbarton,
Who thought he could run like a Spartan.
On the thirty-ninth lap
His braces went snap,
And his face went a red Scottish tartan.

There was a young man from Tralee,
Who was stung in the neck by a wasp.
When asked if it hurt,
He said, 'No, not a bit!
It can do it again if it likes!'

A flea and a fly in a flue,
Were trapped, so they thought 'What to do?'
'Let us fly,' said the flea,
'Let us flee,' said the fly,
So they flew through a flaw in the flue!

An earnest young fisher named Fisher
Once fished from the edge of a fissure.
A fish with a grin
Pulled the fisherman in –
Now they're fishing the fissure for Fisher!

There was a young lady called Hardwick,
By a cricket ball she was struck.
And now you can read on her tombstone:
'Hardwick, hard ball, hard luck'!

There was a young lady from Riga,
Who rode with a smile on a tiger.
They returned from the ride
With the lady inside,
And the smile on the face of the tiger.

Hickory Dickory Dock,
Three mice ran up the clock.
The clock struck one,
And the other two got away with minor injuries ...

There was a young man from Quebec
Who wrapped both his legs round his neck!
But then he forgot
How to undo the knot,
And now he's an absolute wreck!

There once was a writer named Wright,
Who instructed his son to write right;
He said, 'Son, write Wright right.
It is not right to write
Wright as 'rite' – try to write Wright aright!'

There was an old man from Whitehaven,
Whose whiskers had never been shaven;
He said, 'It is best,
For they make a nice nest,
In which I can keep my pet raven!'

There once was a fat boy called Kidd,
Who ate twenty mince pies for a quid.
When asked 'Are you faint?'
He replied, 'No, I ain't,
But I don't feel as well as I did!'

I eat peas with honey,
I've done it all my life.
They do taste kind of funny –
But it keeps them on the knife!

There was an old man from Carlisle,
Who sat down one day on a stile.
The paint it was wet,
So he's sitting there yet;
But he hopes to get off with a file!

There was an old man from Penzance,
Who always wore sheet-iron pants;
He said, 'Some years back,
I sat on a tack,
And I'll never again take a chance!'

An old lady who came from Kilbride,
Ate so many apples – she died!
The apples fermented
Inside the lamented –
Making cider inside 'er inside!

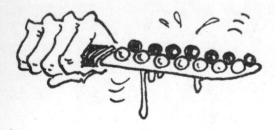

There was a young man from Leeds,
Who swallowed a packet of seeds;
Within just one hour
His nose was a flower
And his head was a riot of weeds!

There was a young man from Bengal,
Who was asked to a fancy-dress ball.
He said he would risk it
And went as a biscuit,
But a dog ate him up in the hall!

There once was a chief of the Sioux,
Who into a gun-barrel blioux
To see if 'twas loaded;
The rifle exploded –
As he should have known it would dioux!

Rolling in the Aisles

'Vicar, come quickly! The church is on fire!'
  'Holy smoke!'

One Sunday the vicar concluded his sermon by saying, 'The preacher for next Sunday will be hung in the porch . . .!'

'Don't you enjoy the sound of church bells?'
  'Sorry?'
  'I said "don't you like the bells?" '
  'Eh?'
  'AREN'T THE BELLS WONDERFUL?'
  'It's no good — I can't hear a word you're saying for those blooming bells!'

'My wife's an angel.'
  'Really? Mine's still alive.'

Sunday School teacher: 'Who sits at the right hand of God?'
Sunday School pupil: 'Er — Mrs God?'

'I didn't see you in church last Sunday, Nigel. I hear you were out playing football instead.'
  'That's not true, vicar. And I've got the fish to prove it.'

Jemima had just returned from her first visit to Sunday School.
  'Well, Jemima,' asked her father, 'did you learn much?'
  'Not a lot,' said the little one. 'I've got to go back next week.'

Young Oliver had heard a sermon in which the preacher, when talking about Man's origins and ultimate destiny, had used the Biblical phrase 'Ashes to ashes, dust to dust'. Oliver returned home and went up to his room; but a few minutes later he came running downstairs and yelled to his mother, 'Mum — you'd better come upstairs!'
  'Why, Oliver?'
  ' 'Cos I just looked under my bed, and there's somebody either coming or going!'

'Father! Father' said the young curate urgently to his parish priest. 'There's an old man in a long white beard sitting at the back of the church — he says he's God! What shall I do?'

'Go and keep an eye on him,' said the older priest, 'and try and look busy!'

The vicar's son was watching his father preparing the next Sunday's sermon.

'How do you know what to say, Daddy?' he asked.

'God tells me,' replied his reverend father.

'Then why do you keep crossing bits out?'

Little Susan was attending church for the very first time.

'What are all those people doing?' she asked her mother.

'Sssh, dear!' replied her mother. 'They're praying.'

'What — with all their clothes on?!'

Two astronauts knocked on the Pearly Gates, and St Peter answered. 'Come in, gentlemen,' said the Archangel. 'Just sit down there while I look up your files.'

'Oh, we don't want to come in,' said the first astronaut.

'You don't?' asked the astonished St Peter. 'What do you want then?'

'Please, sir,' said the second astronaut, 'can we have our capsule back?'

Arriving at a small village the travelling preacher asked a little boy for directions to the local church. The boy duly gave him directions, and the preacher said, 'Thank you, my son. I shall be giving a sermon in the church tonight and I'd like you and your Mummy and Daddy and all your friends to come.'

'What for?' asked the urchin suspiciously.

'Because,' explained the preacher, 'I want to tell you all how to find Heaven.'

'Don't make me laugh!' sneered the brat. 'You didn't even know where the church was!'

Adam was naming all the animals. 'And that', he said to Eve, 'is a rhinoceros'.

'Why call it a rhinoceros?' asked Eve.

'Because,' said the First Man scornfully, 'it looks like a rhinoceros, stupid!'

'Was old Reverend Prendegast a successful missionary?'

'Certainly. He gave the tribesmen in Mbabaland their first taste of Christianity.'

Two ministers were talking, and one said, 'I had a terrible experience last Sunday. Absolutely awful!'

'What was that?' his brother minister asked in concern.

'Well, I dreamed that I was in my pulpit preaching,' said the first minister, 'and when I woke up — I found that I was!'

A priest was appalled to find a small boy sitting at the back of the church playing a pop tune on his mouth-organ. 'That's quite enough of that!' said the priest sternly. 'Don't you know the First Commandment?'

'No, Father,' replied the shaver, 'but you hum it and I'll try to follow you!'

Sunday School teacher: 'Hands up all those who want to go to Heaven? . . . Hands up . . . what about you, Terry? You haven't got your hand up — don't you want to go to Heaven?'
Terry: 'I can't. Me Mum told me to go straight home!'

Everyone in the Primary School was very excited over the forthcoming visit of the bishop. 'Now I want you all on your best behaviour,' said the headmaster, 'and if the bishop should address any of you children, you must speak up and call him My Lord.'

The great day arrived and the saintly bishop beamed upon the assembled tots. To one little boy he said kindly, 'And how old are you, my son?' Confused and over-awed the boy gasped out, 'Oh — er — My God, I'm six!'

A preacher was thrilled when a member of his congregation told him that his sermon had been like the peace and mercy of God. But the good preacher wasn't so pleased when he looked up the quotation in his Bible and found that it read: 'The peace of God passeth all understanding and his mercy endureth for ever'!

A certain preacher was extremely short in stature, but what he lacked in inches he more than made up for in fervour. One Sunday evening he climbed into his pulpit, the top of his head barely visible to the congregation. 'I am the Lamp of the Lord!' he declared. 'I am the Lamp of the Lord!'

At which a woman at the back of the church called out, 'Well, turn your wick up — we can't see you!'

The Reverend Mr Smithers was a missionary, and was sent to a central African country. On arriving at his new post he sent a telegram to his wife in England. Unfortunately it was delivered by mistake to another Mrs Smithers whose husband had died only the day before. Just imagine her horror when she opened the telegram and read: ARRIVED SAFELY THIS MORNING. THE HEAT IS AWFUL!

An elderly pilgrim returning from Lourdes had arrived at Heathrow Airport, and on going through Customs said that he had nothing to declare. 'What's in this bottle?' asked the Customs officer.

'Oh, that's just holy water from the Lourdes spring,' said the pilgrim. But the Customs officer sniffed the contents, dipped in his finger, and licked it.

'This isn't holy water,' he said sternly, 'it's whisky!'

'St Bernadette be praised!' declared the pilgrim piously, 'another miracle!'

'And I'm afraid this is goodbye, God,' said the little girl as she finished her prayers. 'Tomorrow we're moving.'

Of course, Cain wanted to be as popular as his brother, but he turned nasty when he found out he wasn't Abel . . .

How does an airline pilot's child finish his prayers? 'God bless Mummy, God bless Daddy, and God bless me. Over and out.'

'Young Esmeralda, a keen television viewer, was taken to her first church service. When asked by her Grannie how she had enjoyed it, she replied. 'The music and the singing were all right, but I didn't think much of the News.'

'Do you really believe Jonah was swallowed by a whale?'
'When I get to Heaven I'll ask him.'
'But suppose he's in the Other Place?'
'Then you ask him.'

Two comedians were talking, and one said, 'I hear your agent got you a booking in the Vatican. Is that really true?'
'That's quite correct,' said the other, 'but I cancelled.'
'Cancelled?' exclaimed the first comedian. 'You cancelled a booking to entertain the Pope and all the Cardinals?'
'Well, how would you like to do *your* act in Latin?'

'It'd *better* rain,' muttered the kangaroo to his companion as they entered the Ark. 'We've hopped a long way for this.'

'Brother Damien, why is the chapel bell ringing this morning?'
'Because Brother Augustine is pulling the rope, you silly fool!'

What does God have for his tea?
Angel cakes.

What's the easiest way to get to Heaven quickly?
Stand in the fast lane of a motorway.

A little boy went into the confessional box and said to the priest, 'Father, I threw peanuts into the river.' The priest couldn't see too much harm in that, so he gave the lad a light penance. Another boy entered the box and also said, 'Father, I threw peanuts into the river.' The priest was again puzzled, but not wishing to show his confusion sent the second boy away with a light penance. But in came another youngster—he'd thrown peanuts into the river as well—and the next boy, and the next! Then a very tiny mite came in, and the priest said, 'And I suppose you threw peanuts into the river?'
'No, Father,' said the boy, 'I *am* Peanuts!'

The bishop was examining a confirmation class and wanted to make sure the children understood exactly what a bishop was. 'First of all,' he said, 'what am I?' There was a long silence; the children were puzzled by the question. 'Come along now,' repeated his lordship. 'What am I?'

And after a further pause a small voice said tentatively, 'You're a miserable sinner . . .'

In the pulpit was a passionate preacher; his voice rose in a great crescendo of triumph, then fell quavering in terror and pity. His arms flapped and flailed, his face glistened with fervour and the veins stood out upon his forehead, his eyes bulged and his nostrils quivered with righteousness. In the front pew was a small girl attending her first sermon. 'Mummy,' she whispered, having watched the fanatical preacher in growing alarm, 'what shall we do if he gets out?'

The airliner was forty thousand feet above the Atlantic when, to the passengers' horror, an announcement crackled from the cabin loudspeakers. 'This is your captain speaking! I regret to say we have an emergency. Two of our engines have failed. I have every expectation of reaching our destination safely but in the meantime will you please extinguish your cigarettes and fasten your safety-belts? Thank you.' One of the passengers, who was sitting next to a parson, immediately flew into a panic. 'Don't just sit there!' he screamed at his reverend neighbour. 'Do something religious!' So the parson took up a collection . . .

'I want to be good!' declared the penitent in the confessional. 'Can you help me, Father?'

'Of course I can, my son,' said the good priest comfortingly. 'The Lord is merciful.'

'Could you forgive someone who steals £30, Father?'

'Certainly, my son,' said the priest, 'but you must tell me all about this theft.'

'Well,' said the petty crook, 'there was £10 from Woolworth's yesterday and £10 from Tesco's today.'

'But that only makes £20.'

'Oh, I'll be getting the other £10 from Boots tomorrow!'

Little Amy was sent to church with two 10p pieces — one to put in the collection plate and the other to buy herself sweeties. But crossing the road the little girl tripped, and one of the coins dropped out of her hand, rolled along the pavement — and plopped down a grating!

'Sorry, Lord,' she said as she picked herself up. 'There goes your 10p!'

The Salvation Army girl was in the saloon bar with her collecting-tin, which she rattled under the nose of the oldest man in the bar. 'What's this for, then?' he growled.

'I'm collecting for the Lord,' she said.

'You'd better give me the tin, then,' he replied. 'I'll be seein' Him afore you, lass!'

Service With a Smile

- there's a bird in my soup.
That's all right, sir. It's bird's-nest soup.

- there's a dead beetle in my soup.
Yes, sir, they're not very good swimmers.

- there's a fly in my soup!
Well, keep quiet about it or everyone will want one . . .

- bring me a fried egg with finger-marks in it, some luke-warm greasy chips and a portion of watery cabbage.
We don't do food like that, sir!
You did yesterday . . .

- your tie in is my soup!
That's all right, sir, it's not shrinkable.

- this coffee tastes like mud!
I'm not surprised, sir, it was ground only a few minutes ago.

- your thumb's in my soup!
That's all right, sir, it's not hot.

- what's this in my soup?
I dunno, sir, I can't tell one bug from another.

- do you serve crabs?
Sit down, sir – we serve anybody.

- my plate's wet.
That's not wet, sir – that's the soup!

- have you got frogs' legs?
Certainly, sir.
Then hop into the kitchen and get me a steak!

- bring me a glass of milk and a Dover sole.
Fillet?
Yes, to the brim.

- does the pianist play requests?
Yes, sir.
Then ask him to play tiddlewinks till I've finished my meal.

- my bill, please.
How did you find your luncheon, sir?
With a magnifying glass.

- there's a flea in my soup.
I'll tell him to hop it.

- have you got asparagus?
We don't serve sparrers and my name's not Gus!

- I'll have a chop; no – make that a steak.
I'm a waiter, sir; not a bloomin' magician!

– there's a dead fly in my soup!
Yes, sir, it's the hot water that kills 'em.

– this bun tastes of soap.
That's right, sir – it's a bathbun. .

– there a twig in my soup.
Yes, sir, we've got branches everywhere.

– I can't eat this!
Why not, sir?
You haven't given me a knife and fork.

– my knife is blunt and my steak is like leather.
I should strop the knife on the steak then, sir.

– if this is plaice then I'm an idiot.
You're right, sir – it *is* plaice.

– is this all you've got to eat?
No, sir, I'll be having a nice shepherd's pie when I get home.

– I think I'd like a little game.
Draughts or tiddleywinks, sir?

– how long have you been here?
Six months, sir.
Ah, then, it can't be you who took my order.

– there's a fly in my butter.
No there isn't.
I tell you there's a fly in my butter!
And I tell you there isn't; it isn't a fly it's a moth and it isn't butter, it's marge – so there!

– this egg tastes rather strong.
Never mind, sir, the tea's nice and weak.

– I'll have soup and fish.
I'd have the fish first if I were you, sir, it's just on the turn.

– why have you given me my dinner in a feedbag?
The head waiter says you eat like a horse.

– I asked for bread with my dinner.
It's in the sausages, sir.

– you're not fit to serve a pig! – this lobster's only got one claw.
I'm doing my best, sir.   I expect he's been in a fight, sir,
                                Well, bring me the winner!

– bring me tea without milk.
We haven't any milk, sir. How about tea without cream?

– I'll pay my bill now.   – where is my honey?
This pound note's bad, sir.   She left last week, sir.
So was the meal.

– how long will my sausages be?
Oh, about three or four inches if you're lucky.

Don't Make Me Cross

What do you get if you cross . . .
– *a cat and an octagon?*
  An octopus.

– *a bear and a skunk?*
  Winnie the Pooh.

– *a giraffe and a hedgehog?*
  An eight-foot toothbrush.

– *a baby goat and a hedgehog?*
  A stuck-up kid.

– *a bee and a skunk?*
  Something that stings and stinks at the same time.

– *the white of an egg and a pound of gunpowder?*
  A boom-meringue.

– *a snowman and a man-eating shark?*
  Frostbite.

– *a cat and a lemon?*
  A sourpuss.

– *a kangaroo and an elephant?*
  Great big holes all over Australia.

– *an Axminster carpet and an elephant?*
  A great big pile in your sitting-room.

– *a fish and two elephants?*
  Swimming trunks.

In the Madhouse

Things that money can't buy: A button for a coat of paint.
Sheets for an oyster bed.
False teeth for a river's mouth.
Music for a rubber band.
Shoes for a walking stick.
A saddle for a clothes' horse!

A kind-hearted old lady saw a little girl standing in the park crying.
  'What's the matter, dear?' she asked.
  'Rheumatism,' was the unexpected reply.
  'Rheumatism?' exclaimed the old lady. 'At your age?'
  'No,' sobbed the little girl, 'I can't spell it!'

A man went to the optician to have his eyes tested. The optician sat him down and showed him a test card.
  'Can you read that?' asked the optician.
  'No,' said the man.
  The optician moved it closer: 'Now can you read it?'
  'No,' said the the man.
  The optician moved the chart even closer: 'Surely you can read it now?'
  'No,' said the man. 'I can't read.'

'Are you hungry?'
  'Yes, Siam.'
  'Come on, I'll Fiji.'

'I bet I can make you speak like a Red Indian.'
  'How?'
  'That's right!'

Passer-by (to fisherman): 'Is this river good for fish?'
Fisherman: 'It must be. I can't get any of them to leave it!'

Vegetarian: 'I've lived on nothing but vegetables for years.'
Bored listener: 'That's nothing. I've lived on Earth all my life.'

Snake-charmer: 'Be careful with that trunk, porter. It contains a ten-foot snake.'
Porter: 'You can't kid me – snakes don't have any feet.'

A small but saucy boy was on holiday at the seaside. He went down to the beach and said to the Lifesaver, 'Can I swim in the sea?'

'Yes, sonny,' said the Lifesaver.

'That's funny,' said the lad, 'in the bathing pool at home I can't swim a stroke.'

'I'm glad I wasn't born in France.'

'Why?'

'I can't speak French.'

Railway station announcements:

'Will passengers taking the 6.45 train from Platform 6 to Coventry kindly put it back . . .'

'Will the train now standing on Platform 1 please get back on the rails . . .'

'The train now arriving on platforms 5, 6 and 7 is coming in sideways . . .'

Customer: 'You made this suit tighter than my skin.'

Tailor: 'Tighter than your skin? That's impossible.'

Customer: 'Well, I can sit down in my skin but I can't in this suit!'

Helpful passer-by (to stranger): 'Are you lost?'

Stranger: 'No, I'm here. It's the railway station that's lost.'

As two boys were passing the vicarage, the vicar leaned over the wall and showed them a ball.

'Is this yours?' he asked.

'Did it do any damage, vicar?' said one of the boys.

'No,' replied the vicar.

'Then it's mine.'

Harry was given two apples, a small one and a large one, by his Mum. 'Share them with your sister,' she said.

So Harry gave the small one to his little sister and started tucking into the large one.

'Cor!' said his sister. 'If Mum had given them to me I'd have given you the large one and had the small one myself.'

'Well,' said Harry, 'that's what you've got, so what are you worrying about?'

Man in clothes shop: 'Can I try on that blue suit in the window?'

Manager: 'No, sir, you'll have to use the changing-room like everyone else.'

A man in a swimming-bath was on the very top diving-board. He poised, lifted his arms and was about to dive off when the attendant came running up, shouting, 'Don't dive – there's no water in the pool!'

'That's all right,' said the man. 'I can't swim!'

'My uncle's got a wooden leg.'

'That's nothing. My auntie's got a wooden chest.'

Did you hear about the girl who got engaged to a chap and then found out he had a wooden leg? She broke it off, of course . . .

As the judge said to the dentist: 'Do you swear to pull the tooth, the whole tooth, and nothing but the tooth?'

Notice (in a shoe-shop window): Boots and shoes polished inside.

'What happens if you dial 666?'
  'I don't know. What?'
  'A policeman comes along upside down.'

A soap-box orator at Hyde Park corner finished his long-winded speech and then asked for questions.

'Come along, any questions?' he repeated, but again there was no reply. 'Someone among you must have a question?' he insisted.

Eventually a little voice piped up, 'I've got a question, mister.'
'Yes, what is it, little boy?' said the speaker.
'If you've finished with that box you're standing on, can I have it for my Guy Fawkes bonfire?'

A mail-order firm received the following cheeky letter: Dear Sir, please send me the razor as per your advertisement in the paper, for which I enclose a postal order. Yours sincerely, Joe Soap.

P.S. I've forgotten to enclose the postal order but please send me the razor just the same.

The mail-order firm replied as follows: Dear Sir, thank you for your letter. We do not enclose our razor since we feel that a man with a cheek like yours doesn't need one. Yours sincerely . . .

'They're not going to grow bananas any longer.'
  'Really? Why not?'
  'Because they're long enough already.'.

'Just think – a big chocolate ice-cream, a bag of scrumptious toffees and a seat at the pictures for 10p.'
  'Did you get all that for 10p?'
  'No – but just think . . . !'

'I wonder where I got that puncture?'
  'Maybe it was at that last fork in the road . . .'

A boy was sitting on a street corner fishing into a bucket. A kind-hearted old lady passing took pity on him, so she gave him a 5p piece.

'How many have you caught today?' she asked.
'You're the seventh,' said the boy smugly.

What did the speak-your-weight machine say when a very fat lady stepped on it?
  'One at a time, please!'

'It can't go on! It can't go on!'
  'What can't go on?'
  'This baby's vest – it's too small for me.'

'It's gone forever – gone forever, I tell you!'
  'What has?'
  'Yesterday.'

A PT instructor was boasting about his strength. 'I can lift 300 pounds,' he said.
  A weedy-looking individual in the class said, 'That's nothing. I know a woman who can lift 500 pounds.'
  'Where's that?' gasped the instructor.
  'At the bank. She's a cashier!'

Teddy: 'It's no good. I can't do it.'
Instructor: 'Now, then, Teddy, you know what Napoleon said. He said, "There's no such word as can't".'
Teddy: 'I wonder if he ever tried to strike a match on a bar of soap.'

Road sign in an Irish country lane: When this sign is under water, the road is closed to traffic.

At a concert, the boring singer with the tuneless voice announced, 'I should now like to sing "Over The Hills And Far Away".'
  'Thank goodness for that,' whispered someone in the audience 'I thought he was going to stay all evening.'

First railway porter: 'I had a terrific struggle getting a woman's trunk to the Crewe train.'
Second porter: 'Why, was it heavy?'
First porter: 'No. She wanted to go to Portsmouth.'

A simple-minded chap was struggling out of his house with a big table. His neighbour said to him, 'Hello, Harry. Where are you going with that then?'
  And Harry replied, 'I'm taking it to the draper's shop to have it measured for a new table-cloth.'

'It's not worth tuppence – I insist that it's not worth tuppence!'
  'What isn't?'
  'A penny!'

'Do you know all the buses and trains are stopping today?'
  'No, I didn't. Why is that?'
  'To let the passengers off.'

A naughty lad was swimming in a private part of the river when the owner spotted him.

'Hey!' he bawled. 'You can't swim here!'

'I'm not swimming,' the lad shouted back. 'I'm stopping myself sinking!'

A man and his wife had just arrived at Heathrow airport after an exhausting journey from the north of England.

Wearily the husband said, 'I wish I'd brought the piano with me.'

'What on earth for?' his wife demanded.

'I've left the plane tickets on it,' he sighed.

A farmer persuaded one of his cowhands to buy two raffle tickets, for which the draw was to be held that night at a dance. The next day the cowhand asked the farmer who had won the draw.

'Oh, I won the first prize,' said the farmer. 'Aren't I lucky?'

'And who won second prize, farmer?' asked the cowhand.

'My wife won that. Wasn't she lucky?'

'Arr, she were that. And what about third prize?'

'Oh, my daughter won that. Wasn't she lucky? By the way, you haven't paid me for your tickets yet, have you?'

'No,' replied the cowman. 'Aren't I lucky?'

'This match won't light.'

'That's funny – it did this morning.'

'A noise woke me up this morning.'

'What was that?'

'The crack of dawn.'

'If you had two sticks, what would you do to make a fire?'

'Rub them together, I suppose.'

'It's much easier if one of them is a match!'

'Do the buses run on time?'

'Usually, yes.'

'No, they don't. They run on wheels.'

A very fat man started taking violin lessons, and shortly afterwards was stopped by a friend in the street.

'How's the violin progressing, then?' asked the friend.

'Oh, I've given it up,' said the fat man.

'Why's that?' asked his friend.

'Well, my teacher told me to put the violin under my chin – and I couldn't decide which one!'

Notice (in an undertaker's window): Press the bell if you want attention three times.

A boy had invited a friend to stay with him for a few days, but the friend was very frightened of catching cold.

'Are there any draughts in your house?' he asked anxiously.

'I'm afraid not,' was the reply. 'Only chess and ludo.'

Three Chinamen were discussing British television. 'Me likee BBC,' said the first. 'Me likee ITV,' said the second. And the third said, 'Me no telly!'

Bald customer (in barber's shop): 'Is this bottle of hair restorer any good?'
Barber: 'Any good? We had one customer who pulled the cork out with his teeth – next day he had a handlebar moustache!'

Lady passenger: 'I say, conductor, is this a Barking bus?'
Conductor: 'No, lady, it only goes "honk-honk"!'

'Have you ever seen a duchess?'
  'Yes – it's the same as an English "s"!'

Policeman: 'Why did you run away after you'd kicked your ball through that plate-glass window?'
Small boy: ''Cos I couldn't bear to see it go through all that pane (pain).'

Jennifer: 'Are you coming to my party?'
Sandra: 'No, I ain't going.'
Jennifer: 'Now, you know what Miss told us. Not "ain't". It's "I am not going, he is not going, she is not going, they are not going".'
Sandra: 'Blimey, ain't nobody going?'

'Why do Guardsmen catch cold easily?'
  'I don't know.'
  'Because they're always in their bearskins.'

Man (in chemist's shop): 'I'd like some soap, please.'
Assistant: Scented?'
Man: 'No, I'll take it with me.'

'I can tell the time by the sun at any time of the year.'
  'Really? I can tell the time at any hour of the night.'
  'How can you do that?'
  'I get up and look at the bedroom clock.'

To Let: Room for two gentlemen 30ft. x 20ft.

Angry customer: 'These safety matches you sold me won't strike.'
Shop-keeper: 'Well, you can't get matches much safer than that.'

Boss (to cleaner): 'Are you sweeping out the office today?'
Cleaner: 'No, sir, just the dust. I'm leaving the office where it is.'

At one house, when the dustman called round to empty the bins, the occupier had overslept and forgotten to put his bin outside. The dustman rang the bell and banged on the front door. Eventually an upstairs window was opened and a sleepy head looked out.

'Where's yer bin?' asked the dustman.

'I bin asleep,' came the answer. 'Where's *you* bin?'

'My brother's just opened a shop.'

'Really? How's he doing?'

'Six months. He opened it with a crowbar.'

'If I hadn't been in goal we'd have lost by 20 – nil.'

'Oh? What was the score then?'

'Nineteen – nil!'

On a long bus journey, an old man was greatly irritated by the little girl sitting next to him who kept sniffing.

'Have you got a hanky?' he asked crossly.

'Yes,' she replied, 'but my Mum wouldn't like me to lend it to a stranger.'

A lad went into a photographic shop with a photo under his arm.

'Do you do life-size enlargements?' he asked.

'Yes, sonny,' said the shopkeeper.

'Well, see what you can do with this,' said the lad – and plonked down a photograph of Nelson's Column!

'I'll sell you something for 2p that cost me 4p and I'll still make a profit.'

'What's that? It cost you 4p, you'll sell it to to me for 2p and still make a profit?'

'Thats right.'

'All right, here's my 2p. What is it?'

'A used bus ticket.'

At a party, a conjurer was producing egg after egg from a little boy s ear.

'There!' he said proudly. 'I bet your Mother can't produce eggs without hens, can she?'

'Oh yes, she can,' said the boy. 'She keeps ducks.'

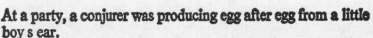

A new golfer was asked by a friend how he got on at his first attempt on the course.

'Seventy-two strokes it took me,' said the new golfer.

'Why, that's fantastic!' said his friend.

'Yes, it wasn't bad, was it,' the golfer agreed. 'And next weekend I'm going to try the second hole.'

A very superior person was walking round an art exhibition, when he paused. 'I suppose this hideous monstrosity is what they call modern art!' he told an attendant.

'No, sir,' replied the attendant, 'that's what they call a mirror.'

Henderson: 'I bet I can tell you the name of your future wife.'

Brown: 'Go on, then.'

Henderson: 'Mrs. Brown.'

'I met a chap yesterday with very long arms. Every time he went up the stairs he trod on them.'

'Gosh! When he went up the stairs he trod on his arms?'

'No, on the stairs.'

A housewife went into a hardware shop and asked for something to help her with her spring-cleaning.

'I've just the thing, madam,' said the salesman. 'This furniture polish is excellent. It'll do half your work for you.'

'Really?' she replied. 'In that case I'll take two tins!'

An old lady was considering buying a squirrel fur coat. 'But will it be all right in the rain?' she asked anxiously.

'Oh certainly, moddom,' said the manager smoothly. 'After all, you've never seen a squirrel with an umbrella, have you?'

A man went into a tailor's shop and saw a man hanging by one arm from the centre of the ceiling.

'What's he doing there?' he asked the tailor.

'Oh, pay no attention,' said the tailor, 'he thinks he's a light-bulb.'

'Well, why don't you tell him he isn't?' asked the startled customer.

'What?' replied the tailor. 'And work in the dark?'

Mr. Brown was reading his evening paper when there came a tremendous banging down the stairs. He jumped up, ran to the hall, and discovered his schoolboy son sprawled on the floor.

'Did you miss a step?' asked his dad.

'No, I caught every blessed one!' came the bitter answer.

A guard was about to signal his train to start when he saw an attractive girl standing on the platform by an open door, talking to another pretty girl inside the carriage.

'Come on, miss!' he shouted. 'Shut the door, please!'

'Oh, I just want to kiss my sister goodbye,' she called back.

'You just shut that door, please,' called the guard, 'and I'll see to the rest.'

A violinist went into a music shop and asked the girl behind the counter for an E string. The girl produced a box of violin strings and said lazily, 'You'd better pick it out for yourself. I can't tell the 'e's from the she's.'

A housewife went into a fish-shop in a fury. 'Those kippers you sold me yesterday were bad!' she complained.

'They can't have been,' said the fish-monger. 'They were only cured last week.'

An angler was interrupted at the river bank by an irate river warden.

'Can't you see that sign?' he roared. 'It says "No Fishing"!'

'And it's dead right,' said the angler calmly. 'I haven't had a bite all day.'

'Do you like my new cap?'

'Yes, very nice.'

'I used to wear a pork-pie hat, but the gravy kept running down my ears . . .'

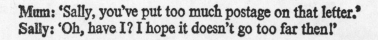

A car-driver stopped in a little country town and asked a passer-by for directions to the station.

'Quickest way to the station from here?' said the local. 'Your best bet is to take a number 73 bus.'

'Are you going to the football match this afternoon?'

'Yes. Are you?'

'No, it's a waste of time. I can tell you the score before the game starts.'

'Can you? What is it, then?'

'Nil – nil.'

Mum: 'Sally, you've put too much postage on that letter.'
Sally: 'Oh, have I? I hope it doesn't go too far then!'

For years an old man had sold newspapers on a windy street corner. One bitterly cold day one of his regular customers said sympathetically, 'Don't you ever catch cold, standing out here in all weathers?'

'No, sir,' replied the old man. 'You see, selling all these papers keeps up the circulation.'

A very shy young man went into an optician's one day to order a new pair of spectacles. Behind the counter was an extremely pretty girl, which reduced the customer to total confusion.

'Can I help you, sir?' she asked, with a ravishing smile.

'Er – yes – er – I want a pair of rim-specked hornicles . . . I mean I want a pair of heck-rimmed spornicles . . . er . . . I mean . . .'

At which point the optician himself came to the rescue. 'It's all right, Miss Jones. What the gentleman wants is a pair of rim-sporned hectacles.'

'You see that chap just getting out of his car on the other side of the street?'

'Yes, what about him?'

'I owe more to him than to anyone else on earth.'

'Really? Who is he?'

'My landlord.'

An old lady was making her very first flight in an airliner. She was highly nervous and insisted on speaking to the captain before take-off.

'You will bring me down safely, won't you?' she asked anxiously.

'Don't worry, madam,' said the captain cheerfully, 'I've never left anyone up there yet.'

'How are your violin lessons progressing?'
   'Not badly at all. I've already mastered the first steps.'
   'I thought you played the violin with your hands.'

'I got the sack last week.'
   'What for?'
   'For good.'

'I hear you've just come back from India.'
   'That's right – I was a guest of a rajah.'
   'Were you really? Did you go hunting?'
   'Oh yes. One day he took me into the jungle to shoot tigers.'
   'Any luck?'
   'Yes – we didn't meet any!'

A policeman discovered a suspicious-looking character lolling up against a doorway.
   'What are you doing here?' the officer demanded.
   'I live here,' said the man. 'I've lost my front door key.'
   'Well, ring the bell, then,' said the policeman.
   'Oh, I did, ten minutes ago.'
   'Perhaps there's no-one in, then,' suggested the officer.
   'Oh yes, my wife and two children are in.'
   'So why not ring again?'
   'No,' said the man, '– let 'em wait!'

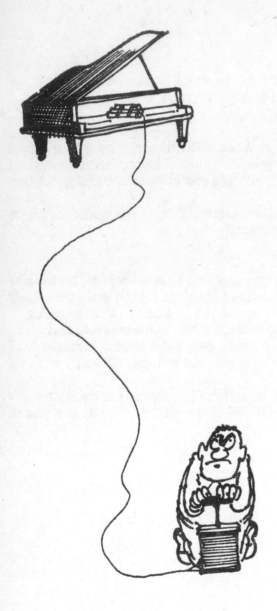

'You know, you always remind me of Charlie Green.'
   'But I'm not a bit like Charlie Green.'
   'Yes, you are. You both owe me 50p.'

Two housewives were looking in the window of a fish-shop.
   'That salmon looks nice, doesn't it, Gertie?' said one.
   'That's not salmon, Elsie,' said the other. 'That's cod blushing at the price they're asking for it!'

'What do you think of this photograph of me?'
   'It makes you look older, frankly.'
   'Oh, well, it'll save the cost of having another one taken later on.'

'How's your snuff shop doing?'
   'Oh, I'm packing it in.'
   'Why?'
   'I'm fed up with pushing my business into other people's noses.'

An irate woman stormed into the greengrocer's. 'Those potatoes you sold me are full of eyes!' she complained.
   'Well, madam,' said the greengrocer, 'you said you wanted enough to see you through the week.'

'I bought a piano twenty years ago and I still can't play it.'
   'Why not?'
   'I can't get the lid open.'

Notice (in a new shop window): Don't go elsewhere and be robbed – try us!

EXTRA COLD SUCK!

The meanest man in Britain went into a garage and asked for a pint of antifreeze. 'Certainly, sir,' said the salesman. 'What sort of car it it for?'

'It's not for a car. I'm going to drink it to save buying myself an overcoat this winter.'

'Did you follow the doctor's diet?'

'Well, I did for a few days, then I got fed up with it. I mean, what's the point of starving to death just to live a few years longer?'

A keen gardener saw his neighbour planting razor-blades in his potato patch. Ever eager to learn something new, he called over the hedge, 'What are you expecting to grow then, Alf?'

'Chips!' was the reply.

A well-dressed man came out of a smart hotel and snapped to the commissionaire, 'You there! Call me a taxi!'

'Certainly, sir,' said the commissionaire politely. 'You are a taxi.'

At the scene of a bank raid the police sergeant came running up to his inspector and said, 'He got away, sir!'

The inspector was furious. 'But I told you to put a man on all the exits!' he roared. 'How could he have got away?'

'He left by one of the entrances, sir!'

'Can I share your sledge?'

'Sure, we'll go halves.'

'Gosh, thanks!'

'I'll have it for downhill and you can have it for uphill.'

'I'd like a fur coat, please.'

'Certainly, moddom. What fur?'

'To keep myself warm, of course.'

'Good morning, sir. I'm applying for the job as handyman.'

'I see. Well, are you handy?'

'Couldn't be more so. I only live next door.'

Fred: 'Here's a riddle for you, Bob. Why did the pigeon cross the road?'

Bob: 'I don't know – why?'

Fred: 'To get his old age pension. Get it?'

Bob: 'No.'

Fred: 'Neither did the pigeon!'

Teacher: 'Where did King John sign the Magna Carta?'

Class joker: 'At the bottom.'

'I once lived on water for eight months.'
  'When was that?'
  'When I was in the Navy.'

Harry was telling his friend about his holiday in Switzerland.
His friend had never been to Switzerland, and asked, 'What did
you think of the scenery?'
  'Oh, I couldn't see much,' Harry admitted. 'There were all
those mountains in the way.'

'How do you spell "'erbert"?'
  'You mean "Herbert", don't you?'
  'No – I've got the "h" down already.'

A woman rang up her greengrocer, to complain that although
she had ordered twelve oranges, he had only delivered eleven.
  'I know, madam' he agreed, 'but one was bad, so I threw it
away.'

'So you are applying for this job emptying gas meters, are you?'
  'That's right, sir.'
  'Well, now, we are offering £25 a week.'
  'Blimey, do I get paid as well?'

'What did you get for Christmas?'
  'A mouth-organ. It's the best present I ever got.'
  'Why?'
  'My Mum gives me 10p a week not to blow it.'

Did you hear about the man who's so lazy he sleeps in his garage
so that he won't have to walk in his sleep?

'What sort of a car has your Dad got?'
  'I can't remember the name. I think it starts with T.'
  'Really? Ours only starts with petrol.'

'I've taken up painting professionally.'
  'Sell anything?'
  'Yes – my car, my telly, my watch . . .'

'What job are you doing now?'
  'I'm a debt-collector.'
  'That's not a very pleasant job, is it?'
  'Oh, I don't know. People are always asking me to call again.'

'What do you mean by telling everyone I'm an idiot?'
  'I'm sorry. I didn't know it was supposed to be a secret.'

First actor: 'What have you been doing lately?'
Second actor: 'Oh, I finished a film last week.'
First actor: 'That's marvellous!'
Second actor: 'Yes – and I get it back from the chemist to-
morrow.'

'Did you hear about the thief who stole two and a half miles of elastic?'

'No.'

'He was put away for a good long stretch.'

A man sitting in a barber's chair noticed that the barber's hands were very dirty. When he commented on this, the barber explained, 'Yes, sir, no-one's been in for a shampoo yet.'

'Have you any invisible ink?'

'Certainly sir. What colour?'

Two mountaineers got into difficulties, and one found himself hanging by his rope over a precipice. While his friend was vainly trying to heave him to safety, the rope began to fray.

At this the one hanging down the cliff-face shouted, 'What happens if the rope breaks?'

'Don't worry,' called his pal. 'I've got another one!'

Judge: 'Prisoner at the bar, how do you plead. Guilty or not guilty?'

Defendant: 'How do I know till I've heard the evidence?'

'Why do you want to work in a bank?'

'Well, I'm told there's money in it.'

A very stout old lady asked a boy scout if he could see her across the road.

'I could see you a mile off!' he grinned.

An extremely tall man with round shoulders, very long arms and one leg six inches shorter than the other went into a tailor's shop.

'I'd like to see a suit that will fit me,' he told the tailor.

'So would I, sir,' the tailor sympathised. 'So would I.'

'Did you read about that chap who invented a gadget for seeing through brick walls?'

'No?'

'He calls it a window.'

A certain little lad was always playing in a neighbour's back yard, much to the neighbour's irritation. One day when the boy was again rushing around in the yard making Red Indian war-whoops, the neighbour leaned out of an upstairs window and yelled, 'Didn't I tell you not to let me catch you there again?'

'Yes,' called the boy, 'but you haven't caught me once yet!'

'Can I borrow that book of yours – How To Become A Millionaire?'

'Sure. Here you are.'

'Thanks – but half the pages are missing.'

'What's the matter? Isn't half a million enough for you?'

'My brother's been practising the violin for ten years.'

'Is he any good?'

'No. It was nine years before he found out he wasn't supposed to blow it.'

'A pound of kiddles, please, butcher.'

'You mean a pound of kidneys.'

'That's what I said, diddle I?'

A lad was proudly showing his expertise on his new bicycle by racing round the block while his Mum stood on the doorstep watching him whizz past.

'Look, Mum – no hands! ... look, Mum – no feet! ... Look, Mum – no teeth!'

'Where do you think you're going?'

'To church.'

'What, with dirt all over your face?'

'No, with Jimmy Green from next door.'

'What do you think of my latest painting? I value your opinion, you know.'

'Frankly, it's worthless.'

'I know, but I'd like to hear it just the same.'

Did you hear about the very well-behaved little boy? Whenever he was especially good his Dad would give him a penny and a pat on the head. By the time he was sixteen he had £17 in the post office and a flat head ...

As a passer-by was walking under a ladder, a brick fell from a hod and hit him on the head, ruining his new bowler.

He looked up at the hod carrier and shouted, 'You clumsy oaf! One of those bricks hit me!'

'You're lucky,' came the reply. 'Look at all the ones that didn't!'

A railway guard dashed out of the station and into a greengrocer's nearby.

'I've lost the pea out of my whistle!' he gasped. 'Can you give me another one – quick!'

The greengrocer only had split peas, so the guard put one of those in his whistle and dashed back to his train.

When he blew his whistle only half of the train moved out ...

'How's your new flat?'
'OK, but it's very small. In fact, we had to scrape the wall-paper off to get all the furniture in.'

'In India I used to chase wild elephants on horse-back.'
'Fancy that! I never knew elephants could ride horses . . .'

'In the park this morning I was surrounded by lions.'
'Lions! In the park?'
'Yes – dandelions!'

'I thought you weren't going to smoke any more.'
'I'm not.'
'But you're smoking as much as ever.'
'Well, that's not more, is it?'

'I bought a big book on body-building and I've been working hard on the exercises for three months.'
'Is it having any effect?'
'It certainly is. Now I can lift the book!'

'What did you do in Blackpool?'
'I went to see the sea.'
'Did the sea see you?'
'Well, it waved at me . . .'

'How's your business coming along?'
'I'm looking for a new cashier.'
'But you only had a new one last week.'
'That's the one I'm looking for.'

At the vicar's tea-party for the choir, the vicar's wife had arranged a super spread with all kinds of goodies. She held out a plate to the smallest choir-boy and said, 'Now, then, Davey, is there any kind of cake you don't like?'
'Yes – stomach ache!' said Davey.

At the height of the battle, a message was sent down the line: *Send reinforcements. Army is advancing on the left flank.* It finally reached Headquarters as: *Send three or four pence. Annie is dancing on wet planks.*

An Irishman at a fairground sat on the roundabout for ride after ride, getting sicker and sicker. Eventually he was positively green so his friend said, 'For goodness' sake, Paddy, will yez come off that thing! It's makin' yez ill!'
'That I will not,' said Paddy, shaking but stubborn. 'The feller that runs this thing owes me ten pounds, and the only way I'll get me money back is by takin' free rides on his machine!'

The meanest man in England stopped a taxi. 'How much to the station?' he asked.
'Fifty pence, sir,' said the taxi-driver.
'And how much for my suitcase?'
'That's five pence,' said the taxi-driver.
'Right,' said the mean man. 'Then take my suitcase to the station. I'll walk.'

'I was shipwrecked once in the Pacific and had to live for a whole week on a tin of sardines.'
  'Goodness, weren't you lucky not to fall off!'

'Here, what have I got in my hands?'
  'A horse and cart.'
  'Oh, you peeped!'

An angry woman swept into the butcher's shop and snapped, 'That joint you sold me was awful!'
  'Why, madam, was it tough?' asked the butcher.
  'Tough!' said the woman. 'I should say it was. Why, I couldn't even get my fork into the gravy!'

'Why are you laughing?'
  'My silly dentist has just pulled one of my teeth out.'
  'I don't see much to laugh about in that.'
  'Ah, but it was the wrong one!'

A man was playing the trumpet in the street when a pal of his happened to walk past.
  'I say, old chap,' the friend exclaimed, 'things must be tough for you if you're reduced to playing in the street!'
  'Oh, I'm not hard up,' said the trumpeter. 'It's my landlady – she won't let me practise in the house.'
  'Oh, I see – do you play by ear?'
  'No, I usually play over there.'

'Are you superstitious?'
  'No.'
  'Then lend me £13.'

'I'm going in for mountaineering.'
  'That's funny, I thought you always went up for mountaineering...'

'My Dad's an exporter.'
  'Is he?'
  'Yes. He used to work for British Rail.'

Old gent (at railway station): 'Porter, I want to go to Glasgow. Shall I take this train?'
Porter: 'If you like, guv'nor – but the engine driver'll be along in a minute.'

What should you do if you split your sides laughing? Run until you get a stitch in them ...

For sale: Piano by lady with elegant carved legs.

'Answer the phone.'
'It's not ringing.'
'Why leave everything till the last minute?'

A snobbish woman was showing a friend round her new house. 'It's very lovely,' her friend admitted, 'but what you need in this big room is a chandelier.'

'I know, my dear,' said her gracious hostess, 'but nobody in the family plays one.'

A car-driver slowed down by the kerb, wound down the window and called to a passer-by, 'Oi! Leatherhead?'

'Fish-face!' came the cheerful answer.

'I'll lend you a quid if you'll promise not to keep it too long.'
'Oh, I won't. I'll spend it right away!'

Auntie Gladys bought herself a new rear-engine continental car. She took an old friend for a spin, but after only half a mile the car broke down. Both women got out and opened up the front of the car.

'Oh, Gladys,' said her friend, 'you've lost your engine!'
'Never mind, dear,' said auntie, 'I've got a spare one in the boot.'

Lost: A guitar with a green hat.

'Dad, Farmer Johnson caught me eating apples in his orchard.'
'I've told you to keep out of there, haven't I? Did he punish you?'
'No, he said I'd been punished enough already. They were cookers.'

Notice (in a shoe-shop window): Anyone can have a fit in this shop.

Fat woman (getting off bus): 'Conductor, this bus was very slow.'
Conductor: 'It'll pick up now you're getting off, Ma!'

River Warden: 'Boy! Can't you see that notice? It says "No Swimming Here".'
Boy: 'Well, it's not true, is it? You come in and see for yourself.'

'Is this a second-hand shop?'
'Yes, sir.'
'Good. Can you fit one on my watch, please?'

Knock! Knock!

– Who's there?
Orange.
Orange who?
Orange you glad I called?

Will you remember me in one day's time?
Of course I will.
Will you remember me in a week's time?
Of course I will.
Will you remember me in a year's time?
Of course I will.
Will you remember me in ten year's time?
Of course I will.
Knock! Knock!
Who's there?
See – you've forgotten already!

– Who's there?
Madam.
Madam who?
Madam finger's caught in the door.

– Who's there?
Boo.
Boo who?
No need to cry – it's only a joke.

– Who's there?
Ammonia.
Ammonia who?
(*Sings*) Ammonia a poor little sparrow . . .

– Who's there?
Olive.
Olive who?
Olive across the road.

– Who's there?
Mummy.
Mummy who?
Mummeasles are better so can I come in?

– Who's there?
Harry.
Harry who?
Harry up and let me in!

– Who's there?
Fanny.
Fanny who?
Fanny the way you keep saying 'Who's there?' every time I knock!

- Who's there?
Lettuce.
Lettuce who?
Lettuce in, won't you?

- Who's there?
York.
York who?
York coming over to our place.

- Who's there?
Alison.
Alison who?
Alison to my radio in the mornings.

- Who's there?
Isabel.
Isabel who?
Isabel broken, 'cos I had to knock?!

- Ring! Ring!
Who's there?
Hurd my.
Hurd my who?
Hurd my hand so I can't knock.

- Who's there?
Marmite.
Marmite who?
Ma might but Pa might not.

- Who's there?
Arthur.
Arthur who?
Arthur any biscuits left?

- Who's there?
Ivor.
Ivor who?
Ivor sore hand from knocking on your door!

- Who's there?
Mister.
Mister who?
Mister last bus home.

- Who's there?
Atch.
Atch who?
Nasty cold you've got.

- Who's there?
Doctor.
Doctor who?
How did you guess?

– Who's there?
Little old lady.
Little old lady who?
I didn't know you could yodel.

– Who's there?
Amanda.
Amanda who?
Amanda fix the television.

– Who's there?
Waiter.
Waiter who?
Waiter minute while I tie my shoelaces up.

– Who's there?
Nicholas.
Nicholas who?
Nicholas girls shouldn't climb trees.

– Who's there?
Walrus.
Walrus who?
Why do you walrus ask that silly question?

– Who's there?
Doris.
Doris who?
Doris locked   that's why I knocked.

– Who's there?
Grannie. Knock! Knock!
Who's there?
Grannie. Knock! Knock!
Who's there?
Grannie. Knock! Knock!
Who's there?
Grannie. Knock! Knock!
Who's there?
Aunt.
Aunt who?
Aunt you glad Grannie's gone?

— Who's there?
William.
William who?
William mind your own business!

— Who's there?
Mary.
Mary who?
Mary Christmas.

— Who's there?
One.
One who?
One-der why you keep asking that?

— Who's there?
Howard.
Howard who?
Howard you like to stand out here in the cold while some
idiot keeps saying 'Who's there . . . ?'

— Who's there?
Max.
Max who?
Max no difference — just open the door!

The Bird-Brain's Reading List

OH NO! NOT AGAIN

SOLITUDE I. MALONE

Parachute Jumping	*by* Willie Maykit
The Inevitable Occurrence	*by* Sue Nora Later
Everybody Out	*by* Rufus Falling
Trouble In Lancashire	*by* Igor Blimey
Laying Carpets	*by* Walter Wall
Caring For Parrots	*by* L.O. Polly
Solitude	*by* I. Malone
The Thirsty Diner	*by* Phillipa Carafe
Brick Laying	*by* C. Ment
Show Jumping	*by* Jim Carner
First In The Form	*by* Hedda De Classe
A Visit To The Dentist	*by* Lord Howard Hertz
Home Haircutting	*by* Shaun Head
End Of Term	*by* C. Myra Port
Shakespeare's Shylock	*by* Judy Fiant
How To Make An Igloo	*by* S. Keemo
Pachyderms	*by* L.E. Fant
Feed Your Dog Properly	*by* Norah Bone
Weight Lifting	*by* Buster Gutt
Writing A Magazine Advice Column	*by* A. Guinea Arnt
Spare the Rod and Spoil the Child	*by* Corporal Punishment
Run For Your Lives	*by* General Panic
Designing Placards	*by* Bill Poster
On The Rocks	*by* Mandy Lifeboat
The Case of the Stolen Chestnut	*by* Nick McConker
Out On Parole	*by* Freda Convict
Escape To The New Forest	*by* Lucinda Woods
Cookery For Beginners	*by* Egon Chips
Riding For Pleasure	*by* G.G. Canters
English Church Architecture	*by* Beverley Minster
Not Too Fast	*by* Ann Dante

The Bank Raid	*by* Dinah Mite
The Millionaire	*by* Ivor Fortune
How To Cross The Road	*by* J. Walker
The Jockey	*by* Willie Winn
The Idiot	*by* M. T. Nutt
Keeping Cheerful	*by* Mona Lott
Home Heating	*by* Arthur Mometer
So Tired	*by* Carrie Mee
The Big Swindle	*by* Hymer Twister
Aching Arms	*by* Belle Ringer

Making Snack Meals	*by* San Widge
Discipline In The Home	*by* Wilma Child Begood
How To Cure Rheumatism	*by* Algy Pan

Differences of Opinion

What's the difference between ...
- *a buffalo and a bison?*
  You can't wash your hands in a buffalo.

- *a jeweller and a jailer?*
  One sells watches and the other watches cells.

- *a baker and a heavy sleeper?*
  One bakes the bread and the other breaks the bed.

- *a butcher and a light sleeper?*
  One weighs a steak and the other stays awake.

- *Hitler and a dog?*
  One goes like this *(raise arm)* and the other goes like this *(raise leg)*.

- *an elephant and a pillar-box?*
  You don't know? Then it's no good sending you to post a letter, is it?

- *a forged pound note and an insane rabbit?*
  One is bad money and the other is a mad bunny.

- *a storm cloud and a child being spanked?*
  One pours with rain and the other roars with pain!

- *a tailor and a horse-trainer?*
  One mends tears and the other tends mares.

- *a railway guard and a teacher?*
  One minds the train and the other trains the mind.

- *an Indian elephant and an African elephant?*
  About three thousand miles.

- *elephants and fleas?*
  Elephants can have fleas but fleas can't have elephants.

Riddle-Tee-Hee

What do you call a 400 kilogram grizzly bear with a bad temper?
  Sir.

What is the most common illness in birds?
  Flu.

What exams are horses good at?
  Hay levels.

Why did the one-eyed chicken cross the road?
  To get to the Bird's Eye shop.

How do you get two whales in a Mini?
  Drive down the motorway. (Two whales = to Wales!)

What can't you do if you put 250 melons in the fridge?
  Shut the door.

Why did the farmer drive over his potato field with a steamroller?
  'Cos he wanted mashed potatoes.

What did the big candle say to the little candle?
  'You're too young to go out.'

What is yellow and flickers?
  A lemon with a loose connection.

What must you be careful not to do when it's raining cats and dogs?
  Step in a poodle.

What happened to the plastic surgeon when he stood by the fire?
  He melted.

Now you see it, now you don't – what is it?
  A black cat walking over a zebra crossing.

Why are 4,840 square yards like a bad tooth?
Because it's an acre.

What is bought by the yard and worn by the foot?
A carpet.

Why did the apple turnover?
'Cos it saw the cheese roll.

If a runner gets athlete's foot, what does a Roman Catholic priest get?
Mistletoe. (Missal-toe!)

Why are whist players aggressive?
'Cos they often lead with a club.

Why does a Scoutmaster have to take a lot of rubbish?
Because he's a Skip.

Where do you get satisfaction from?
A satisfactory.

What cakes do children dislike?
Cakes of soap.

What question always receives the answer Yes?
How do you pronounce Y E S?

Why did the milkmaid sit down?
'Cos she couldn't stand milking.

Who is bigger: Mrs Bigger or her baby?
Her baby, who is always a Little Bigger.

Why does a young lady need the letter Y?
'Cos without it she'd be a young lad.

Why is it dangerous to put the letter 'M' into the fridge?
Because it changes ice into mice.

Why is the sea always restless?
'Cos it's got so many rocks in its bed.

What did one toe say to the next toe?
Don't look now but there's a big heel following us!

Why are your tonsils unhappy?
'Cos they're always down in the mouth.

When is a schoolkid like a rope?
When it's taut.

What's the best place to go to when you're dying?
The living room.

How many coats can you get in an empty wardrobe?
Only one — after that it isn't empty!

Why did the weeping willow weep?
  'Cos it saw the pine tree pine.

How do barbers get to their shops quickly?
  They take short cuts.

Why are dentists unhappy?
  'Cos they're always looking down in the mouth.

Why can't a car play football?
  'Cos it's only got one boot.

Which word is always pronounced wrongly?
  The one that's spelled W R O N G L Y.

Why is the letter T an island?
  'Cos it's in the middle of water.

When were there only three vowels in the alphabet?
  Before U and I were born.

Why is the letter A like a flower?
  'Cos B is always after it.

How does a ship listen?
  Through its engineers.

What do you have when you don't feel well?
  Gloves on your hands.

Who earns a living without doing a day's work?
  A night-porter.

How can you always tell an undertaker?
  By his grave manner.

Why is your nose in the middle of your face?
  'Cos it's the (s)centre.

What did the digital watch say to her mother?
  'Look, Ma! No hands!'

Why are there so few lady pilots?
  'Cos no girl wants to be a plane woman!

Why is perfume always very obedient?
  'Cos it is scent wherever it goes.

Why can the world never come to an end?
  'Cos it's round.

Why is Buckingham Palace cheap to maintain?
  'Cos it's run for a sovereign.

Why is the letter A like noon?
  'Cos it's in the middle of the day.

Why is an airplane like a confidence trickster?
  They both have no visible means of support.

What happened to the man who jumped off a bridge in Paris?
  He went in Seine.

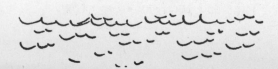

Why did the Communist chicken cross the road?
  'Cos it was a Rhode Island Red.

What pet makes the loudest noise?
  A trum-pet.

What do you always take down when you're run over by a car?
  Its registration number.

Why did the hedgehog cross the road?
  To see his flatmate.

What travels round the world yet stays in one corner?
  A postage stamp.

Why did the cat cross the road?
  'Cos it was stapled to the chicken . . . (ugh!)

What two kinds of fish are needed to make a shoe?
  A sole and an eel.

Where was Rosie when the lights went out?
  In the dark.

What key went to University?
  A Yale.

What flashes by but doesn't move?
  A telegraph pole when you're travelling in a car.

Why was the Boy Scout dizzy?
  He'd done too many good turns.

What tune do you sing in a car?
  A car-toon.

What is full of holes but can hold water?
  A sponge.

What did the bell say when it fell in the water?
  'I'm (w)ringing wet!'

What makes the Tower of Pisa lean?
  It doesn't eat much.

Why are teachers special?
  'Cos they're in a class of their own.

Why are bakers invariably good people?
  'Cos they earn an honest crust.

What happens to the girl who misses the school bus?
  She catches it when she gets home.

Why did the bus stop?
'Cos it saw the zebra crossing.

Did you hear about the red sauce chasing the brown sauce?
  It couldn't ketchup.

Why did the pop singer go to the barber?
  He couldn't stand his hair any longer.

How many days of the week start with the letter T?
  Four: Tuesday, Thursday, today and tomorrow.

How do you get rid of varnish?
   Take away the letter **R**.

What athlete is the warmest in winter?
   The long jumper.

Which roof covers the noisiest tenant?
   The roof of your mouth.

What doesn't ask questions but must always be answered?
   A telephone.

What fish do dogs chase?
   Catfish.

What is open when it's closed and closed when it's open?
   Tower Bridge.

Why is the sea so suspicious?
   'Cos it's been crossed so often.

If a crocodile makes shoes what does a banana make?
   Slippers.

Why did the train go 'ouch!'?
   'Cos it had a tender behind.

What travels faster: heat or cold?
   Heat, because it's easy to catch a cold.

How many balls of string would it take to reach the Moon?
   Just one *HUGE* one!

What is it that even the most careful person overlooks?
   His nose.

On which side of Jack Trot's house did his Beanstalk grow?
   On the outside.

What goes up a chimney down but not down a chimney up?
   An umbrella.

What is a tornado?
   Mother Nature doing the twist.

What do you call a letter when it's dropped down the chimney?
   Blackmail.

Why is a chemistry lesson like a worm in a cornfield?
   They both go in one ear and out the other.

What runs and whistles but can't talk?
   A railway train.

Why is a batsman a coward?
  'Cos he's frightened of a duck.

What jam can't you put on your bread?
  Traffic jam.

What nail can't you hit with a hammer?
  Your fingernail.

'Look, there's a nail!'
  'Where?'
  'On the end of my finger!'

What driver can't drive?
  A screwdriver.

How would you describe beans on toast?
  Skinheads on a raft.

What is the longest word in the dictionary?
  Elastic, because it stretches.

What runs round a garden without moving?
  A fence.

How does an octopus go into battle?
  Fully-armed.

Why did King Kong climb up the Empire State Building?
  To catch a plane.

What do you find in Quality Street?
  Chocolates.

What am I if someone takes away all my letters?
  A postman who's been mugged.

What is the principal part of a lion?
  Its mane.

What should you do if your nose goes on strike?
  Picket.

Who won the World Cup in 1920?
  No one — the first World Cup competition was held in 1930.

What is the best place for a party on board ship?
  Where the funnel be.

What is the softest bed a baby can sleep on?
  Cot-on wool.

A barrel of beer fell on a brewery worker. Why wasn't he hurt?
  'Cos it was full of light ale.

How can you avoid falling hair?
  Jump out of the way.

How can you knock over a full glass without spilling any water?
  Knock over a full glass of milk.

What vegetable do you need a plumber for?
A leek!

Where can you find ice-cream in the Bible?
At the Walls of Jericho.

Have you heard the joke about the wall?
You'd never get over it!

What's the biggest nut in the British Army?
The kernel.

What can never be made right?
Your left ear.

Why did the rabbit cross the road?
To show his girl-friend he had guts.

What can you make that can't be seen?
A noise.

Why is a lion in the desert like Christmas?
'Cos of its Sandy Claws.

What is the best way to cover a cushion?
Sit on it.

What happens if you walk under a cow?
You get a pat on the head.

If twelve make a dozen how many make a million?
Very few.

What are the best things to put in an apple pie?
Your teeth!

What do misers do when it's cold?
Sit round a candle.
What do misers do when it's very cold?
Light it.

What has four eyes and a mouth?
The Mississippi.

What did the idiot do with a flea in his ear?
He shot it.

What gets bigger the more you take away?
A hole.

What is a container that hasn't any hinges but inside has a golden treasure?
An egg.

What whistles when it's hot?
A kettle.

A little thing, a pretty thing, without a top or bottom.
What am I?
A diamond ring.

What is a sausage dog?
A hot dog with no bread.

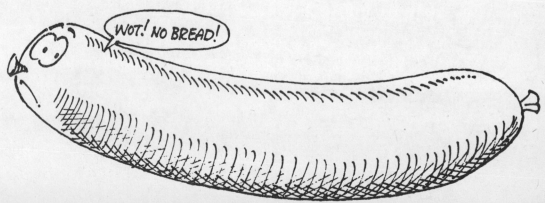

What did Lot do when his wife turned into a pillar of salt?
  He put her in the cellar.

What kind of lights did Noah have on the ark?
  Floodlights.

Why do actors hang around snooker halls?
  'Cos that's where they are sure to get some cues.

What kind of umbrella does a Russian carry when its raining?
  A wet one!

Why was the baby raised on cat's milk?
  'Cos it was a baby kitten.

What is yellow, soft and goes round and round?
  A long-playing omelette.

What is the shortest bridge in the world?
  The bridge of your nose.

What do you call an Irish spider?
  Paddy Longlegs.

What food is impertinent?
  Sauce.

What is a cow that eats grass?
  A lawn-mooer.

What did the French Chef do when a customer fainted?
  Gave her the quiche of life.

Is censorship a good thing or not?
  It depends on whether the result makes censor not.

When are circus acrobats needed in restaurants?
  When tumblers are required on the tables.

If we get honey from a bee, what do we get from a wasp?
  Waspberry jam.

Who sailed the Seven Seas looking for rubbish and blubber?
  Binbag the Whaler.

Why did the simpleton bury his car battery?
  'Cos the mechanic told him it was dead.

What do you get in Friday papers?
  Fish and chips. (Fri-day)

Why did the stupid postman get the sack?
  To put his stupid letters in.

Why was the United Nations worried when a waiter dropped his tray?
  'Cos it was the fall of Turkey, China was broken and Greece was overthrown!

What is purple and 4,000 miles long?
The Grape Wall of China.

Why did the Lone Ranger take a hammer to bed?
So's he could hit the hay.

Who was Mexico's most famous fat man?
Pauncho Villa.

What will happen to you at Christmas?
Yule be happy.

What clothes do lawyers wear in court?
Lawsuits.

What's rich and goes putt-putt?
A sunburned golf-pro.

What is big, has four wheels and flies?
A rubbish cart.

Why did the antelope?
Nobody gnu.

What is the fastest vegetable in the world?
A runner bean!

Why did the scientist have his phone cut off?
'Cos he wanted to win the Nobel prize.

What did the man say when he stepped on a choc bar?
'I've set foot on Mars!'

What bow can't you tie?
A rainbow.

Why is the Eiffel tower so called?
'Cos from the top you sure get an eye-ful!

What is the hottest part of the Sun?
Page three!

What would you say to a German barber?
'Good morning, Herr Dresser!'

How does a professional hypnotist travel?
By public transport.

Why was Cleopatra so cantankerous?
She was Queen of denial.

What is the smallest ant in the world?
An infant.

What is the definition of a minimum?
A woman with only one child.

What is always behind time?
The back of a clock.

Why should you always have plenty of clocks in the house?
Because time is precious.

Why should Elijah's parents be remembered by all business people?
Because they made a prophet.

Why did the father call two of his sons Edward?
'Cos two Eds are better than one.

What do you call someone who steals pigs?
A ham-burglar.

What did Queen Guinevere say when she fell in love?
'Arthur any more at home like you?'

Did Cain hate his brother for ever?
No, just for as long as he was Abel.

What is black and white and has eight wheels?
A nun on roller skates.

Where were chips first fried?
In Greece.

What soup do Irish cannibals like best?
The broth of a boy.

Why are goldfish gold?
So they won't go rusty.

How did the glow-worm feel when it backed into a fan?
Delighted.

What is a mermaid?
A deep-she fish.

What did the guests sing at the Eskimo's coming-of-age party?
'Freeze A Jolly Good Fellow . . .'

What is the definition of 'debate'?
It's something dat lures de fish.

What is Shakespeare's most popular play in the Orient?
Asia Like It.

What will a wise man say on the Last Day?
'Armageddon out of here . . .'

What is yellow and goes click-click?
A ball-point banana.

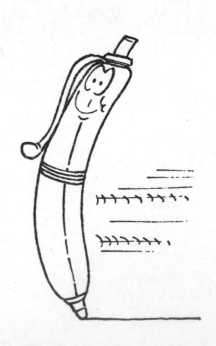

What is Father Christmas's wife called?
Mrs Christmas.

What did Mrs Christmas say to her husband during the storm?
'Come and look at the reindeer.'

'Why are you taking that steel wool home?'
'I'm going to knit myself a car.'

Did you hear about the stupid water-polo player?
His horse drowned . . .

Did you hear the joke about the roof?
It's way above your head.

What happened to the idiot who sat on the floor?
She fell off.

Did you hear about the stupid tap-dancer?
He fell in the sink.

Why did the bald-headed man look out of the window?
To get some fresh 'air.

Where does Tarzan buy his clothes?
At a Jungle Sale.

What did Tarzan say when the tiger started chewing on his leg?
AAAAAAAAAAAAAAAAA! (Give Tarzan yell)

What lives in a pod and is a Kung Fu expert?
Bruce Pea.

Why are you tired on April Fool's Day?
'Cos you've just had a thirty-one days' March.

Why are adults boring?
'Cos they're groan-ups.

Do sailors go on safaris?
Not safaris I know.

What drink do jungle big cats prefer?
Lyons quick brew.

What's big, hairy and can fly?
King Kongcorde.

What has a horn and drives?
A car.

What do cannibal children like playing best?
Swallow my leader.

What do Eskimos use for money?
Ice lolly.

What kind of warmth do sheep enjoy in winter?
Central bleating.

Why did Henry VIII have so many wives?
He liked to chop and change.

What kinds of cans are there in Mexico?
Mexicans.

How would you define a stick of rhubarb?
A stick of celery with high blood-pressure.

Why did the fireman wear red trousers?
His blue ones were at the cleaners.

What does a pig use to write his letters with?
Pen and oink.

What's a good place for water-skiing?
A sloping lake.

We all know that a nun rolling down a hill goes black-and-white-and-black-and-white, but what is black-and-white and goes ha-ha? The nun that pushed her!

Where would you find a stupid shop-lifter?
Squashed under Tesco's.

What was Beethoven's favourite fruit? (Sing to the opening four notes of Beethoven's Fifth Symphony:)
Banana-naaaa!

Why do some women wear curlers at night?
So they can wake up curly in the morning.

Have you heard the joke about the dog that walked twice from Land's End to John O'Groats?
No, neither have I . . .

What pop group kills household germs?
The Bleach Boys.

What did the policeman have in his sandwiches?
Traffic jam.

Why did the cockerel cross the road?
To show he wasn't chicken.

How do you take a sick pig to hospital?
In a hambulance.

Where do you take a sick dog?
To the dogtor.

Who invented fire?
Some bright spark . . .

What do you get if you give sugar and egg-whites to a monkey?
Meringue Outan.

What happened to the man who slept with his head under the pillow?
When he woke up he found the fairies had taken all his teeth out.

What do miners play in the pit?
Mine-opoly.

What do you call a potato that insults the farmer?
A fresh vegetable.

What's yellow and goes round and round?
A banana in a washing machine.

Why couldn't the sailors play cards?
'Cos the captain was standing on the deck.

What's black and white and extremely difficult?
An A-level exam paper.

What happened to the man who dreamed he was eating a giant marshmallow?
When he woke up his pillow had disappeared.

If you drop a white hat into the Red Sea, how does it come out?
 Wet.

What's green and white and bounces?
 A spring onion.

How do you make gold soup?
 Use fourteen carats.

Where do bees go for transport?
 The buzz-stop.

What's white and climbs trees?
 A fridge — I lied about it climbing trees.

What's white and blue and climbs trees?
 A fridge wearing denims. (And I'm still lying about it climbing trees.)

What vegetable plays snooker?
 A cue-cumber.

If you put a crowd of Mastermind contestants in a London Underground train, what have you got?
 A Tube of Smarties.

How do pixies eat?
 By gobblin'.

Why did the orange stop rolling down the hill?
 It ran out of juice.

How do you cut through the waves?
 With a sea-saw.

How can you put on weight easily?
 Eat an entire peach and you'll immediately gain a stone.

Do robots have brothers?
 No, only tran*sisters*.

Who makes suits and eats spinach?
 Popeye the Tailorman.

Why couldn't Cinderella go to the ball?
 'Cos it had a puncture.

Preserve wild-life — pickle a squirrel.

What is the crocodile's favourite game?
 Snap.

If King Kong went to Hong Kong to play ping-pong and died, what would they put on his coffin?
 A lid.

When a lemon calls for assistance, what does it want?
 Lemonade.

Amaze Your Friends

An easy trick at a party is to say that you will go out of room, and in your absence you want any lady present and any gentleman present to place a coin on the table – and you will be able to tell which coin belongs to the man and which to the woman! The secret is that when you come back into the room you must pick up each of the coins; one will feel warmer than the other – this is the man's, since the coin will have been warmed by his body. The woman's coin, on the other hand, will have been in her handbag and so will be quite cold.

You can make a matchbox appear to rise of its own accord by shutting it over a fold of skin on your knuckle. Try it and see!

Invite a friend to breathe on your magic mirror to see what it will tell him. As he breathes on the mirror, sure enough a ghostly message appears! The secret of this is simplicity itself: before your friend enters the room simply mark the mirror with whatever message you wish him to read (i.e. 'You are a silly fool!') *with your finger*. Believe it or not, this will not show up until he breathes on it!

The following story is a good one to tell at parties:

'I am going to tell you a story about three little ducks. Will you help me? Thank you. Now these three little ducks were called – (*here you hold up one finger*) Quack, Quack-Quack (*hold up two fingers*) and Quack-Quack-Quack (*hold up three fingers*). Shall we try that again? Three little ducks called Quack (*one finger*), Quack-Quack (*two fingers*) and Quack-Quack-Quack (*three fingers*)'.

'Now, one day these three little ducks decided to go into the country to collect some mushrooms, to make a lovely mushroom soup. So out they went, and collected a huge basketful of mushrooms; they went home and made their lovely mushroom soup. But in the middle of the night – (*hold up one finger*) – fell ill! So (*two fingers*) . . . said to (*three fingers*) . . . "you'd better go and get the doctor".

'Well, the doctor came and examined (*one finger*), and said, "Oh, he's just got a touch of indigestion, he'll be all right in the morning. Just give him these pills. And so, greatly relieved, (*two fingers*) . . . and (*three fingers*) . . . gave (*one finger*) the pills. But by the time morning came, (*one finger*) had died! (*Aaaaah!*) At which (*two fingers*) . . . said to (*three fingers*) . . . "I think that doctor must have been a bit of a (*one finger*)! Thank you."

Say to a friend who is wearing a coat or a jacket, 'I bet you can't button your coat up.' When he has fastened the buttons, which he will do immediately to prove you wrong, you then say, 'There, I told you you couldn't button it *up*' – because everyone buttons from the top *down*.

How to tie a knot in a piece of string without letting go of the ends: fold your arms, pick up the string with an end in each hand, then unfold your arms. Hey presto – a knot is made!

Put ten matches on the table and invite a friend to make a monkey from them. When he fails, simply arrange the matches into the word 'APE', using two matches for the top of the letter P. Similarly, seven matches can be used to make an hotel. It may seem impossible, until you use the seven matches to spell out the word 'INN' – which is a kind of hotel, isn't it?'

Challenge a friend to pick up a brush without touching it; your solution is to produce a second brush which you push firmly down onto the bristles of the first!

Make a fist, place a playing card on the back of your hand and a coin on the card. Then announce that you will remove the card without touching the coin. The solution? You simply flick the card with your left hand. If you get the angle right (it needs a slightly downward flick) the card will go sailing away but the coin will remain.

Patsy: 'I bet I can make you say "black".'
Mike: 'Go on, then.'
Patsy: 'What are colours of the Union Jack?'
Mike: 'Red, white and blue.'
Patsy: 'There you are. I told you I could make you say "blue".'
Mike: 'No – you said you couldn't make me say "black".'
Patsy: 'And you've just said it, haven't you?'

Tell a friend that you have 11 fingers. When he scoffs at this claim, count from 1 to 10 on your fingers; then count backwards, saying, '10, 9, 8, 7, 6 – and 5 fingers on the other hand makes 11!'

A mystifying illusion is to tell your friends that you can push a chalk cross through a solid table. You take a piece of chalk, draw a small cross on a table or chair, then put one hand under the table while pushing hard on the cross with the other. After a few seconds, the cross on the top is gone and – lo and behold! – there is a little chalk cross on the plam of your other hand.

The secret is very simple. Before starting you draw a small chalk cross on the nail of your second finger. Although the palm of your hand can be examined closely and even washed, no-one ever thinks of looking at your nails. So while this hand is under the table or chair, you just close your fist, press hard and the chalk cross will be transferred to the ball of your thumb. The hand on top of course simply rubs the chalk cross out.

This one is simply astounding to anyone not in the know: to begin you show round a skeleton cut out of cardboard and coloured white, and about 12" in height – it helps if the limbs can be jointed with staples. This can be handled and examined by your audience. You then place the skeleton upright between the legs of a table or chair at one end of the room – and the skeleton not only stands unaided but dances to your command! You can then pick up the skeleton, again hand it round for examination and repeat the trick as often as required.

The secret is this: before the start of your party, you push a drawing-pin into the back of each of the two legs of the table or chair under which your skeleton is to dance. These pins should be placed at about the height of the skeleton's shoulders. You then attach a piece of black cotton to one of the drawing-pins, and take it across to the other drawing-pin. The cotton is not attached to the second drawing-pin – it merely rests on it, and continues to the nearset chair. In this chair is sitting your accomplice . . . now you can see how the skeleton dances. As you turn to place the skeleton beneath the table or chair, your accomplice picks up the other end of the cotton and pulls it taut. You place the arms of the skeleton behind the cotton, and step back. On the command, 'Skeleton, dance!' your accomplice merely has to jerk the cotton very gently – and your skeleton does just that!

You can be sure that, if the lights are lowered, and your skeleton is carefully painted, the cotton will not be seen.

The following coin trick was demonstrated to the author by his father over a period of five or six years without the secret displaying itself: so you can try it with confidence! The effect is this:

You pick up a coin and show it for examination. You then place your elbow on a table with your arm bent and slap the coin on to your forearm, rubbing it up and down between your wrist and elbow with four fingers of the other hand. You take away one finger, still rubbing, then another, then another, and finally take away the remaining finger to show that the coin has disappeared! The coin (which can be marked to show there is no substitution) can then be produced from your ear, or your pocket, or wherever you choose.

The secret is the old illusionist technique of mis-direction. When you first start to rub the coin on your arm, you 'accidentally' drop it; you pick it up and again start to rub –and again you 'accidentally' drop it. The third time you pick it up with the *other hand*, i.e. the hand which does not do the rubbing. Swiftly however you slap the empty hand against your arm and start to rub – I can guarantee that this will not be spotted. I have even tried it on grown-ups and fooled them! With the coin in your other hand, you can then produce it from wherever you like.

Here's a wheeze that's bound to catch someone. Ask them to write down on a piece of paper eleven thousand, eleven hundred and eleven. The correct answer is 12111 – but you'll nearly always be given the wrong one!

Another party trick: you announce to the company that you will divine any object in the room that they care to choose. You pick on one of the company as spokesman and leave the room. When you return the spokesman says, 'Is it the television set? Is it the clock on the mantelpiece? Is it the mirror on the wall?' – and so on, until he mentions the article chosen, which you instantly identify.

The secret is that the spokesman is an accomplice. As you leave the room you quite naturally put your hand on the door to shut it. The number of fingers displayed as you do this will indicate to him or her when to indicate the chosen article. In other words, if you show three fingers, then the article chosen by the company will be the third one named by the spokesman. Very simple, but remarkably effective.

Try this one on a friend, and you can be sure you'll catch him or her out.

'What does T O spell?'

'To.'

'And what does T O O spell?'

'Too.'

'What does T W O spell?'

'Two.'

'And what is the second day of the week?'

'Tuesday (or, trying to be clever, Toosday).'

'No – Monday is the second day of the week!'

Another party wheeze: put a glass of water under one of your Dad's hats and announce that you will drink the water without touching the hat! Amidst sounds of disbelief, you crouch down behind the hat – hiding your face from view and make slurping sounds as though drinking. Then you stand up and say, 'There you are!' Someone is bound to lift the hat to see whether the water is gone from the glass. As soon as this happens you calmly pick up the glass and drink *without touching the hat* – as promised!

You can continue with this gag: place the empty glass on the table upside down. Then place on the table three matches and invite one of the parties to place one of the matches on top of the glass using only the other two matches. After some difficulty, he will do this. 'But,' you will say, 'I told you to put the match on the top of the glass – and you've put it on the bottom!'

You can then show everyone a small coloured disc of cardboard and three egg-cups. You say that you will turn your back – or even go out of the room – while the disc is placed under one of the egg-cups. When you return you will be able to tell which one the disc is under. The secret is that beforehand you have stuck a hair on to the disc with some gum; the hair which will be undetectable to anyone not in the secret, will stick out from underneath the egg-cup (provided you don't make the disc too small) enabling you to work the trick instantly. Take a little time over it, though – you don't want to make it look too easy!

Ask a pal if he can write 'fifty miles under the sea' in four words. When he admits defeat, show him the solution: $\frac{\text{the sea}}{\text{fifty miles}}$

Easy when you know how, eh?

Try this one on your Mum or Dad. Say, 'I bet I can get you to clasp your hands together so that you won't be able to leave the room without undoing them?' When this challenge is accepted, you just get your victim to clasp his or her hands together round a piano leg or the leg of the telly stand or any heavy piece of furniture. Sure enough, they won't be able to leave the room without unclasping their hands!

Here's a neat trick: take three handkerchiefs, one coloured and the other two white. Tie them together with the coloured one at the end, and then ask a friend whether he can put the coloured handkerchief *between* the white ones without untying any knots. When he is unable to do so, you demonstrate how it is done by simply tying the free ends of the handkerchiefs together. You now have a circle of hankies, and the coloured one is between the white ones!

Take a piece of paper and a pencil and announce to a friend, 'I can write with my left ear!' When he challenges you to do so, simply take up the pencil and write 'with my left ear'!

Tie a pencil to one end of a piece of string and hold it up by the other end. Now you state that you will cut through the string but the pencil will not fall to the floor. To perform this amazing feat you simply tie a loop in the string, and then cut through the loop!

Ask a pal whether he can take half away from something and leave more? When he fails to think of anything – as you can be sure he will – you write down the word: HALFPENNY. Then all you have to do is to scratch through HALF with your pencil, leaving PENNY – which is more than you started with!

A similar wheeze is to announce that you can sing underwater. When challenged to prove this unlikely boast, you merely sing the words 'under water' to a popular tune! ('Daisy, Daisy' is a good one for this.)

Everyone knows that there are 26 letters in the alphabet, but you can prove that there are only 11 letters in the alphabet. And how do you do this? Quite simply – by counting out the letters as you write 't-h-e a-l-p-h-a-b-e-t'!

Mystify a pal by saying that you are about to show him or her something which has never been seen before by human eyes and will never be seen again. You then open a peanut shell and swallow the peanut!

If a man is locked in a prison cell with only a wooden chair, how can he get out?

First of all he rubs his hands together till they're sore; then he takes the saw and saws the chair in half. Two halves make a whole, so he crawls through the hole and then shouts till he is hoarse. Then all he has to do is to jump on the horse and gallop away!

Here's a super party wheeze: put three sweets on the table and cover them with three hats. Lift the first hat, pick up the sweet and eat it; do the same with the second sweet and the third. Now for the magic! You say to the assembled company, 'And now, ladies and gentlemen, which hat would you like to be covering the three sweets?' And when someone unsuspectingly points to one of the hats, you simply pick it up and put it on your head!

Here's a game that you can always win. Put 16 matches on the table and challenge a friend to remove either one or two matches, you will then also remove one or two; then it is his turn again, then yours and so on. The point of the game is that the loser is the one who has to take the last match. So how do you always win?

First, your challenger must always *start first*; second, if he takes one match, you must take *two* and if he takes two matches you must take *one*. In this way he will always be the one to take the last match and so lose the game!

Cut a small hole in a piece of paper and challenge a friend to push his finger through the centre of the paper. When he fails to do so, simply roll the paper up into a cylinder and push your finger down the centre of the roll!

How to cut a square in a piece of paper with one snip of the scissors. Fold the paper in two and then in two again. Now all you have to do is to cut straight across the folded corner. Unfold the paper and there is a perfect square!

Ask a friend to take a coin out of his pocket and hold it tightly in his hand: by concentrating hard with your hand on his or her head you will be able to tell the date. After screwing your eyes up, with every appearance of racking your brains you eventually say, 'Yes . . . I have it, I think . . . the date is –' And then you give today's date!

This is bound to catch somebody out: ask which of the following two statements is correct – the yolk of an egg *are* white or the yolk of an egg *is* white? Almost certainly you will be told that 'the yolk of an egg *is* white' is correct; whereupon you point out that the yolk of an egg is yellow . . . !

Another challenge: ask a friend to add 2 to 91 and make it less? It sounds impossible, until you write it this way: $\frac{91}{2}$ ($9\frac{1}{2}$)!

If you put seven matches on the table, how can you take away one and leave none? By simply arranging the six remaining matches into the word NIL!

Here's a neat trick: put three matchboxes on the table and explain that only one of them has matches in it. Pick up each box in turn and shake it – only one will rattle. You then change the three boxes round rapidly and challenge the company present to guess which is the box with the matches in. No-one will ever get it right. And why is this? Because none of the boxes has any matches in it! How do you get one to rattle, then? You have *another* box with some matches in it attached to your arm with a rubber band (you must keep your jacket on for this trick of course), so that when you shake a box with that hand your audience will hear a rattle. To demonstrate the two 'empty' boxes you just shake them with the other hand.

You can bet your bottom dollar you can catch a pal out with this gag. Say to him, 'There's only one way of making money.' And when he says, 'What's that, then?' as he certainly will, your swift reply is, 'I thought *you* wouldn't know it!'

You can be sure of getting a laugh at your party with this trick. Take an ordinary object, such as a book or a newspaper, and announce to a guest that you will place it in full view of everyone else, but that you will hypnotise him so that he will not be able to see it.

Then, having made a few suitable passes in front of his face, you simply place the object on his head. In that position, of course, everyone will be able to see it but the person underneath. Make sure that there are no mirrors around though, or the tables may be turned on you!

This card trick will make your friends' eyes pop out with amazement. The effect is this: you ask one of your friends to think of a pack of cards. You then ask him to tell you his preference as to colour – red or black. Now ask him which suit he would prefer – if he chooses black he must decide between clubs or spades. Then you ask whether he would like a picture card or a pip card. If he chooses a picture card, you continue as follows.

'We'll divide the picture cards into two pairs – Jack and Queen and King and Ace. Which do you choose? The Jack and Queen? Right – now let's take them one at a time. Do you choose the Jack *or* the Queen? The Jack – very well, that leaves the Queen. And you earlier chose Clubs, didn't you? So you have now selected the Queen of Clubs. Would you look in the left-hand pocket of your jacket, please?'

And sure enough, the Queen of Clubs will be found in the left-hand pocket of your friend's jacket – a card chosen at random by himself!

How to do it? The secret is that the card to be discovered is planted by you in advance. It can be any card – say, the two of hearts – which you will slip into your friend's jacket pocket, or put in the leaves of a book in a cupboard, or seal in an envelope, or anywhere you fancy. Now, the way you ask the questions is all-important, for although you appear to offer a choice, in fact you lead the questioning *in the required direction all the time*. Let's try it with the two of hearts:

'Which colour do you choose – red or black?'

'Black.'

'Very well, that leaves red. Hearts or diamonds?'

'Hearts.'

'Hearts. Now, will you have pip cards or picture cards?'

'Picture cards.'

'That leaves pip cards. Now, I'll divide them up into two: two to five, and six to ten. Which half will you have?'

'Two to five.'

'And now I'll divide those into two pairs: two and three, four and five. Which do you choose?'

'Four and five.'

'That leaves two and three. Which of those cards will you choose?'

'Two.'

'The two of hearts – and here it is!'

Do you see now how the questioning leads on to the card? If your friend makes the correct choice for the card you have pre-selected, you just carry on. If, however, he makes the wrong choice, you just say, 'Very well, that leaves –' and you carry on with the right choice.

This trick is an absolute baffler, but don't do it more than once or the secret will become apparent!

The zany wireless-operator's alphabetical code (to be used when spelling words or names over the telephone):

A	for 'Orses	(hay for horses)
B	for Mutton	(beef or mutton)
C	for Yourself	(see for yourself)
D	for Ential	(differential – part of a car)
E	for Lution	(evolution)
F	for Vescence	(effervescence)
G	for Police	(chief of police)
H	for Himself	(each for himself)
I	for Eadache	(I've a headache)
J	for Oranges	(Jaffa oranges)
K	for Dweller	(cave dweller)
L	for Leather	('ell for leather)
M	for Sis	(emphasis)
N	for Mation	(information)
O	for The Wings Of A Dove	(song title)
P	for Pifer	(Picked a Peck of Pickled Peffers)
Q	for Billiards	(cue for billiards)
R	for Mo	(half a mo)
S	for Ofarim	(Esther Ofarim, a singer)
T	for Two	(Tea for two)
U	for Me	(you for me)
V	for La France	(vive la France!)
W	for quits	(double you for quits)
X	for Breakfast	(eggs for breakfast)
Y	for the Luvva Mike	(why for the Love of Mike?)
Z	for Breezes	(zephyr breezes)

Cross Purposes

What do you get if you cross...

—*a skunk and an owl?*
A bird that smells but doesn't give a hoot!

—*a cow and a camel?*
Lumpy milkshakes!

—*a sheep-dog and a bunch of daisies?*
Collie-flowers!

—*a parrot and an alligator?*
Something that bites your head off and says 'Who's a pretty boy?!'

—*a parrot and an elephant?*
Something that tells everything it remembers.

—*an elephant and peanut-butter?*
Either peanut-butter that never forgets or an elephant that sticks to the roof of your mouth.

—*a sheep-dog and a plate of jelly?*
Collie-wobbles!

—*a football team and ice-cream?*
Aston Vanilla.

—*a zebra and a donkey?*
A zeedonk.

—*a kangaroo and a mink?*
A fur jumper with pockets.

—*a sheep and a rainstorm?*
A wet blanket.

—*a pig and a zebra?*
Striped sausages.

—*a centipede and a parrot?*
A walkie-talkie.

—*a cow and a duck?*
Queam Quackers.

Lucky Dip

Another country lad was being interviewed for a farm labourer's job.

'You must be fit,' said the farmer. 'Have you had any illnesses?'

'No, sir,' said the lad.

'Any accidents?'

'No, sir.'

'But you walked in here on crutches,' said the farmer. 'Surely you must have had an accident?'

'Oh, that!' replied the lad. 'Oi were tossed by a bull – but it warn't no accident, sir. He did it on purpose!'

PROBLEM SOLVED

Two Irishmen bought two horses at a sale in County Cork. Both the horses were very similar in appearance, so Pat said to Mike, 'How shall we tell which horse is whose?'

'Oi tell you what,' said Mike, 'we'll bob the tail of one of them.'

But by a mistake the tails of both horses were bobbed, so they were still in the same predicament.

'Oi know the answer,' said Pat. 'You take the whoite one and Oi'll have the black one!'

'Can I help you, caller?' said the telephone operator.

'Yes, get me Interpol. Quick!'

'You'll have to dial the Overseas operator, caller.'

'Oh, very well.' The caller dialled again.

'Overseas operator. Can I help you?'

'Yes, I want Interpol. Quick. It's important!'

'Do you have the number, caller?'

'No, I don't. But please hurry!'

'You'll have to speak to Directory Enquiries in Paris, caller. I'll connect you.'

'Thank you. Hurry, please!' There was a longish pause and then a French voice said, 'Can I 'elp you, caller?'

'Yes, give me the number of Interpol. And hurry, please, I'm getting desperate!'

'One moment, monsieur ... the number is Paris 28945.'

'Thanks.' And the number is dialled frantically.

'Allo?'

'Is that Interpol?'

'Oui, monsieur.'

'Thank heavens for that! Listen – I want to send some flowers to my mother ...!'

A Catholic priest and a Rabbi were discussing their respective financial arrangements. 'A third of the money we collect in the plate,' said the priest, 'goes to the Pope in Rome, a third goes to the bishop and the rest we can keep for ourselves.'

'I see, I see,' said the Rabbi. 'We do things a little differently. All the money we collect in the plate I put in a blanket; then my wife, my sons and myself take a corner each. We pray and then we toss all the money high in the air. Whatever God wants for Himself he keeps and whatever falls back on the blanket *we* keep!'

What did the fireman's wife get for Christmas?
A ladder in her stocking.

Which Member of Parliament has the biggest head?
The one with the biggest hat!

Why did the cowboy die with his boots on?
'Cos he didn't want to stub his toes when he kicked the bucket.

What did the judge say to his wife when he came home?
'It's been another trying day.'

'What does a boy do when he wears his trousers out?
Wears them in again.

How many famous people were born in Dundee?
None — only babies.

'Doctor! Doctor! I think I need glasses!'
'You certainly do, madam. This is a fish and chip snop!'

'Doctor! Doctor! I feel like a ladder!'
'Keep calm and let me take it one step at a time.'

What did one chick say to the other chick when it found an orange in their nest?
'Look at the orange Mama laid!' (Orange Marmelade)

What did the little eye say to the big eye?
'Aye, aye, Captain!'

What did one flea on Robinson Crusoe's knee say to the other flea on Robinson Crusoe's knee?
'Bye for now — I'll see you on Friday!'

An Anglican minister and a taxi-driver both died at the same time, but to his chagrin the minister discovered that the taxi-driver had been sent to Heaven while he was consigned to the other place. 'Why should this be?' the aggrieved clergyman complained to St Peter. 'After all, I must have prayed to the Lord far more than that taxi-driver.'

'That may well be so,' replied St Peter. 'However, each time you gave a service everyone fell asleep, but when that taxi-driver gave *his* service everyone prayed!'

In which Biblical story is tennis mentioned?
When Moses served in Pharaoh's court . . .

Sunday School teacher: Mavis, why should we pray for grace?
Mavis: Er, 'cos she's a very naughty little girl, Miss?

Thieves who broke into a church were terrified to hear, as they approached the vestry in search of gold plate, a deep voice saying, 'I'm going to eat your arms . . . then your legs . . . then your head . . . and then your body!' With a shriek they hurtled back out through the window whence they had entered, tumbled down the ladder and scurried off as fast as their legs would carry them. Meanwhile, back at the vestry, the vicar was finishing the last of his favourite jelly-babies . . . 'I'm going to eat your arms . . .'

Did you hear about the little boy who was christened Glug-Glug?
The vicar dropped him in the font.

'I say, waiter! There's a fly in my soup!'
'Well, throw him a doughnut — they make super lifebelts!'

'I say, waiter! There's a button in my lunch!'
'Well, you did ask for a jacket potato . . . !'

What would you do if an elephant sat in front of you at the cinema?
Miss most of the film.

Why do elephants have flat feet?
From jumping out of tall trees.

Is the squirt from an elephant's trunk very powerful?
Of course — a jumbo jet can keep five hundred people in the air for hours at a time.

How do you make an elephant sandwich?
First of all you get a *very* large loaf . . .

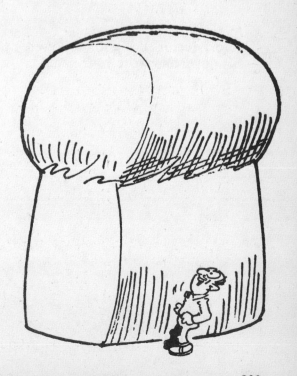

'Doctor, doctor! I want to lose 20lb of excess fat.'
  'Right – I'll amputate your head.'

'Doctor, doctor! I'm having trouble with my breathing.'
  'I'll soon put a stop to that.'

'Doctor, doctor! Can you cure my acne?'
  'I'm making no rash promises.'

'Doctor, doctor! I'm becoming invisible!'
  'Yes, I can see you're not all there.'

'Doctor, doctor! You've taken out my adenoids, my tonsils, my gall-bladder, my varicose veins and my appendix, but I still don't feel well!'
  'That's quite enough out of you.'

'Doctor, doctor! I feel like a sheep!'
  'That's baaaaaad!'

'Doctor, doctor! I feel like an apple!'
  'We must get to the core of this.'

'Doctor, doctor! I feel like an orange!'
  'Have you tried playing squash?'

'Doctor, doctor! I feel like an electric wire!'
'How shocking!'

'Doctor, doctor! I feel like a dog!'
  'Sit!'

'Doctor, doctor! I've just swallowed a pencil!'
  'Sit down and write your name.'

A Scotsman paying his first visit to the zoo stopped by one of the cages.
  'An' whut animal would that be?' he asked the keeper.
  'That's a moose, sir, from Canada,' came the reply.
  'A moose!' exclaimed the Scotsman. 'Hoots – they must ha' rats like elephants over there!'

One keen John Travolta fan went to the barber's and asked for a John Travolta hair-style. The barber sat him down and began to wield the scissors enthusiastically – rather too enthusiastically, thought the customer.

'Are you sure you know what I mean by a John Travolta hair-style?' he asked.

'Certainly, sir, don't you worry,' said the barber confidently, snipping away. The customer became increasingly worried as his hair became shorter and shorter; when the barber then took up an electric razor and, in one swift movement, shaved a bald patch right across his head from ear to ear, he became positively frantic.

'What are you doing?' he yelled, 'I thought you said you knew what a John Travolta hair-style was?'

'And so I do,' said the indignant barber, 'I saw him in *The King And I* fourteen times!'

Young Chris was definitely more than a bit thick; when his pal asked him how he had enjoyed his day at the zoo, he replied, 'It was a rotten swizz! I saw a sign that said "To the Monkeys", so I followed it and I saw the monkeys. Then I saw another sign that said "To the Bears", so I followed that and I saw the bears. But when I followed a sign that said "To the Exit", I found myself out in the street."

A farmer bought a new cart-horse on Hire Purchase; after a week he took it back to the dealer and complained.

'He does his work well enough,' said the farmer, 'but he won't hold his head up and I think there must be something wrong with him.'

'Don't worry about him not holding his head up,' explained the dealer, 'it's just his pride – he will when he's paid for!'

The box-office clerk at the theatre went to the manager's office to tell him that there were two horses in the foyer.

'Two horses?' exclaimed the manager in surprise. 'What on earth do they want?'

'Two stalls for Monday night.'

A circus proprietor caught his animal trainer thrashing one of the eleven performing elephants mercilessly. 'Stop that!' he yelled, 'What do you think you're doing, beating a valuable animal like that?'

'Coming out of the ring this afternoon he slipped, guv,' said the trainer.

'That's no reason to punish him so severely.'

'Oh, no? When he slipped he pulled the tails out of your other ten elephants!'

What do you think of Dracula films?
  Fangtastic!

What does a ghost take for a bad cold?
  Coffin drops.

What are a ghoul's best friend?
  Demons.

The trial had been constantly interrupted by scenes of rowdyism in the public gallery, and the judge had had enough. 'The next person who interrupts the proceedings will be thrown out of my court!' he said severely, at which the defendant yelled, 'Hooray!'

'You are charged with stealing a television set.'
  'I only took it as a joke, your honour.'
  'Where did you take it?'
  'To Glasgow.'
  'That's what I'd call taking a joke too far. Fined £100.'

'How did you get on in court yesterday?'
  'Oh, fine ...'

'Oh don't talk to me about lawyers,' sighed the widow. 'I've had so much trouble settling my late husband's estate that I sometimes wish he hadn't died ...'

'Where are your rear lights?' said the traffic cop to the motorist.
  The motorist looked round and started. 'Never mind my rear lights,' he said, 'where's my trailer?!'

'Did you actually *see* my client bite off his neighbour's nose?' asked defending counsel.
  'Well, I didn't actually see him bite it off,' admitted the witness, 'but I saw him spit it out!'

Mr Smith and Mr Brown were up before the magistrate for fighting, and Smith was fined £20.

  '£20, your honour?' he said bitterly, 'but I was just defending myself – Brown bit half my ear off!'

  'And you, Brown,' said the magistrate, 'are bound over to keep the peace for a year.'

  'Oh, I can't do that, your honour,' replied Brown, 'I threw it away!'

A fishmonger was painting *Fresh Fish Sold Here Today* above his shop when a passer-by said to him, 'you don't want to put *Today*, do you? I mean, you won't be selling it yesterday or tomorrow, will you?'

  'No, I suppose not,' said the fishmonger.

  'And then you don't want *Here* either – you're not selling it anywhere else, are you?'

  'No, that's quite right,' agreed the fishmonger.

  'And then why put *Sold*?' continued the helpful man. 'You're not going to give it away, are you?'

  'Of course I'm not,' said the fishmonger.

  'And then why say *Fresh* – after all, you wouldn't sell it if it weren't fresh, would you?'

  'I certainly wouldn't,' said the fishmonger. 'I must thank you for saving me so much trouble.'

  'Just one final thing,' said the man. 'You don't need *Fish* either – I could smell it two streets away!'

FOR SALE!

What does the Indian ghost live in?
  A creepy teepee.

When the man ghost met the lady ghost was it love at first fright?

Who brings the Monsters their babies?
  Frankenstork.

How do ghosts get through locked doors?
  They use skeleton keys.

Where do ghosts go at Christmas time?
  To see the Phantomime.

Where does Dracula always stay when he's in New York?
  In the Vampire State Building.

The new and very miserable liftboy on his first morning at work failed to recognise the managing director. 'Don't you know who I am, boy?' roared the offended boss.
  'No,' snivelled the wretched youth.
  'You don't? How long have you been here?'
  'All bloomin' mornin' . . .!'

That afternoon the liftboy was required to take the managing director from the twentieth floor to the ground floor. In the lad's inexpert hands the lift roared down the shaft and came to a shuddering, clattering halt at the bottom. 'Er – was that stop too quick, sir?' he asked nervously.
  'No, not at all,' said the managing director heavily. 'I always wear my trousers round my ankles!'

'So you want a job with us, do you?' the boss asked the school-leaver. 'What's your name?'
  'Roy Castle, sir.'
  'Roy Castle, eh?' said the manager jocularly. 'Well, that's a well-known name, isn't it?'
  'It should be,' said the lad proudly. 'I've been delivering papers round here for years!'

'Have you any experience with machines?' the foreman asked the youth.
  'Yeah – slot and pin-ball!'

'You're late for work again Lamport!'
  'Yes, I'm sorry, sir. I overslept.'
  'I thought I told you to get an alarm-clock?'
  'I did, sir, but there are nine of us in our family.'
  'What's that got to do with it?'
  'The alarm was only set for eight!'

'Doctor, I'm getting very forgetful.'
'I see, Mr. Bloggs. Won't you take a chair?'
'Thanks – take a what?'
'A chair. Now, when did you first notice this trouble?'
'What trouble?'

'Doctor, how can I cure myself of sleepwalking?'
'Sprinkle tin-tacks on your bedroom floor.'

'Here, Nick, what's your big brother doing now that he's left school?'
'He's taking French, German and Italian.'
'Gosh! That must take a lot of studying'
'No – he's a liftboy in the Hotel International.'

'Would you rather a lion ate you or a gorilla?'
'I'd rather the lion ate the gorilla . . .'

Susie: 'My baby brother's only a year old and he's been walking for six months!'
Annie: 'Really? He must be very tired.'

'Are you writing a thank-you letter to Grandpa like I told you?'
'Yes, Mum.'
'Your handwriting seems very large.'
'Well, Grandpa's deaf, so I'm writing very loud.'

'You're very late in coming from school, aren't you?'
'I stayed in for fencing lessons, Dad.'
'Right – tomorrow you can help me mend the one behind the garage.'

Joey Brown was having afternoon tea with his Grandma.
'Would you like some bread and butter, Joey?' she asked.
'Yes, thank you, Grandma,' he said.
'That's a good boy,' said Grandma. 'I like to hear you saying "thank you".'
'If you want to hear me say it again,' added Joey, 'you might put some jam on it!'

Why did the ghost go to the astrologer?
'Cos he wanted to see his horrorscope.

Why are ghosts cowards?
'Cos they've got no guts.

A distraught mum rushed into the back yard, where eight-year-old Tommy was banging on the bottom of an old upturned tin bath with a poker.
'What *do* you think you're playing at?' she demanded.
'I'm just entertaining the baby,' explained Tommy.
'Where is the baby?' asked his Mum.
'Under the bath.'

Office junior: 'Can I have tomorrow afternoon off, sir? It's my grandmother's funeral.'
Manager: 'Come off it, boy. Didn't you have an afternoon off a couple of months ago because your grandmother died?
Office junior: 'Yes, but Grandad married again.'

'Your mother has been living with us for six years now,' said the long-suffering wife to her husband. 'I really think it's time she moved out and found a place of her own.'

'*My* mother?' said her bewildered husband, 'I thought she was *your* mother!'

'My husband is a man of rare gifts.'
'That's nice.'
'He hasn't given me a present in twenty-five years of marriage ...'

Q: Under British law, what is the maximum penalty for bigamy?
A: Two mothers-in-law.

'Last week when I cut my hand badly, my mother-in-law cried over me.'
'She's fond of you, is she?'
'No – she just wanted to get salt into the wound.'

Husband: Why can't you make bread like my mother?
Wife: I would if you could make dough like your father!

Doctor: 'Your system needs toning up. What you should do is take a nice cold bath every morning.'
Patient: 'Oh, I do, doctor.'
Doctor: 'You do?'
Patient: 'Yes, every morning I take a nice cold bath and I fill it with nice warm water!'

A little girl attending the school clinic started crying as the doctor approached her.
'I'm only going to take your pulse,' the doctor explained.
'But don't I need it?' sobbed the little girl.

Doctor: 'Now just step on the scales. There, you see? Look at this chart – you're overweight.'
Patient: 'No, I'm not. I'm just six inches too short.'

A doctor advised a very fat man to take up golf for exercise. 'That's no good to me,' said the patient, 'I've tried it before. If I put the ball where I can hit it I can't see it, and if I put it where I can see it I can't hit it!'

Customer: Ironmonger, have you got two inch nails?
Ironmonger: Yes, madam.
Customer: Scratch my back, will you?

'I'd like some really tight jeans.'
  'Certainly, sir. Will you walk this way?'
  'If they're as tight as yours I'll probably have to.'

The old lady walked into a chemist's shop and bought a packet of mothballs. The next day she returned – and again bought a packet of moth balls. On the third day she did the same and when she appeared the fourth day and asked yet again for a packet of mothballs the chemist could not restrain his curiosity. 'You must have a lot of moths, madam?' he queried.
  'Yes, I have,' she nodded, 'and I don't know what I'm going to do. I've been throwing these balls at them for three days now and I haven't hit one yet!'

A woman rushed into an ironmonger's shop and said, 'Can I have a mousetrap, please? And will you be quick – I've a bus to catch.'
  'Sorry, madam,' said the assistant, 'we don't sell 'em that big!'

A man dashed into a cafe and said to the woman behind the counter, 'Can you give me a glass of water, please?'
  'Here you are, love,' she said, handing it over. But to her astonishment the man ran out of the cafe without drinking it. Two minutes later he was back with the empty glass. 'Can I have another glass of water, please?'
  'Certainly, love,' she said in kindly fashion. 'But why don't you drink it here?'
  'Oh, it's not for drinking,' he said. 'My house is on fire!'

'Here's your Christmas present. A box of your favourite chocs.'
  'Coo, thanks! But it's half-empty!'
  'Well, they're my favourite chocs, too ...'

Little Susie had made a creche for Christmas with the shepherds and the animals and the Holy Family, and her handiwork was being admired by a fond aunt. 'But what's that thing in the corner?' asked Auntie Gladys.
  'Oh, that's the telly,' replied Susie proudly.

Only a week after Christmas an irate Mum stormed into the toy-shop. 'I'm bringing back this unbreakable toy fire-engine,' she said to the man behind the counter. 'It's useless!'
  'Surely your son hasn't broken it already?' he asked.
  'No, he's broken all his *other* toys with it!'

What did the big bus say to the little bus?
  'You're too young to be driving.'

*What did the big fly say to the little fly after they were both
caught in a fly-paper?*
  'This is a sticky problem!'

What did the woman with a bad cold say to the chemist?
  'I need a box of a-a-atishoos!'

Harry was always very sentimental about Christmas. Every
year he'd take his socks off and stand them up by the fireplace.

Why does Father Christmas come down chimneys?
  Because they soot him.

What's this?

A fountain-pen nib.

'I never had a sledge when I was a kid. We were too poor.'
  'What a shame! What did you do when it snowed?'
  'Slid down the hills on my cousin.'

'For our next Christmas dinner I'm going to cross a chicken
with an octopus.'
  'What on earth for?'
  'So we can all have a leg each.'

As the funeral cortège reached the top of the hill the rear door
of the hearse came open. To the horror of the mourners the
coffin slid out, and then proceeded to bounce and clatter its
way right down the hill! At the bottom of the hill its speed
carried it right through the open doorway of a chemist's shop
where, before the appalled gaze of the assistant, it crashed
into the counter causing the lid to spring open. 'For goodness'
sake,' said the corpse, 'give me something to stop this coffin
…'

Customer: This loaf is lovely and warm!
Baker: So it should be, madam. The cat's been sitting on it all
morning!

Did you hear about Paddy who opened a shop next to the
Chinese Takeaway? He called it an Irish Bring-back …

'Do you write with your right hand or your left hand?'
'Well, I usually write with a pencil . . .'

An old lady saw a little boy walking from the river with a fishing rod and a jar of tiddlers.

'You're a very naughty boy to go fishing on the Sabbath,' she said.

'Well, it serves 'em right for chasing after worms,' said the lad.

A Cockney boy was staying in the country for the first time. One evening while out for a walk with a new village friend he heard an owl hoot.

'Wassat?' he cried, startled.

'It's only an owl,' said the village boy, laughing.

'I know it's an 'owl,' said the town boy, 'but 'oo's 'owling?'

A man climbing a cliff got stuck and called for help. When a rescue team arrived, the leader shouted to him, 'Can't you get down the same way you climbed up?'

'No, I can't,' shouted the frightened man. 'I came up head first!'

A farmer asked his Irish shepherd whether he had counted the sheep that morning.

'Oi did indaid, sor,' said the Irishman. 'Oi counted up to nineteen, but one of the craytures ran so fast Oi couldn't count him at all, at all.'

Notice (in a butcher's window): John Smith butchers pigs like his father.

Old Grannie Harbottle was a very stubborn and independent-minded lady. It didn't matter how cold it was she would insist on getting the coal in her nightie! Even in the depths of winter there she'd be – down the garden, in the shed, getting the coal in her nightie!! One Christmas the neighbours all clubbed together to buy her a shovel but she said her nightie held more

'Butcher, have you got a sheep's head?'
'No, it's just the way I part my hair.'

'Give me a half-pound of bacon, please, and make it lean.'
'Certainly, madam – which way?'

Barber: Tell me, sir, when you came in here were you wearing a red scarf?
Customer: No, I wasn't.
Barber: Blimey, I've cut your throat!

'Before I can accept a cheque, madam,' said the shop assistant, 'you will have to identify yourself.'

'Very well,' said the customer, taking a mirror from her handbag and peering into it. 'Yes, it's me.'

'So you're looking for a job, eh?' said the shopkeeper. 'Do you like hard work?'

'No, sir.'

'I'll take you on – that's the first honest answer I've had this morning!'

Central heating has ruined Christmas – how can Father Christmas slide down radiators?

Who is the meanest man in the world? The father who goes out of the house on Christmas Eve, fires a gun, comes back in and says to his children:

'No presents this Christmas – Father Christmas has shot himself!'

A school-leaver was being interviewed for a job as an office boy.

'You'll get five pounds a week to start off with,' said the boss, 'and then after six months you'll get ten pounds a week.'

'Rightho,' said the lad. 'I'll come back in six months.'

A tramp knocked on the back door of a house and asked for a bite to eat.

'Go away,' said the lady of the house. 'I never feed tramps.'

'That's all right, lady,' said the tramp. 'I'll feed myself.'

The manager of a shop was ticking off one of his staff.

'I saw you arguing with a customer,' he said crossly. 'Will you please remember that in my shop the customer is always right. Do you understand?'

'Yes, sir,' said the assistant. 'The customer is always right.'

'Now, what were you arguing about?'

'Well, sir, he said you were an idiot.'

'I say, Ginger, why does your bike always have flat tyres?'

'So's I can reach the pedals.'

A small girl went into the post office and said to the man behind the counter, 'If I put a threepenny stamp on this letter, will it go to Burnley?'

'Yes, it will,' said the man.

'That's funny,' replied the little girl, 'because I've addressed it to Plymouth.'

An American tourist was visiting a quaint country village, and got talking to an old man in the local pub.

'And have you lived here all your life, sir?' asked the American.

'Not yet, m'dear,' said the villager wisely.

If it takes a football team 45 minutes to eat a ham, how long will it take three football teams to eat half a ham?

It depends on whether they are professional or 'am-a-chewers' [amateurs]!

A chap went into the police-station and put a dead cat on the counter.

'Somebody threw this into my front garden,' he complained.

'Rightho, sir,' said the desk sergeant. 'You come back in six months and if no-one's claimed it you can keep it.'

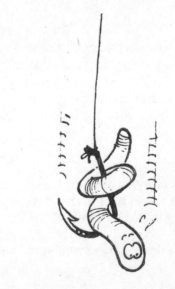

'I once travelled from Edinburgh to Bristol without a ticket.'

'How did you manage that?'

'I walked.'

'Little girl, did you catch that big fish all by yourself?'

'No, I had a little worm to help me.'

'What's a Grecian urn?'

'I dunno.'

'About £15 a week . . .'

A tramp stopped a passer-by and said, 'Give us 25p for a cup of tea, guv?'

'Tea doesn't cost 25p!' exclaimed the outraged gent.

'I know,' said the tramp, 'but I'm expecting company.'

'Did your watch stop when you dropped it on the pavement?'

'Of course it did. Did you expect it to go right through, you fool?'

Barber: 'How would you like your hair cut, sir?'
Customer: 'Off!'

A little boy knocked on the door of his friend's house. When his friend's mother answered, he said, 'Can Julian come out to play, please?'

'No, I'm afraid not,' said Julian's Mum. 'It's too wet.'

'Well, then,' asked the lad, 'can his football come out to play?'

Two boys were talking about the various illnesses and accidents they had suffered.

'Once I couldn't walk for a year,' said the first.

'When was that?' asked the second.

'When I was a baby.'

'If you found a pound note, would you keep it?'

'No, vicar.'

'That's a good boy. What would you do with it?'

'I'd spend it.'

'Oi! You can't fish here!'

'I'm not fishing. I'm giving my pet worm a bath.'

A car-driver stopped in a small village and called to a passer-by, 'Excuse me, can you tell me where this road goes to?'

'It don't go nowhere,' grinned the local. 'It stays right where it is.'

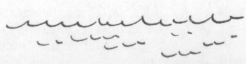

An old lady saw a little boy with a fishing-rod over his shoulder and a jar of tadpoles in his hand walking through the park one Sunday.

'Little boy,' she called, 'don't you know you shouldn't go fishing on a Sunday.'

'I'm not going fishing, missus,' he called back. 'I'm going home.'

'Is it difficult to get to be a professor?'
'Oh, no. You can do it by degrees.'

'I don't think much of this mirror,' said the small child.
'Why not?'
'Well, every time I try to look at something my face gets in the way.'

'I say, your umbrella's seen better days, hasn't it?'
'Yes, it's had its ups and downs.'

'What are you going to do when you grow up, young man?'
'Grow a beard so I won't have so much face to wash.'

'Farmer Giles, why do you have two barrels on your shotgun?'
'So that if I miss the fox with the first I can get him with the other.'
'Why not fire with the other first, then?'

'We had my Grannie for Christmas dinner last year.'
'Really? We had turkey.'

'I tell you what I like about Christmas. Kissing girls under the mistletoe.'
'I prefer kissing them under the nose.'

One unfortunate girl was so ugly that at Christmas time the boys used to hang her up and kiss the mistletoe ...

The new office-boy came into his boss's office and said, 'I think you're wanted on the phone, sir.'
'What d'you mean, you *think*?' demanded the boss.
'Well, sir, the phone rang, I answered it and a voice said, "Is that you, you old fool?"'

Overheard in a very crowded train: 'Would you mind taking your elbow out of my ribs?'
'Certainly – if you'll take your pipe out of my mouth.'

'What did you get on your birthday?'
'A year older.'

Lost: Watch belonging to a gentleman engraved 'first prize'.

'Can you stand on your head?'
   'I've tried, but I can't get my feet up high enough . . .'

'I wish to return this cricket bat. It's useless.'
   'Oh? What's wrong with it, sir?'
   'Every time I've been in to bat with it I've been out first ball.'

'I saw six men standing under an umbrella and none of them got wet.'
   'Must have been a big umbrella.'
   'No. It wasn't raining.'

A visitor to a museum was stopped at the entrance by an attendant who said, 'Leave your umbrella in the cloakroom, please, sir.'
   'But I haven't got an umbrella,' protested the visitor.
   'Then you can't come in, sir,' said the attendant. 'I have strict instructions that people cannot come in without leaving their umbrellas in the cloak-room.'

'How did you hurt your foot?'
   'Tim fell on it.'
   'Tim who?'
   'Tim-ber.'

'I've got a wonder watch. Only cost £2.'
   'What's a wonder watch?'
   'Every time I look at it I wonder if it's still going.'

'I wish I'd lived in olden times.'
   'Why?'
   'There wouldn't be so much history to learn.'

A tramp knocked at a kitchen door and asked for food.
   'Didn't I give you some pie a week ago?' said the lady of the house.
   'Yus, lady,' said the tramp, 'but I'm all right again now.'

'What's your name, little girl?'
   'Bessie.'
   'I know that. I mean what's your last name?'
   'I dunno – I'm not married yet.'

. A visitor to Ireland asked a farm labourer the time.

'Sure, it's twelve o'clock, yer honour,' answered the Irishman.

'Only twelve?' queried the traveller. 'I thought it was much later than that.'

'Oh, no, sir, it never gets later than that in these parts.'

'How's that?'

'Well, sir, after twelve o'clock it goes back to one.'

'You're from Scotland, aren't you?'

'Aye.'

'What does "I dinna ken" mean?'

'I don't know.'

'Well, if you're Scottish, you ought to!'

'Your Dad's shaved his beard off again. That's the third time this year, isn't it?'

'Yes, it's my mum. She's stuffing a cushion.'

A lodger was complaining about the food to his landlady. 'I didn't like that pie, Mrs. Maggs.'

Mrs. Maggs was furious. 'I've been making pies since before you were born!' she said angrily.

'Perhaps that was one of them,' said the lodger feelingly.

A woman went into a newsagent's and asked, 'Do you keep stationery?'

'No, madam,' said the salesman. 'I usually go home for my lunch.'

One housewife had a kitchen so small that she could only use condensed milk.

A woman who had not been feeling well went to see the doctor, while her husband waited for her. When she eventually came out of the doctor's surgery, he said, 'Well, what's the diagnosis?'

'The doctor says I'm underweight.'

'Well, have a plum. If you swallow it whole you'll put on a stone.'

A guide was taking a party of visitors round a stately home. They stopped in front of a large grandfather clock and the guide said, 'This clock is 350 years old, and the big hand is twelve inches long.'

Before he could say another word, a little lad piped up, 'If it's twelve inches long, it's not a hand. It's a foot.'

'I bought my wife a wonderful present for Christmas – a mink outfit.'

'Really?'

'Two steel traps and a gun.'

George was born on 24 December. He said he wanted to be home in time for Christmas.

As a be-jewelled duchess descended from her limousine, a dirty old tramp sidled up to her and said, 'Excuse me, lady, I haven't eaten for a month.'

'Well, my dear man,' the dowager replied, 'you must *force* yourself!'

Old lady: 'Where are you going to, my little man?'
Small boy: 'I'm going to the football match.'
Old lady: 'Oh, you're a supporter, are you? Is it very exciting for you when they win?'
Small boy: 'I don't know. I've only been going for two seasons.'

Lost: An umbrella by a lady with two broken ribs.

'What's your new house like?'
'Oh, it's all right, I suppose. But my bedroom's so cold and so small – and every time I open the door the light goes on.'

An old man and a young lad were sitting on opposite benches in the park. Suddenly the old man leaned across and shouted, 'It's no use your talking to me from over there. I'm deaf.'

'I'm not talking to you,' the boy shouted back. 'I'm chewing bubblegum.'

'Do you notice any change in me?'
'No. Why?'
'I've just swallowed a penny.'

'I've just finished painting your portrait. There, don't you think it looks like you?'
'Er . . . well . . . it probably looks better from a distance.'
'I told you it was like you!'

Two little girls were discussing their arithmetic lessons.
'Why do we always stop our multiplication tables at 12?' asked one.
The other had the answer. ''Cos it's unlucky to have 13 at table,' she replied confidently.

'Do you mind my smoking these cigars?'
'Not if you don't mind my being sick.'

Inscribed on the tombstone of a hypochondriac: *I TOLD YOU I WAS ILL.*

A man rushed into a bank and stuck two fingers through the grill.
'This is a muck-up!' he hissed to the startled cashier.
'Don't you mean a stick-up?' she said.
'No,' replied the bandit, 'it's a muck-up. I've forgotten my gun.'

'I say, ticket-inspector, why did you punch a hole in my ticket?'
'So you can go through, sir.'

A country policeman cycling down a lane was astounded to see a hiker walking along bent under the weight of a large signpost which read *To Plymouth*.
"Allo, 'allo, 'allo!' said the policeman, dismounting. 'What are you up to with that, then?'
'I'm walking to Plymouth, constable,' explained the hiker, 'and I don't want to lose my way.'

'Are you a mechanic?'
'No, I'm a MacTavish.'

Mrs. Lard, who was extremely stout, was visiting her friend Mrs. Ellis one day, when Mrs. Ellis's little girl said, "Mrs. Lard, would you get down on your hands and knees, please? Teacher says I've got to draw an elephant.'

'How many fish have you caught today?'
'When I get another I'll have one.'

A surly-looking tramp knocked on the kitchen door and demanded something to eat. The woman of the house was a bit frightened, but she said, 'If I give you a piece of my home-made apple pie, will you promise to go away and not come back?'
'Well, you know your cooking better than I do lady', said the tramp.

'Can you fight?'
'No.'
'Put 'em up, then – you coward!'

A man went into a furniture shop and said that he wanted to buy a mattress.
'Spring mattress, sir?' asked the manager.
'No,' said the customer. 'One I can use all year round.'

An American tourist found himself in a sleepy little country village, and asked one of the locals the age of the oldest inhabitant.
'Well, zur,' replied the villager, 'we bain't got one now. He died last week.'

'My Dad's got a leading position in a circus.'
'Great! What's he do?'
'He leads the elephants in.'

A much-travelled explorer was talking about the huge mosquitoes of the African jungle.
'Were they vicious?' asked one of his listeners.
'No,' the explorer replied casually, 'they'd eat out of your hand.'

A neighbour bumped into little Diana playing in the street well after dark.

'Hello, Diana,' said the neighbour. 'Isn't it time little girls were in bed?'

'I dunno,' said Diana. 'I haven't got any little girls.'

An Irish navvy was instructed by his equally Irish foreman to dig a hole in the road.

'And phwhat shall Oi do wit' the earth, sor?' he asked.

'Don't be daft, Mick,' said the foreman, 'Sure, ye jist dig anither hole an' bury it.'

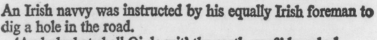

A burglar, new to the life of crime, nervously held up a pawn-broker.

'Hands up or I'll shoot!' he cried.

'I'll give you £20 for the revolver,' said the quick-thinking pawn-broker.

'I say, porter, where is this train going to?'

'This train goes to Liverpool in ten minutes, madam.'

'Good gracious! Last time I went to Liverpool it took four hours.'

A nervous young mountaineer looked up the steep cliff which his guide was proposing that they should climb.

'Do people often fall off the top?' he asked anxiously.

'No,' said the guide arily. 'Once is usually enough.'

'Would you like a duck egg for tea?'

'Only if you "quack" it for me.'

For sale: Large crystal vase by a lady slightly cracked.

Lost: School scarf by small boy with green and blue stripes.

'Jemima, how many more times have I to tell you that it's very rude to keep reaching over the table for cakes. Haven't you got a tongue in your head?'

'Yes, but my arm's longer.'

'Who are you?'

'I'm the piano-tuner, madam.'

'I didn't order a piano-tuner.'

'No, madam, but your neighbours did.'

'Take a week's notice. You're sacked.'

'But I haven't done anything!'

'That's why you're sacked.'

Sign at the boundary to an Irish country town: 'Corrigan welcomes careful drivers. One man is knocked down in Corrigan every thirty minutes – and he's getting mighty tired of it.'

A hiker stopped an old farmhand in a country lane and asked, 'How far is it to Shaftesbury?'

'Ten mile as the crow flies,' came the answer.

'And how far when he walks?' asked the hiker wearily.

A school-leaver was being interviewed for a job. 'Do you think you'd make a good book-keeper?' asked the boss.

'Oh, yes, sir,' came the keen reply. 'I've sometimes kept library books for years and years.'

On the ocean liner a passenger was hanging over the rail, suffering acutely from seasickness. A steward approached him to see if he could assist in any way, but the passenger just groaned and said, 'Oh, I feel so ill. What shall I do?'

'Don't worry, sir,' the steward sympathised, 'You'll soon find out.'

What's this?

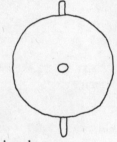

A Mexican riding a bicycle.

At an exhibition, a famous artist was asked by a gushing young lady, 'Do your pictures have a big sale?'

'Only when I draw pretty boats,' was the freezing reply.

For sale: A cow that gives 5 quarts of milk a day, a set of golf clubs, a brown overcoat and a complete set of Shakespeare.

The nervous passenger was being reassured by the ship's steward.

'Don't worry, sir,' he said, 'we may be in the middle of the Atlantic, but we're only two miles from land.'

'Only two miles,' queried the passenger.

'Yes, sir,' said the steward. 'Straight down.'

Oh No!

What did the big tap say to the small tap?
  'You little squirt!'

What did the small tap say to the big tap?
  'You big drip!'

What did one witch say to the other witch when inviting her to supper?
  'You'll just have to take pot luck!'

What did one chimney say to the other chimney?
  'I'm going out tonight — can I borrow your soot?'

What did one sardine say to the other sardine?
  'Move over — you're squashing me!'

What did one ear say to the other ear?
  'Just between us we need a haircut.'

What did the chick say when she came out of the shell?
  'What an egg-sperience!'

What did the bull say after his famous visit to the china shop?
  'I've just had a smashing time!'

What did the boy candle say to the girl candle?
  'Let's go out together!'

What did one eye say to the other eye?
  'Between you and me, something smells!'

What did the girl magnet say to the boy magnet?
  'I find you very attractive.'

What did the big clock hand say to the little clock hand?
  'I'll be back in an hour.'

What did the egg say to the Kenwood mixer?
  'I know when I'm beaten.'

What did the calculator say to the bank clerk?
  'You can count on me.'

What did the mother crow say to the nestling?
  'If you gotta crow, you gotta crow!'

What did the young porcupine say to the cactus?
  'Is that you, Daddy?'

What did one lift say to the other lift?
  'I think I'm going down with something!'

What did one tonsil say to the other tonsil?
  'You'd better get dressed — the doctor's taking us out tonight!'

What did one wall say to the other wall?
  'I'll meet you at the corner.'

What did the orange say to the lemon?
  'Hello, lemon . . .'

What did the dog say to the cat?
  'Woof Woof!' (What else?!)

What did one flea say to the other flea?
  'Shall we walk or take a cat?'

What did the boy octopus say to the girl octopus?
  (Sing) 'I wanna hold your hand, your hand, your hand, your hand . . .!'

What did the bald man say to the comb?
  'I'll never part with you.'

What did one salt-cellar say to the other salt-cellar after a fight?
  'Shake!'

What did the Daddy Shoe say to the Baby Shoe?
  'You'll do in a pinch!'

What did the girl bulb say to the boy switch?
  'Boy, do you turn me on!'

What did the big fountain say to the little fountain?
  'You're too young to drink.'

What did the beaver say to the tree?
  'It's been nice gnawing you.'

What did the King Egg say to the Bad Egg?
  'I'm going to have you eggsecuted.'

What did the Headmaster Egg say to the Pupil Egg?
  'I'm going to eggspel you.'

How did the Mother Babana spoil the Baby Banana?
    She left him in the sun too long.

Which capital city cheats at exams?
    Peking.

What do you call a flea that lives in an idiot's ear?
    A space invader.

Why did the woman take a load of hay to bed?
    To feed her nightmare.

What is Kojak's favourite washing powder?
    Bald Automatic.

What do cats prefer for breakfast?
    Mice Crispies.

What's red, has wheels, and lies on its back?
    A dead bus.

What's yellow and goes slam-slam-slam-slam?
    A four-door banana.

Why did the idiot jump out of the window?
    To try out his new spring suit.

Why did the idiot spring out of the window?
    To try out his new jump suit.

What did the Baby Corn say to the Mother Corn?
    'Where's Pop Corn?'

Did you hear about the Irish Kamikaze pilot?
    He flew ninety-nine missions . . .

What did one angel say to the other angel?
    'Halo there!'

Did you hear about the idiot Morris dancer?
    He fell off the bonnet.

What did the picture say to the wall?
    'First they frame me and then they hang me!'

What do ants take when they are ill?
    Antibiotics.

Where do astronauts park their space vehicles?
    On meet-eorites.

What's furry and minty?
    A Polo bear.

What's black and white and noisy?
    A zebra with a drum-kit.

If you want to know where the sun goes after it has set, just stay up all night and it will finally dawn on you!

What's yellow and leaps from cake to cake?
Tarzipan.

What's the fastest thing in water?
A motor-pike.

Hear about the world's worst athlete? He ran a bath and came in second.

What's very intelligent and loves boating?
A row-bot.

How do you kill an Aberdonian?
Throw a 5p piece under a bus.

Where do snowmen go to dance?
A snowball.

Did you hear about the terrorist who tried to blow up a bus?
He burnt his lips on the exhaust pipe.

What's black and white and bounces?
A penguin on a pogo-stick. *Or* An india-rubber nun.

What do you call a sleeping heifer?
A young bulldozer.

Shall I tell you the joke about the postcard that hadn't been stamped? No, you'd never get it.

What pipes are never played in Scotland?
Hose-pipes.

Did you hear about the idiot who had a brain transplant?
The brain rejected him!

Why do so many Irish people emigrate?
Because MacGillicuddy Reeks!

Why did the idiot have his sundial floodlit?
So's he could tell the time at night.

How do you cope with a gas leak?
Put a bucket under it.

What fish are other fish most scared of?
  Jack the Kipper.

What would you call a goods train loaded with sweets?
  A Chew-Chew train.

What comes out of a wardrobe at one hundred miles an hour?
  Stirling Moth.

What goes 'Click-click — have I done it?'
  A blind man doing the Rubik Cube.

Why didn't the banana snore?
  'Cos it was afraid to wake up the rest of the bunch.

What jacket is always burning?
  A blazer.

What looks like half a loaf of bread?
  The other half.

What makes a tree noisy?
  Its bark.

Who is the biggest gangster in the sea?
  Al Caprawn.

What pantomime story is set in a chemist's shop?
  Puss in Boots.

What do you call ants who run away very fast to get married?
  Ant-elopers.

What is black and swings through trees?
  Tarzan's coalman.

Why is a bee's hair always sticky?
  'Cos it uses a honeycomb.

What does Luke Skywalker shave with?
  A laser blade.

What fruit starts with the letter N?
  A 'nana.

What do you get if you drop a piano on an army camp?
  A flat major.

What happened to the hyena who swallowed an Oxo cube?
  He made a laughing stock of himself.

What do frogs drink?
  Croaka Cola.

Where would you weigh a pie?
  (Sing) Somewhere over the rainbow, weigh a pie . . .
(way up high!)

Who is in cowboy films and is always broke?
  Skint Eastwood.